D0421466

GEOGRAPHIES OF MUSLIM IDENTITIES

Re-materialising Cultural Geography

Dr Mark Boyle, Department of Geography, University of Strathclyde, UK and Professor Donald Mitchell, Maxwell School, Syracuse University, USA

Nearly 25 years has elapsed since Peter Jackson's seminal call to integrate cultural geography back into the heart of social geography. During this time, a wealth of research has been published which has improved our understanding of how culture both plays a part in and – in turn – is shaped by social relations based on class, gender, race, ethnicity, nationality, disability, age, sexuality and so on. In spite of the achievements of this mountain of scholarship, the task of grounding culture in its proper social contexts remains in its infancy. This series therefore seeks to promote the continued significance of exploring the dialectical relations which exist between culture, social relations and space and place. Its overall aim is to make a contribution to the consolidation, development and promotion of the ongoing project of re-materialising cultural geography.

The series will publish outstanding original research monographs and edited collections which make strong and clear contributions to the furtherance of the re-materialisation agenda. Work which foregrounds the role of culture in shaping relations of domination and resistance will be particularly welcomed. Both theoretically reflexive contributions charting the progress and prospects of the agenda, and theoretically informed case studies will be sought:

1) the re-materialising agenda - progress and prospects: including the location of the agenda within the broader development of human geography; reflexive accounts of the main achievements to date; outstanding research agendas yet to be explored; methodological innovations and new approaches to field work; and responses to the challenges posed by non-representational theory and theories of performativity.

2) Theoretically informed case studies within the tradition: including work on new links between culutre, capital and social exclusion; changing concepts of masculinity and femininity; nationalism, cosmopoloitanism, colonial and postcolonial identities, diaspora and hybridity; the rescaling of territorial identities, the new regionalism and localism, and the rise of supranational political bodies; sexuality and space; disability and the production of and navigation around the built environment.

Geographies of Muslim Identities
Diaspora, Gender and Belonging

Edited by

CARA AITCHISON
University of the West of England, UK
PETER HOPKINS
University of Newcastle Upon Tyne, UK
and
MEI-PO KWAN
Ohio State University, USA

ASHGATE

© Editors and Contributors 2007

All rights reserved. No part of this publication may be reproduced, stored in a retrieval system or transmitted in any form or by any means, electronic, mechanical, photocopying, recording or otherwise without the prior permission of the publisher.

The editors and contributors have asserted their moral right under the Copyright, Designs and Patents Act, 1988, to be identified as the editors and contributors of this work.

Published by
Ashgate Publishing Limited
Gower House
Croft Road
Aldershot
Hampshire GU11 3HR
England

Ashgate Publishing Company
Suite 420
101 Cherry Street
Burlington, VT 05401-4405
USA

Ashgate website: http://www.ashgate.com

British Library Cataloguing in Publication Data
Geographies of Muslim identities : diaspora, gender and
    belonging. - (Re-materialising cultural geography)
    1. Muslims - Non-Muslim countries 2. Ethnicity
    3. Islamophobia 4. Women in Islam 5. Gender
    I. Aitchison, Cara II. Hopkins, Peter III. Kwan, Mei-Po
    305.6'97

Library of Congress Cataloging-in-Publication Data
Geographies of Muslim identities : diaspora, gender and belonging / edited by Cara
Aitchison, Peter Hopkins and Mei-Po Kwan.
        p. cm.
    Includes index.
    ISBN 978-0-7546-4888-8
    1. Muslims--Non-Muslim countries. 2. Ethnicity. 3. Islamophobia. 4. Women in
Islam. 5. Gender. I. Aitchison, Cara. II. Hopkins, Peter (Peter
E.) III. Kwan, Mei-Po.

    BP52.5.G46 2007
    305.6'97--dc22

                                                                    2007001509

ISBN: 978-0-7546-4888-8

Printed and bound in Great Britain by Antony Rowe Ltd, Chippenham, Wiltshire.

Contents

List of Figures

Notes on Contributors

Cara Carmichael Aitchison is Professor in Human Geography and Director of the Centre for Leisure, Tourism and Society at the University of the West England, Bristol, UK.

Patricia Ehrkamp is Assistant Professor in the Department of Geography at the University of Kentucky, USA.

Eileen Green is Professor of Sociology and Director of the Centre for Social and Policy Research in the School of Social Sciences and Law at the University of Teeside, Middlesbrough, UK.

Peter E. Hopkins is a Lecturer in Social Geography, University of Newcastle Upon Tyne, UK

Tess Kay is a Senior Research Fellow in the Institute of Youth Sport, School of Sport and Exercise Sciences at Loughborough University, UK

Mei-Po Kwan is Distinguished Professor of Social and Behavioral Sciences in the Department of Geography at Ohio State University, USA.

Gabriele Marranci is a Lecturer in the Anthropology of Religion in the School of Divinity, History and Philosophy, University of Aberdeen, UK.

Cameron McAuliffe is based in the Urban Research Centre at the University, of Western Sydney, Sydney, Australia.

Sadiq Mir is a Research Associate in the Department of Geography at King's College London, UK.

William C. Rowe is an Assistant Professor in the Department of Geography and Anthropology and in the International Studies Program, Louisiana State University, Baton Rouge, Louisiana.

Carrie Singleton is a Senior Researcher in the Centre for Social and Policy Research in the School of Social Sciences and Law at the University of Teeside, Middlesbrough, UK.

Sonia van Wichelen is a Postdoctoral Fellow at the Center for Cultural Sociology, Yale University, New Haven, USA.

Samuel Zalanga is an Associate Professor of Sociology in the Department of Anthropology and Sociology at Bethel University, Saint Paul, Minnesota, USA.

Chapter 1

Introduction:
Geographies of Muslim Identities

Peter E. Hopkins, Mei-Po Kwan and Cara Carmichael Aitchison

Introduction

Following the terrorist attacks of September 11th 2001 in New York, there were feelings of 'shock, anger [and] fear' (Flint, 2002: 77) alongside recognition of the global and local nature of the events (Smith, 2001). As Fred Halliday (2002: 31) observed:

> The crisis unleashed by the events of 11 September is one that is global and all-encompassing. It is global in the sense that it binds many different countries into conflict, most obviously the USA and parts of the Muslim world. It is all-encompassing in that, more than any other international crisis yet seen, it affects a multiplicity of life's levels, political, economic, cultural and psychological.

> (Halliday, 2002: 31)

More recently too, the bombings in Bali on October 12th 2002, the Madrid train bombings of 11th March 2004 and bombings on the London underground on July 7th 2005 have all contributed to these discourses of danger, fear and risk (Bauman, 2006; Beck, 1992, 1999). Furthermore, these events also share an association with terrorists and suicide bombers who are almost always identified as being Islamic. In recent years, markers and signifiers of Muslim identities have increasingly come to signify 'the Other'; resulting in many Muslims becoming 'the victims of discrimination, harassment, racial and religious profiling, and verbal and physical assault' (Peek, 2003: 271).

Despite the demonisation of Muslims and their associated bodily marking and dress, Islam is by no means a homogenous category. As Halliday, 1999: 897) notes "Islam' tells us only one part of how these people live and see the world: and that 'Islam may vary greatly". Tariq Modood (2003: 100), for example, has sought to clarify the diversity and heterogeneity of the category 'Muslim':

> Muslims are not, however, a homogenous group. Some Muslims are devout but apolitical; some are political but do not see their politics as being 'Islamic' (indeed, may even be anti-Islamic). Some identify more with a nationality of origin, such as Turkish; others with the nationality of settlement and perhaps citizenship, such as French. Some prioritise fundraising for mosques, other campaign against discrimination, unemployment or Zionism. For some, Ayatollah Khomeini is a hero and Osama bin Laden an inspiration;

for others, the same may be said of Kemal Ataturk or Margaret Thatcher, who created a swathe of Asian millionaires in Britain, brought in Arab capital and was one of the first to call for NATO action to protect Muslims in Kosovo. The category 'Muslim', then, is as internally diverse as 'Christian' or 'Belgian' or 'middle-class ', or any other category helpful in ordering our understanding ...

(Modood, 2003: 100)

A key aim of this book is to demonstrate, highlight and explore the diversities of Muslim identities, their geographical specificity and variation, and the ways in which markers of Muslim identities are resisted, contested and manipulated in various ways across time and space.

The places where Muslim identities are negotiated, celebrated or resisted matter to how these identities are experienced by Muslims and non-Muslims alike. The geographies of Muslim identities, be they based around neighbourhood connections, national affiliations or regional associations, are important to the ways in which these identities are experienced in everyday lives. Clearly then '... place matters if we want to understand the way social identities are formed, reproduced and marked off by one another' (Smith, 1999: 139). Tied in with the importance of place and the significance of locality are other markers of social difference: 'aside from contestations over meanings, the politics of religious spaces are also tied up with gender, race and class politics, and politics between nations' (Kong, 2001: 217). So, alongside the influence of place and locality on Muslim identities, are other identities that influence people's opportunities, life course trajectories and everyday experiences. Thus, the second aim of this book is to identify and explore the ways in which Muslim identities and geographies interact with, produce, reproduce and rework other significant markers of identity such as gender, race and class.

The chapters in this book focus on experiences of the *Geographies of Muslim Identities* in the context of diaspora, gender and issues of belonging. Whilst geography forms the central underpinning discipline to the collection the contribution of other disciplines and subject fields including sociology, social anthropology, political economy, media studies, gender studies and leisure studies is evident. Through theoretically-informed empirical research many of the chapters seek to challenge dominant understandings of, and associations with, Muslim identities. Overall, this collection brings together research conducted across five continents, in a range of urban, rural, regional and national contexts, and with different social groups and people possessing different forms of Muslim identities.

Muslim Identities: Diaspora Spaces and Communities

The first part of the book explores the transnational experiences of Muslims and the complex hybrid cultures that have developed across diasporic communities. Experiences of migration and mobility are important to the construction, negotiation and contestation of various identities, including religious identities. As Rachel Silvey (2005: 138) argues, migration is a socially embedded process. It reflects and reinforces social organization along multiple axes of differences (including gender, race, class, nation, sexuality, and religion). As migrants often maintain multiple ties to their countries of origin, they create new transnational cultural and social spaces for themselves (Ehrkamp, 2005). Yet these ties are not the only, or even the most important, sources of migrants' identities because their experiences are also shaped by the social networks they establish in their new place of residence, by the larger social and economic milieu of the destination country, by state policies and actions, and by the media's representations of migrant groups. The authors of the four chapters in this section examine the ways in which Muslim identities have been negotiated in new environments and cultures. They explore the movement of peoples from Pakistan to Scotland, Iran to the U.K., Canada, and Australia, Turkey to Germany, and South Asia to Northern Ireland.

Chapter two, 'Beyond the Mosque: Turkish Immigrants and the Practice and Politics of Islam in Duisburg-Marxloh, Germany', by **Patricia Ehrkamp** examines the transnational experience of Turkish immigrants and how they shape the neighbourhood and establish it as their home. She explores the ways in which Islam is practiced and lived by the Turkish immigrants in a neighbourhood, and how these immigrants engage in contestations and struggles over religious meaning and place. The study found that Turkish immigrants in Germany consist of a heterogeneous group with different migration biographies. Their Islamic practices and cultural expressions are far more complex and diverse than the public discourse at the national level suggests. Further, these cultural practices undergo constant change as the lives of Turkish immigrants unfold in German neighbourhoods and cities. Ehrkamp concludes that negotiations of identities and belonging are highly complex, that it is necessary to view identities in more differentiated ways that move beyond the well-known registers of race, class and gender, and that we need to take into consideration the multiplicities of human subjectivity.

Chapter three, by **Cameron McAuliffe** makes an important methodological contribution to understandings of the geographies of Muslim identities, by exploring the contested ways in which diasporic Iranian Muslims are visually represented and how these representations link with gender, age and nation. Based on research with the children of Iranian migrants in Sydney, London and Vancouver, he explores how visual representations of Iran and Muslims in the media intricately shape their experiences of racism. McAuliffe argues that photographs and illustrations that accompany articles about Iran often construct an inscrutable Muslim 'threat'. These visual representations also serve to construct a monolithic Islamic Iran and lead to popular understandings of Iranians as a homogeneous group. The study found that the extent to which the children of Iranian migrants are perceived as 'Muslim' and experience racism depends heavily on how closely they resemble the stereotypical Muslim images in media representations.

Just as global migration and mobility are important to the geographies of Muslim identities, so too are local and regional experiences. Local experiences of negotiating Muslim identities, creating Muslim space and managing other identities alongside this, are significant in helping to understand the experience of being Muslim in various places. Muslim identities are often assumed to be connected to traditional Muslim spaces such as areas of Muslim settlement in cities or areas near mosques or shops where halal meat can be purchased. It is important for geographers to understand the complexity and multiplicity of ways in which Muslim identities are experienced in such locations. As such, in chapter 4, **Sadiq Mir's** challenges the tradition in social geography that associates immigrant communities with the inner-city by focusing upon the middle-class professional identities of Muslims in suburban Glasgow in Scotland, UK. His analysis combines economic and cultural geography in order to explore the new suburban Muslim identities inhabited by his respondents. Mir examines the effects of the suburbanization of the Pakistani community in Glasgow on the cultural landscape and social geography of the city. The study found that the identities of the young and professional suburban Pakistanis are more in line with a middle-class Scottish suburbanite identity (as house-proud homeowners who send their children to good schools, etc.) than a distinctly 'Pakistani' identity. It reveals the diverse, complex, and professionalizing identities of Scottish-born Pakistanis as a crucial influencing factor in the community's dispersal from areas of the city centre to more affluent suburbs. The study thus calls into question the stereotypical and dominant understandings of Britain's black and minority ethnic communities and their perceived association with economic and social marginality or threat.

The final chapter in this section, chapter five, is by **Gabriele Marranci** who explores the processes through which Muslim migrant women in Northern Ireland construct their identity. He argues that a sense of identity is an outcome of the symbolic communication of one's emotional commitment through which a person experiences her/his autobiographical self. According to Marranci, personal identity can be viewed as a 'circuit' connecting the autobiographical-self to the environment and its stability can be disrupted by changes in the environment which may challenge the circuit that composes our identity. Based upon three years of ethnographic work with seventy-six Muslim women, he found that Muslim women in Northern Ireland have developed specific acts of identity through Islamic rhetoric despite facing difficulties integrating within the Northern Ireland community. Through their 'acts of identites', these women were able to foster a sense of being part of Northern Irish society without feeling challenged by its western values and Christian sectarian environment.

Muslim Identities: Gender, Place and Culture

Muslim women have received much attention from geographers interested in the interaction between religion, gender and place (Bowlby *et al.*, 1998, Dwyer, 1999, Falah and Nagel, 2005). As Caroline Nagel (2000: 63) has observed, 'it is difficult to find another group of women (especially one defined in religious terms) that has generated a similar degree of scrutiny and interest'. However, as Claire Dwyer (1998: 53) has emphasised, there has often been a tendency to represent Muslim women as the 'passive victims of oppressive cultures' and as the 'embodiment of a repressive and 'fundamentalist' religion'. This growing body of research has focussed on issues of domesticity, familial relationships and changing patterns of employment rather than exploring the myriad components that make up the culture of everyday life including leisure, sport and the media and the ways in which such cultural forms and processes inform Muslim identities (see for example, Mohammad, 1999; Dwyer, 1999).

In chapter six **Sonja van Wichelen** offers a detailed analysis of the inter-relationships between gender and the media in the representation and re-inscription of Muslim identities and bodies in post-Suharto Indonesia. Her exploration focuses on the mass-mediated but historically situated images and debates relating to the wearing of the veil by Muslim women and the practice of polygamy by Muslim men. Van Wichelen argues that different socio-political periods in Indonesian history have allocated different meanings to the praxis of veiling and polygamy and that such praxis can be seen as part of the process and practice of 'Islamization' in Indonesia. She discusses the increasing visibility of veiled women in public spaces and in the 'mediatized landscapes' of urban centres by exploring two dominant discourses of veiled bodies: the consumerist discourse prevailing in the middle and upper classes and the politicized discourse which appears more frequently in the lower middle class stratum. Van Wichelen then contrasts her findings relating to the veiling of women with the debate surrounding the practice of polygamy by men. She concludes that, while the representations of veiling reaffirm 'Muslimness' rather than femininity, the act of being polygamous appears to reaffirm masculinity rather than Muslim identity. Van Wichelen's chapter thus introduces us to the complex intersections and entanglements of gender and religion in the formation of identity whilst not losing site of the influences of nationality, spatiality and class relations.

In chapter seven **Eileen Green and Carrie Singleton** explore the inter-relationships between gender, leisure and Muslim identities in relation to the growing discourse of fear and risk through their detailed study of young South Asian women's perceptions of risk and risk management strategies in leisure settings in a town in the North-East of England. They argue that whilst there is a wealth of knowledge within the social sciences relating to 'risk society' (Beck, 1992; Giddens, 1991), there is limited research exploring the experiences of young women and the ways in which they manage aspects of risk as part of their everyday leisure lives (Pain, 2001). Through their exploration of the ways in which women create, negotiate and maintain 'safe' spaces for leisure, Green and Singleton argue that leisure, as both embodied and spatially located, can be developed and managed to offer secure and appropriate environments in which young women develop networks of belonging and friendship. As such, leisure is seen as both a site and process in the production, legitimisation, representation and reworking of Muslim identities that intersect gender, sexuality, ethnicity, 'race' and class in everyday life (Aitchison, 2003; 2007).

Kay, in chapter eight, then examines the role of sport as a vehicle for enhancing the social inclusion of young Muslim women within education. Her chapter outlines the workings of an outreach project undertaken in Loughborough in England where an 'Education and Sport' Development Worker was appointed to run an activity programme for female Muslim youth within the town. The chapter explores the role of sport in relation to the Muslim faith and the challenges facing the delivery of female only sport-related programmes. The chapter seeks to contribute to our understandings of being a young Muslim woman in England by drawing attention to family diversity and the dynamics of intra-family relationships as a core component of ethnic identity. Like many of the other chapters in this book, Kay seeks to offer new and nuanced insights into the ways in which Muslim women conduct their day-to-day lives in the context of the varied and sometimes contradictory influences of their religion, the culture of their family's country of origin and their exposure to western values and expectations. Thus, the three chapters in this section each provide evidence, explorations and explanations of the complex and dynamic inter-relationships between Muslim identities, gender, place and culture.

Muslim Identities: Belonging, Attachment and Change

The processes of migration that have been discussed, along with the gendered construction and contestation of Muslim identities, influence the senses of belonging and attachment experienced by Muslims in different places. As Lily Kong (2001: 226) has observed, 'religion, like class and race, must be a matter for historical and place-specific analysis rather than taken as *a priori* theory'. So, understanding the historical development, contestations and changes in Muslim places and landscapes are important to understanding the contemporary nature of the geographies of Muslim identities. Furthermore, Muslim identities also intersect and interact with other identifications, based on, for example, everyday experiences of nationality, caste, gender, age and so on. Political circumstances, economic development and cultural change on the local, national and transnational levels also influence the ways in which senses of belonging, attachment and change are experienced by those identifying as Islamic.

Focusing on post-Soviet central Asia in Chapter nine, **William Rowe** explores this issue in relation to the historical development and transformation of Muslim identities in the region, and the political tensions and ambiguities associated with these changes. He provides a detailed account of the history of Islam in Central Asia, exploring the ways in which the spread of Islam in the region connected with broader political changes, power struggles and economic development. Rowe demonstrates how tensions between Islamic ideologies and government intentions encouraged many Muslims to adapt their religious practices by focusing upon the familial and personal spaces of everyday life. Furthermore, Rowe also discusses religious practices – marriage, burial, architecture – and the ways in which these are responded to, ignored or resisted by government policies and broader societal ideologies.

The geographies of Muslim identities also interact with and influence the development of neighbourhood change, national development and global events. As such, the particular religious connections and affiliations of certain places are likely to influence the extent to which they progress, develop or stagnate. In Chapter ten **Samuel Zalanga** contributes to our understanding in this area by exploring the ways in which economic development in Malaysia and Nigeria interacts with Muslim identities, politics and nationalism. He demonstrates the ways in which geography, locality and culture interact with markers of social difference such as caste, ethnic group and class affiliations. The comparative approach adopted by Zalanga places emphasis on the ways in which everyday religious conduct influences economic, political and social change. Overall, he emphasises the ways in which different factors – political economic, social – influence the ways in which Muslim identities are experienced, and how these identities relate to historical change, economic development and the importance of space and time.

Along with historical influence and development of Muslim identities over time, it is also important to understand contemporary experiences. Furthermore, although a number of chapters in this collection explore Muslim women's experiences, it is also important to understand '… the way in which religious place holds different meanings and exerts different influences on such different constitutions as women, children, teenagers and the elderly' (Kong, 2001: 227). In response to this, **Peter Hopkins**, in the final chapter, challenges the focus of much work in the geographies of Muslim identities by exploring the experiences of young Muslim men following the events of September 11th 2001. In addition to exploring their masculine focus on sport and peer-group, this chapter highlights ways in which the nature of 'the street' changed following September 11th 2001 because of the increased chance of the young men experiencing racism, discrimination and Islamophobia.

The Geographies of Muslim Identities

The various research projects, geographical foci and methods of analysis covered in this collection is evidence of the fact that geographers are starting to take religion, and in this case Islam, seriously, and are approaching this work informed by a wide range of theoretical and methodological approaches. Alongside 'race', class, gender, disability and age, religion is an important marker of identity, a determinant of economic and political circumstances, and an influence over how people experience their everyday geographies. Caroline Nagel (2005: 13) recently noted that 'religion remains curiously absent from many academic accounts of cultural transformation, especially in the discipline of geography'. This collection challenges this absence by providing a series of thought-provoking accounts of the ways in which the geographies of Muslim identities are experienced through gendered, diasporic processes and evaluating how such experiences are linked to emotions and realities of attachment and belonging.

The collection also advances the significance of the *geographies* of Muslim identities. Many studies within the social sciences have explored ways in which Muslim identities are constructed, performed and articulated but the significance of place, the importance of locality, and the role of space in shaping Muslim identities are often neglected by such work (Alexander, 2000). The authors in this collection make important contributions to our understandings of the ways in which place matters in the production and performance of Muslim identities, and their intersections with gender, diaspora and belonging. Muslim identities are influenced by global processes, national politics and regional development strategies, as well as by the ways in which everyday spaces, such as the street, home and mosque, are experienced in a range of emotional, spiritual, inclusive and exclusionary ways. Clearly, geography matters to the construction and contestation of Muslim identities, and this collection exemplifies this through a series of insights into specific local, regional and national contexts all of which emphasise the importance of place and time as significant influences over how Islam is experienced, lived out and practiced on an everyday basis.

References

Aitchison, C.C. (2003) *Gender and Leisure: Social and Cultural Identities*, London, Routledge.

Aitchison, C.C. (ed.) (2007) *Sport and Gender Identities: Masculinities, Femininities and Sexualities*, London, Routledge.

Alexander, C. (2000) *The Asian Gang: Ethnicity, Identity, Masculinity,* Oxford: Berg.

Bauman, Z. (2006) *Liquid Fear*, Polity, Cambridge.

Beck, U. (1992) *Risk Society: Towards a New Modernity*, Sage, London.

Beck, U. (1999) *World Risk Society*, Polity, Cambridge.

Bowlby, S. Lloyd Evans, S. Mohammad, R (1998) Becoming a Paid Worker, in T. Skelton, and G. Valentine (eds) *Cool Places: Geographies of Youth Cultures,* London: Routledge, 229-248.

Brah, A. (1996) *Cartographies of Diaspora,* London: Routledge.

Dwyer, C. (1998) Contested identities: challenging dominant representations of young British Muslim women, in T. Skelton and G. Valentine (Eds) *Cool Places: Geographies of Youth Cultures,* London: Routledge, 50-64.

Dwyer, C. (1999) Contradictions of community: questions of identity for young British Muslim women, *Environment and Planning A*, 31 (1), 53-68.

Ehrkamp, P. (2005) Placing identities: Transnational practices and local attachments of Turkish immigrants in Germany, *Journal of Ethnic and Migration Studies*, 31 (2), 345-364.

Falah, GW. Nagel, C. (eds) (2005) *Geographies of Muslim women,* London: Guilford Press.

Flint, C. (2002) Initial thoughts towards political geographies in the wake of September 11th 2001: an introduction, *Arab World Geographer,* 4 (2), 77-80.

Halliday, F. (1999) 'Islamophobia' reconsidered, *Ethnic and Racial Studies,* 22 (5), 892-902.

Halliday, F. (2002) *Two Hours that Shook the World: September 11, 2001: Causes and Consequences,* London: Saqi Books.

Kong, L. (2001) Mapping 'new' geographies of religion: politics and poetics in modernity, *Progress in Human Geography*, 25 (2), 211-233.

Modood, T. (2003) Muslims and the politics of difference, *Political Quarterly*, 71 (1), 100-115.

Mohammad, R. (1999) Marginalisation, Islamism and the Production of the 'Other's' 'Other', *Gender, Place and Culture,* 6 (3), 221-240.

Nagel, C. (2001) Contemporary Scholarship and the Demystification - and Re-mystification - of "Muslim Women", *The Arab World Geographer*, 4 (1), 63-72.

Nagel, C. (2005) Introduction. GW. Falah and C. Nagel (eds) (2005) *Geographies of*

Muslim Women, London: Guilford Press, 1-15.

Pain, R. (2001) Gender, race, age and fear in the city, *Urban Studies* 38 , 899-913.

Peek, LA. (2003) Reactions and Response: Muslim Students' Experiences on New York City Campuses Post 9/11, *Journal of Muslim Minority Affairs* 23 (3), 271-283.

Silvey, R. (2005) Border, embodiment, and mobility: feminist migration studies in geography, in L. Nelson and J.Seager (eds), *A Companion to Feminist Geography,* Oxford: Blackwell, 138-149.

Smith, SJ. (1999) The cultural politics of difference, in D. Massey, J. Allen and P. Sarre, (eds) *Human Geography Today,* Cambridge: Polity Press, 129-150.

Chapter 2

Beyond the Mosque: Turkish Immigrants and the Practice and Politics of Islam in Duisburg-Marxloh, Germany

Patricia Ehrkamp

Introduction

On November 21, 2004, more than 20,000 people, predominantly of Turkish origin, gathered in Cologne, Germany, to demonstrate for the peaceful coexistence of Muslims and non-Muslims in Germany. Prompted by anti-Muslim violence following the religiously motivated murder of Dutch filmmaker Theo van Gogh, the highly publicized demonstration sought to establish Islam as an accepted religion in Germany, and to dispel assumptions that being Muslim and being at home in Germany were contradictory and irreconcilable identities. German politicians present at the demonstration rushed to affirm that Islam and Christianity ought to be respectful of one another and that there was room for both religions in Germany. Moreover, some politicians sought to emphasize Islam as a permanent fixture in German society. Many politicians stressed the importance of Islam as a 'guestworker' religion in Germany (Der Tagesspiegel, 2004), revealing how Islam has become associated with the permanent settlement of Turkish guestworkers in German cities. In numerous accounts, being Turkish is conflated with being Muslim although only about two thirds of Germany's immigrant population from Turkey describe themselves as Muslims.

In recent years, Islam has been central to German political and public debates about the integration of immigrants primarily of Turkish origin. Certain segments of German society and polity, especially the Green Party and the Social Democrats, welcomed Turkish immigrants' religious expressions as integral to a multicultural outlook for German society. However, highly publicized attempts by Turkish Muslim organizations in Berlin and elsewhere in Germany to establish Islamic instruction in public schools have provoked profound opposition to Islam in Germany. Debates about Muslim women wearing headscarves abound and in 2000, the two German *Bundesländer* (states) of Baden-Württemberg and Niedersachsen (Lower Saxony) passed laws that prohibit Muslim teachers from wearing headscarves in schools. Lower Saxony's Minister of Education and Culture, Renate Jürgens-Pieper, justified her attempts to ban Islamic practices such as wearing the veil by arguing that 'the headscarf is not a necessary article of clothing. It has often become a sort of weapon with which women show that they are Muslim' (Die Zeit, 1998).

Expressions of Islamophobia are often related to the transnational connections that Turkish immigrants create and maintain with their country and places of origin. The widespread availability of Turkish mass media such as satellite television and newspapers and their distribution and visibility in Germany has contributed to the impression that transnational influences have become stronger in recent years and that they have increasingly shaped urban space (Çağlar, 2001). While most immigrants' transnational practices are characterized by friendship and kinship networks, there are also institutional ties that fuel perceptions of Islam as a transnational force that influences immigrants in Germany. For example, as part of its transnational engagement in Germany, the Turkish government's Presidency for Religious Affairs supports DITIB (Diyanet İşleri Türk Islam Birliği – Turkish Islamic Union of the Institute for Religion), an umbrella organization of several Diyanet mosque associations in Germany (Lemmen, 2000). DITIB has ties to the Turkish state, and numerous spiritual leaders of mosques in Germany are selected by the Turkish Presidency for Religious Affairs DIB (*Diyanet Isleri Bakanligi*) that also determines spiritual leaders' qualifications and ensures that their teachings do not contradict or undermine Turkish secularism (Lemmen, 2000).

Beyond such institutional ties, Turkish immigrants' transnational practices have changed German society and altered German cities. Turkish restaurants, teahouses, green grocers and import/export stores are now part and parcel of urban life in Germany. Religious institutions and communal places such as mosques have become integral fixtures of Germany's urban landscapes. These changes to the urban landscape reflect that former Turkish guestworkers have come to stay permanently (Ehrkamp, 2005). Turkish immigrants have increasingly made their voices heard in local and national politics as well as in their civic actions and through institutions of civil society, a number of which are religious organizations (Ehrkamp and Leitner, 2003). Hence, Turkish Muslims and Turkish immigrants more broadly have been claiming their right to stay in Germany, and to participate in German society.

Immigrants from Turkey living in Germany form a heterogeneous population with different migration biographies. Presently, they comprise four generations, the first of which migrated from various regions in Turkey. In addition to the guestworkers recruited in the 1960s, family unification, political turmoil, as well as the persecution of Kurds brought numerous other migrants and refugees from Turkey to Germany. Additionally, the immigrant population from Turkey differs in terms of level of education and political beliefs, and they belong to different ethnic groups and communities of faith. Similarly, their religious practices and beliefs are highly heterogeneous and often intersect with political persuasions, which have at times led to conflicts between subgroups of the Turkish population.

Public discourses at the national level that homogenize Islam and Turkish immigrants fail to consider the multiple differences that exist among immigrants from Turkey and the complexities of immigrants' religious identities and practices (Ehrkamp, 2002). In this chapter, I argue that immigrants' Islamic practices and cultural expressions more generally are far more diverse and complex than monolithic accounts at the national level make them seem. I consider the ways that Turkish immigrants have transformed German society and urban space in order to better accommodate their needs and cultural practices. Rather than being static, these cultural practices undergo constant reiterations in immigrants' everyday lives in German neighbourhoods and cities.

Transnationalism, Religious Identities and Urban Space

Along with the acceleration of globalization and migration, transnational contacts contribute heavily to constructions of migrants' identities. By maintaining multiple ties to their countries of origin, immigrants create new transnational social and cultural spaces for themselves (Faist, 2000), and develop identities across national borders and societies (Glick Schiller, Basch *et al.*, 1992). In order to capture the multiple points of attachment and identification that span across borders, scholars have resorted to describing transnational identities as diasporic (Anthias, 1998). Immigrants continue to maintain ties to their country of origin, but it would be wrong to conceive of these connections as quasi-natural sources of identity because immigrants' experiences are also influenced by local contacts in their new place of residence (Ehrkamp, 2005), by state discourses and actions (Clifford, 1994) and by economic structures and conditions at the national scale that in turn are embedded in processes of economic and cultural globalization (Anderson, 1991).

Religious affiliations and identities have received particular attention in studies of transnationalism and diasporas. Such research focuses on the ways that processes of globalization create and transform transnational religious communities and imaginations (Casanova, 2001). Bowen (2004: 879-80), for example, argues that Islam also 'creates and implies the existence and legitimacy of a global public space ... that ... cannot be reduced to a dimension of migration or of transnational religious movements'. Bowen examines the ways that Islam is (re)interpreted in diaspora, thus emphasizing the spiritual and intellectual space of Islam as diaspora. In contrast, Mandaville (2001a) is interested in the changing nature of Muslim subjectivities in diaspora. Paying particular attention to the political community of Islam, he shows how the transnational realm of Islam might act as a potential space of resistance in which community boundaries and identities are re-articulated.

Yet other research examines more closely the ways that Islam is de-territorialized and re-territorialized through processes of migration and settlement of Muslims as religious minorities in Western Europe (Saint-Blancat, 2002). These studies conceptualize Islam as hybrid and fluid as Muslims negotiate their identities in different contexts and across different societies. This research is particularly helpful in understanding contemporary migrants' experiences and the ways in which Muslim identities and subjectivities are constructed in relation to different places and communities (Dwyer, 1999; 2000). The formation of Islamic identities in Western Europe (Schmidt, 2004; Husain and O'Brien, 2000; Mandaville, 2001a) receives particular attention as Muslim migrants seek to establish themselves in the countries of settlement. Some of this work highlights the problems of integration that Muslims face in the light of Islamophobia and prohibitions of veiling (El Hamel, 2002; Talhami, 2004); while others emphasize that political interpretation of Islam hinder the integration of second and third generation immigrants (Heitmeyer, Mueller *et al.*, 1997).

In Germany, much recent research has focused on the appeal that emanates from Islamism and fundamentalist interpretations of Islam for Turkish immigrants of the second and third generation (Heitmeyer, Mueller *et al.*, 1997; Schiffauer, 1999; Schiffauer, 2001). Schiffauer (2001) shows that young Turkish men in particular are attracted to extremist groups as they vie for acceptance in their Turkish communities and in German society without being considered to be *Deutschländer* (Germanlanders), that is, as having severed their ties to Turkey. The complexities of identities and negotiations of belonging show that it is necessary to view identities in more differentiated ways that move beyond the well-known registers of race, class and gender, and to take into consideration the multiplicities of the human subject (Nagar, 1997a).

Religious identities, as Nagar (1997a; 1997b) points out, are closely related to place (Nagar and Leitner, 1998; Fortier, 1999). In her study of Asians in Dar es Salaam, Nagar shows how communal places are produced through differentiation and exclusion (Nagar, 1997a). Communal places are particularly important for creating a sense of attachment, and a sense of home: they are part and parcel of enacting identities (Fortier, 1999; 2000). Since these identities are multiple, space and places may be contradictory. As they are sites that reinforce identity and empower groups, they may simultaneously be oppressive for subgroups of a community, for example women (Nagar, 2000) or members of lower and less powerful castes (Nagar, 1997b).

It is therefore essential to understand the importance of particular places and urban space in the ways that religious identities are negotiated. Kong (2001b) identifies several ways in which power and politics shape the meaning and the creation of secular and sacred spaces, arguing that the creation of religious places and space need to be understood as exertions of power. It is particularly crucial here not to neglect the power of the state and secular forces that determine which spaces are to be sacred, and in what ways (Kong, 2001a).

Exertions of power need to be understood as part of struggles over meaning and power rather than as fixing power in space (Abu-Lughod, 1990). As Nagar (2000) has demonstrated, the establishment of religious places themselves does not prevent acts of resistance or counter-hegemonic practices. Hence, there are deeply rooted interconnections between religion and (identity) politics in which geographic research is interested. According to Kong, 'the politics surrounding meaning investment in religious places take various forms: tensions between secular and sacred meanings, inter-religious contestations in multi-religious communities, politics between nations, intra-religious conflicts, and gender, class and race politics' (Kong, 2001a: 215).

In the remainder of this chapter I explore such contestations and struggles over religious meaning and place. I focus on a neighbourhood in Germany to examine more closely the ways in which Islam is practiced, lived, and contested within the local immigrant population from Turkey. As the discussions in the following sections show, Turkish immigrants' identities are multiple and shaped by a variety of factors. Religious identities can only be understood in the specific contexts of immigrants' everyday lives that significantly impinge on the ways that identities are constructed, contested, and lived.

Duisburg-Marxloh and its Changing Urban Landscape

Duisburg-Marxloh is a neighbourhood in Germany's heavy industrial Ruhr conglomeration. Located close to the Rhine River, the neighbourhood's urban landscape, all illustrated in (see Fig. 2.1), remains dominated by heavy industries although economic restructuring in the 1990s led to the downscaling of local production sites and caused thousands of jobs to be lost. Two blast furnaces, a nearby coking plant and company housing, however, are remnants of Marxloh's industrial past and present.

Figure 2.1: The industrial landscape surrounding Marxloh

Marxloh's Turkish population first grew when German corporations recruited Turkish guestworkers in the 1960s to work in heavy industries and coal mining. In the 1970s, family members from Turkey followed the original guestworkers. In the 1980s and 1990s, a wave of political refugees from the Turkish left and Kurdish asylum seekers joined the guestworkers and their families. The diverse migration biographies of immigrants from Turkey are but one indicator of the vast heterogeneity of Marxloh's immigrant population. In addition to their biographies, immigrants differ by age, gender, generation, region of origin, political persuasion, and religious orientation, all of which are reflected in immigrants' identities, cultural practices, and the ways that they use and shape neighbourhood space.

Marxloh's urban landscape bears the imprint of its immigrant population from Turkey. Numerous import/export stores for textiles and jewellery, three green grocers, *Döner Kebap* (Turkish fast food restaurants) and other Turkish restaurants, a Turkish bakery and countless other Turkish businesses dominate the commercial streetscape. Several specialized Turkish physicians, a tax consulting service, driving schools and real estate agencies further complete the picture of a thriving Turkish immigrant economy in the neighbourhood.

Numerous communal places that serve the local immigrant population further define Marxloh's urban landscape. More than 25 teahouses provide Turkish men in the neighbourhood with space for socializing. In addition to the local communal places maintained by different Turkish and Kurdish communities in Marxloh, there are also religious places such as mosques and places of worship that facilitate cultural practices and the expression of religious identities.

The following analysis is based on ethnographic research conducted over a period of ten months, six month of which I lived in Marxloh and was a frequent guest in residents' homes, institutions, and communal places, apart from being able to observe behaviour in public space. I conducted formal intensive interviews with 59 Turkish, Kurdish and German residents using a sampling technique that aimed to represent the diversity of the local population along such axes as gender, age, generation, political affiliation and religion. In addition to interviews with residents, the study included expert interviews and more than 200 informal conversations in different neighbourhood settings of Marxloh to further explore the heterogeneity of the local population.

The Practice and Politics of Islam in Marxloh

Religious practices and cultural expressions are important aspects of everyday life in Marxloh as the local Turkish population seeks to shape the neighbourhood and establish it as their home. Different interpretations of Islam and the ways that religious practices shape public and private spaces also serve to structure exclusion of others in the neighbourhood and elicit contestations that I explore in the following sections.

Religious Communities in Marxloh

Over the past few decades, mosques have become integral elements of Marxloh's urban landscape. Six *Moscheevereine* (mosque associations) maintain mosques in the neighbourhood. They cater to different communities although occasionally the members of a particular mosque association will attend prayer at a different mosque. It is noteworthy that there are mosque associations whose relationships with other religious associations are strained. For instance, one local mosque association formed after splitting from another mosque association because of disputes over the handling of financial affairs and donations.

Often, immigrants alter the use of existing buildings for communal places. For example, a store that previously sold wallpaper and paint is now home to one of the local mosque communities, and serves as a mosque (see Fig. 2.2). Other mosques are only recognizable by a small sign that reveals the particular building's new use.

Figure 2.2: Merkez Camii, one of Marxloh's six mosques

While these religious places seem rather inconspicuous in the urban landscape, they are important sites of identification and integral to Turkish immigrants' religious identities. There are important differences between these various mosques and mosque associations. *Moscheevereine* vary according to their organizational structure and their interpretation of Islam. The largest of the local mosques is affiliated with the Germany-wide *Diyanet Isleri Türk Birligi* (Diyanet Turkish Islamic Union) that has its headquarters in Cologne and forms part of the Turkish Presidency for Religious Affairs' efforts of supporting Turkish citizens abroad. Marxloh's Diyanet mosque has a membership of approximately 500 households (Diyanet Moscheeverein, 1998). In addition to regular prayers and Koran instruction, the mosque association maintains a teahouse and provides homework help for local youth.

Another important local (Sunni) community is IGMG/Milli Görüş, which is also part of a Germany-wide hierarchical organization with close transnational organizational ties to Turkey (Lemmen, 2000). It is important to mention Milli Görüş because its national organization in Germany has been accused numerous times of anti-democratic Islamist objectives, and has been under observation by the German *Verfassungsschutz* (anti-terror organization of the Ministry of the Interior) for its political activities which the German government deems anti-democratic (Bundesministerium des Innern, 1999). The organization's publication, Milli Gazete, serves as the major outlet for Islamist propaganda. Additionally, Milli Görüş is considered the religious arm of the Turkish Welfare Party (MHP) of Metin Kaplan, a right-wing Turkish political party that was banned in Turkey and Germany (Ögelman, Money *et al.*, 2002). Hence, this local community is deeply embedded in the transnational social field (Glick Schiller, Basch *et al.*, 1995; Faist, 2000) that the organizational structures and political activities of the broader association create.

In addition to Sunni *Moscheevereine*, the Alevi-Bektaşi community maintains a *Cem Evi* (house of worship) in Marxloh. Alevism is an Anatolian form of religious practice that many scholars deem to have derived from Shi'a Islam (Geaves, 2003) Alevis are not formally recognized as a religious minority in Turkey, and have often been persecuted and suffered violent attacks (Geaves, 2003; Kosnick, 2004). Between 18 to 25 million of Turkish nationals are Alevis (Kosnick, 2004). Among Turkish immigrants in Germany it is estimated that about 35 percent consider themselves Alevi. Similarly, the local Alevi-Bektaşi community in Marxloh states that they represent about a third of the local Turkish population. Located in the space of a former nightclub, Marxloh's Alevi *Cem Evi* serves as a centre for both religious practice and expression, especially for the weekly *Cem* that is celebrated on Thursday evenings. Similar to some of the local mosques, the Alevi *Cem Evi* accommodates a teahouse located in the back of the building that mostly caters to the older men in the community. However, the *Cem Evi* also serves as a communal place and hangout space for Alevi youth who meet there on Sunday afternoons for social gatherings.

The Practice of Islam: Mosques and Beyond

As much as communal places contribute to establishing a common sense of community and belonging in their members, different mosque associations highlight the diversity of faiths and religious practices among Marxloh's Muslim population. Mosque associations' national or transnational organizational ties to umbrella organizations or the Turkish state and other Turkish institutions were of little importance to local immigrants in their choice of affiliation. While most immigrants that participated in this study maintained strong ties to friends and family in Turkey and often vacationed there, they did not consider their affiliation with a particular mosque as part of their transnational ties. Instead, interviewees deemed the interpretation of Islam in a particular *Moscheeverein* to be crucial to their affiliation, and many immigrants reported that family members introduced them to their local community. Hanife, a woman in her thirties and mother of three, sent her son to Koran school at the early age of six in an attempt to foster his sense of belonging to the local mosque association. She relied heavily on her father's connections in order to place her son in the Koran school at a rather early age, and proudly reported that her father's standing in the community helped her son get into the program:

My son... is still too young for the mosque... but I talked to the hoças [religious leaders]... And they said, yes, well, okay, we do that. Because my father has been a member of this community for a very long time, and that's why they tolerated this [admitting her son at young age]. Normally, well, they would not accept such young children.

(Hanife, aged 31, interview, August 1999)

Hanife further described the centrality of the mosque and its religious community for establishing a sense of home and belonging in her extended family. In mentioning her father's role in getting her son into Koran instruction early on, she depicts how much the community values stability, and how length of tenure as a member within the community contributes to higher social standing and greater influence.

In addition to worship, ritual washings, and Koran instruction, local mosques serve a variety of purposes beyond immediate religious practice. Mosques serve as communal places, and larger local mosques include teahouses that offer space for members of the community (usually male) to socialize. Several local mosque associations also offer homework tutoring for children, and some have after-school programs or sewing classes for women. Sevim, a 32-year-old woman, described the mosque's functions as follows:

Well, most of the time, we go there for prayers, and I also send my children there daily, my older children, I mean, to study the Koran. To study the religion, and, um, I and my husband, in general, usually go there to pray, and to social occasions, when there is something [events]. Then we really like to be there.

(Sevim, aged 32, interview, August 1999)

For Sevim, the mosque is essentially a place of worship and the centre of her spiritual and social life, although her family also tried to pray at home five times a day. Religion is not simply a matter of visiting the mosque. This became clear when talking to Osman, a 21 years old in his last year of vocational school training. While he said he attempted to go to the mosque for Friday prayer or on important religious holidays he rarely went there in actuality, and most of his religious practices took place at home. Osman described his faith and prayer as ways of connecting with his family, in particular with his father who had died six years earlier:

I read the Koran every Thursday. [Only these particular verses:] Yasem, that's the name. That's for people who died. [You read these verses] in order to save their spirit from hell. Because, well, they say, every Thursday night, towards midnight, the dead [bodies] come. Well, that's the spirits [ghosts] that circle above the house and wait for someone from the family, one is sufficient, to open the Koran and read these 2-3 pages, that is, three sheets, six pages. I do that. And fasting, of course, but other than that, praying regularly, I don't. I don't have the time.

(Osman, aged 21, interview, April 2000)

Osman's religious practice is thus guided by pragmatism and his desire to reconnect with his father, and most of his religious practice takes place in the private space of his home rather than in the mosque. Religious practice thus varies greatly, not only in the actual practices local immigrants engage in but also in the sites and spaces where worship takes place.

But not all of Marxloh's Muslim residents actively practiced Islam. Many members of the second and third generation of immigrants hardly ever went to the mosque or even prayed at home regularly. For these generations, going to the mosque was a practice that their parents and/or grandparents engaged in rather than part of their everyday life. Ferdane, a woman in her early thirties, for example, while describing herself as a Muslim, distanced herself quite harshly from those who went to the mosque. She explained that her parents' generation, and in particular men who had retired from work, turned to the mosques as a new center for their life. She said:

Well, for many it is like this, during their work life, well, …there was no time for prayer and such things. Yes, maybe it wasn't just that. It is also, it [going to the mosque] keeps them [first generation men] grounded. They have company, cohesion … in the mosque they can get together and chat.

(Ferdane, aged 31, interview, August 1998)

Ferdane's comment highlights the heterogeneity of the local Turkish population. Generational differences overlap and intersect with differences in interpretation of Islam, and in religious practice. As I show in the following section, these differences are also intertwined with the politics of religious expression and interpretation, as some Sunni Muslims contest others' interpretations as well as the political ambitions and prescriptions of certain communities.

Contested Interpretations of Islam

There are significant distinctions between different mosque associations and other communities of faith that divide the local population. For Alp, a member of the original guestworker generation in his early sixties, only one local mosque was acceptable. When asked which mosque he belonged to he replied:

...only Diyanet! Only *Warbruckstrasse* [street address that interchangeably is used as the name for the mosque]. That's the only one you can go to. The others are not good. Way too strict. There is too much force. Religion is not force.

(Alp, personal conversation, February 2000)

He referred to other local mosque associations in Marxloh that he considered fundamentalist and whose interpretation of Islam he found to be too restrictive. In Alp's family, women were free not to wear headscarves and he prided himself on the fact that women in his family made their own decisions about their private and professional lives. His only daughter chose her husband whom she met while on vacation in Turkey, and brought him to Germany. She also deemed other Islamic associations in Marxloh problematic, in particular Milli Görüş, and shared an anecdote about plans she had made with a friend for New Year's Eve celebration when she was younger:

A few years back, my [girl-] friend and I were invited to a couple of parties. I said, "Well, let's go to the first place for a while, and then move on to the second party. We'll have fun. I'll get a bottle of champagne that we can bring to the party". My friend was shocked, and answered that that was absolutely impossible, and that we could not bring alcohol to that party at all. These people are not allowed to have any fun! You can't do this, don't do that. Everything is forbidden, and will result in punishment. I don't get it!

(Ferdane, interview, August 1998)

Clearly, Ferdane challenges what she perceives as the punitive character of her friend's community and is not comfortable with the ways that her friend's community prescribes ways of life that she does not share. In contrast to Ferdane's depiction, Fatma reacted very strongly to criticism directed at Milli Görüş and other religious communities. While Fatma neither wears a headscarf nor describes herself as particularly religious, her mother is veiled, and her parents are members of the local Milli Görüş community. In her interview, Fatma found the bad reputation that Milli Görüş had earned in the German public and among other Turks unfair, and she protested against the criticism levelled at Milli Görüş by other Turkish immigrants:

These people [other Turks in Marxloh] should not talk badly about Milli Görüş at all. They should look and see what people from that community have achieved. Their children are all getting an education, and the families are staying together. There are not such problems like other families in Marxloh have. People don't drink or take drugs and are good people. Children respect their parents and go to school.

(Fatma, aged 32, interview, March 2000)

Hence, challenges arise even between Sunni Muslims belonging to different communities in Marxloh, as various disputes play out in personal friendships as well as in particular spaces. Religious practice is not limited to belonging to a particular mosque community or the practice of going to the mosque or not. Instead, religious persuasion influences the spaces of everyday life beyond religious places and also shapes the lives of those who are not immediate members of a particular community.

Young Turkish women in particular felt that Muslim identities and expectations raised by Sunni Muslim communities significantly shaped neighbourhood space beyond the site of mosques, and affected their everyday lives in undesirable ways. The Turkish women in their twenties and early thirties that I interviewed, for example, noted they did not feel free to dress any way they wanted to in Marxloh. One young woman said that she did not dare wear a mini-skirt or a tank top in Marxloh, even when she was accompanied by her husband. Others felt pressured to wear a headscarf in public although they would not wear one if they were free to choose how to dress and practice Islam. These women all found older Turkish Muslim women, and especially those wearing scarves, to be particularly adamant about the way they expected younger women to dress, thereby extending Islamic space into the neighbourhood's public space rather than confining it to their communal places and private homes. As I suggest in what follows, this notion of Sunni practices 'taking over' spaces beyond private homes and communal places also affects religious minorities among Turkish immigrants.

Local/Transnational Identity Politics

Disagreements about religious differences abound in the everyday lives of Marxloh's residents. Some local immigrants attribute a number of religious, ethnic, and political differences to the immigration experience rather than to differences that also exist in Turkey. For example, Hanife who considers herself a Muslim (without further qualification) suggested that Alevis and Kurds were the ones who created divisions among the Turkish population:

Patricia: You are a Sunni Muslim, then?

Hanife: Um, yes. Says them.

Patricia: Says them?

Hanife: Say the Kurds, the Alevis. We don't differentiate/divide like that, you know? But they do that, they say, they are Alevis, we are Sunnis, like that. I only learned this word [Sunni] in Germany. And my parents say, too, they did not know that before [in Turkey]. But since the Alevis have been setting themselves apart, and have, have said, we are Alevis, we are not, no Sunnis, we are not like you, [raising her voice] we are different, that's how we got to know that [Sunnism, Alevism]. And that's just how it is.

In the above interview segment, Hanife clearly distances herself from other groups of immigrants, while using their practice and politics of difference to accuse them of causing dividing lines between Muslims. Interestingly, Hanife characterizes this othering among Turkish immigrants as a phenomenon of their migration to Germany since neither she nor her parents were aware of such differences while living in Turkey. In Hanife's opinion, it is the minority Alevi community that creates tensions by insisting that their religion and culture is different from that of Sunni Muslims.

Hanife's family migrated to Germany well before religious and ethnic minorities in Turkey were attempting to receive official minority status and the protection of their minority rights. This may be one of the reasons why Hanife and her family attribute differences between Muslims to living in Germany. Similarly, Bozkurt, a second generation immigrant noted that differences between migrants' religious and ethnic identities in Germany emerged over time. He said:

It isn't like that with the older people. Honestly not. Many of the first generation, you can ask them, they don't even know what 'Alevi' means... For example in Erzinjan, there are many Alevis. They live there, live in my village as well. They come and go, and even sometimes marry each other [intermarry with other religious groups]. There is no problem! Only because now there are some boneheads here, they want a little bit of power.

(Bozkurt, aged 34, interview, March 2000)

Clearly, Bozkurt was attuned to the power struggles between different groups, struggles that he deemed counterproductive to improving the situation of immigrants in Marxloh and more generally in Germany, which he mentioned later in our interview. However his comments, as with those of Hanife, need to be understood with regard to his position as a member of the Sunni majority in the local Turkish population. Members of the Turkish Sunni majority have the luxury of not making distinctions between Turkish immigrants in order to assert their identities because they are part of the dominant religious group. In addition, Sunni Turks are often oblivious to the persecution and oppression that Alevis have faced in Turkey, or try to downplay such oppression, which becomes evident in Bozkurt's statement that "there is no problem".

Contrary to such depictions, Alevis among Marxloh's Turkish population maintain that indeed there were problems that arose from their minority status. Alevis interviewed for this study clearly sought to set themselves apart from Sunni Muslims and insisted that their religious practice and community differed tremendously from Sunni Islam. One example they cited numerous times was that women and men were not gender-segregated during worship at the *Cem*. More importantly, local Alevis expressed how much they felt oppressed both in Turkey and in Germany. Alevi experiences in Turkey were shaped by their minority status and various states of oppression over the course of several centuries (Geaves, 2003). Alevis' fears and perceptions of disempowerment were heightened by violent attacks on Alevi leaders and communal places in Turkish cities during the 1990s. These events in Turkey affected the lives of Marxloh's Alevi community, which demonstrates how strong transnational ties affect local everyday life and identities of Alevis in Germany.

For Alevis, being part of a minority group among Turkish immigrants in Germany brought additional challenges to their position as immigrants in Marxloh. A number of Alevis reported that they had faced direct confrontation by other immigrants from Turkey, especially because religious identities intersect and overlap with ethnic identities and political persuasions. Fikriye, the 20 year old daughter of a native German mother and Turkish father, commented on her Alevi faith after a heated discussion with several other young Turks, some of whom were conservative Sunnis and members of the Grey Wolves, the youth organization of MHP, a nationalist Turkish party. Two young men had challenged her in the conversation, in part by mocking her for wearing a golden sword on her necklace. One of the young men had asked if Fikriye "was siding with the Kurds these days," about which she said later:

> I wear Ali's sword because I am an Alevi [woman], that's my faith. When Kaya makes these comments about Kurds, I feel insulted, too, because many Kurds are Alevis, and I'm not sure if he means Kurds or Alevis. Why does he think that he is better and needs to tell everyone what they should or shouldn't do anyway?

(Fikriye, aged 20, interview, April 2000)

Fikriye was furious because Kaya ascribed an ethnicity to her that she did not identify with herself. Lumping together Alevi faith and Kurdish ethnicity reveals Kaya's political persuasions, and his verbal assault on Fikriye needs to be understood as an exertion of power. Fikriye's reaction to Kaya's attack against Kurds highlights the close links and intersections between religious, ethnic, and particularly political identities of Turkish immigrants. Since many of Germany's Turkish immigrants came from Southeast Turkey, a region of great ethnic, religious and political diversity, different identities and political persuasions intersect and become entangled as immigrants negotiate their local lives. The tremendous differences in immigrant identifications render visible the complexities of migrants' lives in the transnational era.

Alevis more generally found their everyday lives to be difficult because Sunni Turkish immigrants asserted their majority position in Marxloh, as well as in Germany more broadly. As Kosnick (2004) has shown, Alevis in Germany struggle to make their voices heard in a number of ways. Members of the local Alevi- Bektaşi association described how their children who were attending Turkish courses in schools had to learn about Turkey's dominant Sunni religion rather than being able to learn about the Alevi faith (WAZ, 1995). Parents and community representatives found this to be problematic because it perpetuated and fostered Sunni Muslim dominance. Indications of such difficulties and Alevis' struggles to overcome them were manifested in demonstrations and commemorative marches in Marxloh's streets. Alevis in Marxloh used their local religious association and the public space of the neighbourhood for political expression geared towards raising awareness for their problems as minority among Turkish immigrants in Germany *and* as religious minority in Turkey. Problems in Marxloh are thus deeply intertwined with transnational politics and connections. The local Alevi community's attempts to promote their community of faith as a religious minority, while simultaneously seeking acceptance in Germany and Turkey, highlights the multiple scales at which Alevi identity politics operate. As Ehrkamp and Leitner (2003) suggest, immigrants may use civil rights granted to them by the receiving society to make their causes public and to challenge the state of origin, which may well contribute to perceptions that differences between migrants are a phenomenon of the immigration situation.

However, not only local Alevis are affected by and contest the dominance of Sunni Muslim practices in their neighbourhood. One Turkish couple, refugees from the Turkish state's oppression of Kurds and the political left in the 1980s and 1990s, and self-described atheists reported that they felt that Sunni Muslim practice was taking over the neighbourhood, including their private lives. In our interview, they discussed the ways that their daughter had been influenced by her Turkish teacher in school. The teacher had taught the pupils the Sunni practice of kissing parents' hands in order to receive gifts and sweets on *Seker Bayramı* (Festival of Breaking the Fast), the day that marks the end of the month of Ramadan. Accordingly, Ali and Zehra's daughter woke up her rather surprised parents by kissing their hands. Ali and Zehra reported that they were initially confused because they were not accustomed to this practice. They found out from their daughter that her teacher (who Ali and Zehra deemed a Sunni Muslim) had taught them that the act of kissing their parents' hands was a Turkish rather than an Islamic practice, thereby (either inadvertently or expressly) implying that all Turks were Sunni Muslims who needed to behave accordingly.

This story reflects two important issues. First, the teacher, a member of the Sunni majority among Turkish immigrants, simply assumed that there was no reason to differentiate between being Turkish and being Muslim. The teacher's attitude reflects her comfortable position as part of the majority, whom seldom need to reflect on their own identities. Secondly, it shows another way of creating a Muslim space, here in a Turkish language classroom (that by extension affects and changes Ali and Zehra's home space), thus confirming how much the creation of religious space is an exertion of power (Kong, 2001a) that elicits contestations and resistance.

Conclusions

While homogenizing discourses at the national scale in Germany often depict Turkish immigrants as Muslims without paying much attention to the great heterogeneity and conflicting identities of Germany's immigrant population, the local case study reveals important differences in immigrants' lived experiences, and varying interpretations of Islam. The local practice and politics of Islam vary according to gender, generation, and belonging to particular Sunni mosque associations or the Alevi community. Family ties and particular interpretations of Islam determine local immigrants' affiliations with different religious associations. But interviews with second and third generation Muslims reveal that they often do not practice Islam at all. Contrary to what Heitmeyer *et al.* (1997) suggest, this shows that Islam and/or Islamism may not necessarily be attractive for younger Turkish immigrants. Although many young Turkish immigrants practice Islam, young women often disagree with the ways that Islamic practice and discourse shape the neighbourhood in ways that restrict their freedom of expression and dress.

While communal places such as mosques play an important role in religious practices as Turkish immigrants enact local belonging to their communities, the practice of Sunni Islam or Alevism is not limited to communal places. Many local immigrants choose not to actively practice Islam, while others limit their religious practice to the private home in attempts to connect with family members. Hence, the spaces of religious practice vary.

As the dominant Sunni population's interpretation and practice of Islam spill out from communal places and private homes, they come to define neighbourhood space as 'Muslim', which needs to be understood as exertions of power (Kong, 2001). Alevis and Atheists contest and resist such exertions of power in public neighbourhood space and schools. Such contestations of Sunni practices brought about by Alevis and Atheists complicate simplistic notions of religious identities and places. For Atheists, the contestation of Islam is about their ability to live their local lives and define their home space away from the influence of Islam. For Alevis, experiencing exertions of power in the local neighbourhood is deeply entangled with experiences of oppression in Turkey. The local and transnational scales are articulated in religious practices and identity politics. As Alevis use the local space to make the situation of Alevis in Turkey known, they engage in multi-scalar practices (Ehrkamp and Leitner, 2003) that politicize religious identities.

Transnational ties and connections influence the politics of Islam in Marxloh although many interviewees did not deem these ties important for their local practice of Islam. Most local faith-based associations are deeply embedded in wider national and transnational organizations and networks as the examples of Diyanet and Milli Görüş show, and interpretations of Islam taught and practiced in local communities are directly linked to the wider organizations. The transnational politics of Islam become especially important for the local Alevi community that finds their lives in Marxloh and Germany to be influenced by dominant Muslim groups.

Hence, in the context of transnational migration, the creation of religious places and sacred space needs to be examined not only in relation to the current place of migrants' residence, but also in relation to ties and connections with the country of origin and religious politics there. In particular, it is important to pay attention to the specificities and spatialities of everyday life at different scales to understand how geographies of Muslim identities are lived, expressed, and contested.

Acknowledgements

This research was supported by an NSF Dissertation Improvement Grant (BCS-0000282) as well as by grants from the AAG and the University of Minnesota. The research would not have been possible without the generosity and hospitality of Marxloh's residents. Ole R. Gram and Mei-Po Kwan provided helpful comments on earlier versions of this chapter. All remaining errors are mine.

References

Abu-Lughod, L. (1990) The romance of resistance: tracing transformations of power through Bedouin women, *American Ethnologist*, 17 (1), 41-55.
Anderson, K. (1991) *Vancouver's Chinatown: Racial Discourse in Canada, 1875-1980*, Montreal, Buffalo: McGill-Queen's University Press.
Anthias, F. (1998) Evaluating 'diaspora': beyond ethnicity?, *Sociology*, 32 (3), 557-580.
Bowen, J.R. (2004) Beyond migration: Islam as a transnational public space, *Journal*

of Ethnic and Migration Studies, 30 (5), 879-894.

Çağlar, A.S. (2001) Constraining metaphors and the transnationalisation of spaces in Berlin', *Journal of Ethnic and Migration Studies*, 27 (4), 610-613.

Casanova, J. (2001) Religion, the New Millenium, and globalization (2000 Presidential Address), *Sociology of Religion*, 62 (4), 415-441.

Clifford, J. (1994) Diasporas, *Cultural Anthropology*, 9 (3), 302-338.

Der Tagesspiegel Online (2004) Islam-Demo für den Frieden in Köln', *Der Tagesspiegel Berlin* (Online Edition) http://ww.tagesspiegel.de/tso/aktuell/artikel. asp? TextID=44449; last accessed March 10, 2005.

Die Zeit (1998) Worte der Woche, *Die Zeit*, Hamburg, 3.

Diyanet Moscheeverein (1998) *Diyanet Merkez Camii Pollmann - Wer sind wir? Mit diesem Faltblatt stellen wir uns ganz kurz vor*, Duisburg-Marxloh, Germany: Diyanet-Moscheeverein.

Dwyer, C. (1999) Contradictions of community: questions of identity for young British Muslim women, *Environment and Planning A*, 31 (1), 53-68.

Dwyer, C. (2000) Negotiating diasporic identities: young British South Asian Muslim women, *Women's Studies International Forum,* 23 (4), 475-486.

Ehrkamp, P. (2002) Turkish immigrants' politics of belonging: identity, assimilation discourse and the transformation of urban space in Duisburg-Marxloh, Germany, unpublished Ph.D. dissertation, geography. Minneapolis, University of Minnesota, p. 240.

Ehrkamp, P. (2005) Placing identities: transnational practices and local attachments of Turkish immigrants in Germany, *Journal of Ethnic and Migration Studie*s, 31 (2), 345-364.

Ehrkamp, P. and H. Leitner (2003) Beyond national citizenship: Turkish immigrants and the (re)construction of citizenship in Germany, *Urban Geography*, 24 (2), 127-146.

El Hamel, C. (2002) Muslim diaspora in Western Europe: the Islamic headscarf (hijab), the media and Muslims' integration in France, *Citizenship Studies*, 6 (3), 293-308.

Faist, T. (2000) Transnationalization in international migration: implications for the study of citizenship and culture, *Ethnic and Racial Studies*, 23 (2), 189-222.

Fortier, A.-M. (1999) Re-membering places and the performance of belonging(s), *Theory, Culture & Society*, 16 (1), 41-64.

Fortier, A.-M. (2000) *Migrant Belongings. Memory, Space, Identity*, Oxford and New York: Berg.

Geaves, R. (2003) Religion and ethnicity: community formation in the British Alevi community, *NUMEN*, 50 (1), 52-70.

Glick Schiller, N., L. Basch, C. Blanc-Szanton (1992) Towards a definition of transnationalism, in N. Glick Schiller *et al.* (eds), *Toward a Transnational Perspective on Migration*, New York: New York Academy of Sciences, pp. 1-24.

Glick Schiller, N., L. Basch, C. Blanc-Szanton (1995) From immigrant to transmigrant: theorizing transnational migration, *Anthropological Quarterly*, 68 (1), 48-64.

Heitmeyer, W., J. Mueller, H. Schroeder (1997) *Verlockender Fundamentalismus*,

Frankfurt: Edition Suhrkamp.

Husain, F. and M. O'Brien (2000) Muslim communities in Europe: Reconstruction and transformation, *Current Sociology*, 48 (4), 1-13.

Kong, L. (2001a) Mapping 'new' geographies of religion: politics and poetics in modernity, *Progress in Human Geography*, 25 (2), 211-233.

Kong, L. (2001b) Religion and technology: refiguring space, place, identity and community, *Area*, 33 (4), 401-413.

Kosnick, K. (2004) "Speaking in One's Own Voice": representational strategies of Alevi Turkish migrants on open-access television in Berlin, *Journal of Ethnic and Migration Studies*, 30 (5), 979-994.

Leitner, H. (2004) Local lives, transitional ties, and the meaning of citizenship: Somali histories and herstories from small town America, *Bildhaan – An International Journal of Somali Studies,* 4, 44-64.

Lemmen, T. (2000) *Islamische Organisationen in Deutschland*, Bonn: Friedrich-Ebert-Stiftung.

Mandaville, P. (2001a) Reimagining Islam in diaspora: the politics of mediated community, *Gazette*, 63 (2-3), 169-186.

Mandaville, P. (2001b) *Transnational Muslim Politics: Reimagining the Umma*, London and New York: Routledge.

Nagar, R. (1997a) Communal places and the politics of multiple identities: The case of Tanzanian Asians, *Ecumene*, 4 (1), 3-25.

Nagar, R. (1997b) The making of Hindu communal organizations, places, and identities in postcolonial Dar es Salaam, *Environment and Planning D: Society and Space*, 15 (6), 707-730.

Nagar, R. (2000) "I'd rather be rude than ruled": gender, place and communal politics among South Asian communities in Dar es Salaam, *Women's Studies International Forum*, 23 (5), 571-585.

Nagar, R. and H. Leitner (1998) Contesting social relations in communal places: Identity politics among Asian communities in Dar es Salaam in R. Fincher and J.M. Jacobs (eds), *Cities of Difference*, New York: The Guilford Press, pp. 226-251.

Ögelman, N., J. Money, et al. (2002) Immigrant cohesion and political access in influencing foreign policy, *SAIS Review*, 22 (2), 145-165.

Saint-Blancat, C. (2002) Islam in diaspora: between reterritorialization and extraterritoriality, *International Journal of Urban and Regional Research*, 26 (1), 138-151.

Schiffauer, W. (1999) Islamism in the Diaspora: the fascination of political Islam among second generation German Turks, *Transnational Communities Programme Working Paper Series*, 99.

Schiffauer, W. (2001) Auf der Suche nach Anerkennung im Spagat zwischen zwei Kulturen, *Der Bürger im Staat*, 51 (4), 226-232.

Talhami, G.H. (2004) European, Muslim and female, *Middle East Policy*, 11 (2), 152-168.

WAZ (Westdeutsche Allgemeine Zeitung) Ausgabe Duisburg-Nord (1995), *Alevitischer Kulturverein trauert um Kemal Davir*, December 13.

Chapter 3

Visible Minorities: Constructing and Deconstructing the 'Muslim Iranian' Diaspora

Cameron McAuliffe

Introduction

One of the strongest visual signifiers in contemporary geopolitics is the Muslim veil. Whether it is the *burkha* of an Afghan woman, the *chador* of the women of Iran and other 'Middle Eastern' states, or the headscarves of French schoolgirls, the Muslim veil has become, in political and wider public discourse, a readily recognisable and increasingly deployed marker of difference. This chapter looks at the way visual representations of Islam are being used to construct particular ideas about Muslims and their religion and how these representations are selectively consumed by those who are constructed as Muslim. Beyond the analysis of the form and impact of representations of Islam in a Western context, this chapter also explores how representations of religion are tied to national discourses of belonging and how this limits our understanding of racism[1] towards Muslims. In terms of the geographies of Muslim identities, representations of Islam in the media typically construct discourses of belonging set at the scale of the nation producing dialectical tensions between religious nationals and informing a territorial relationship to religion, one that is felt in the nations of the West despite their avowed secularism.

Following the seminal work of Edward Said (1978, 1997) there has been a great deal of research undertaken on Muslim representations in the mainstream Western media. In particular, contemporary research has focused on the demonisation of Muslims in the West (see Parekh *et al.*, 2000; Richardson, 2001, 2004; Hafez, 2000, 2000a; Poole, 2000; Roushanzamir, 2004; Bell, 1992; Brasted, 2001; Wilkins and Downing, 2002; Macmaster and Lewis, 1998; Lueg, 1995; Glass, 1996; El-Farra, 1996; Runnymede Trust, 1997). Much of this research, which relates to wider issues of racism in the press, centres on the construction of a monolithic Islam set in contest with the West, broadly within Said's discourse of Orientalism, and concurrent with critiques of Huntington's (1993) flawed thesis of a 'Clash of Civilisations'.

---

1   Racism here is taken to include all acts of intolerance based on 'race', religion and ethnicity. In this chapter there is no room to go into this debate over the applicability of the term 'racism' to acts of religious minority intolerance. It is enough to say that the boundaries of race and religion are blurred and that intolerance against one of these often implies intolerance against the other.

Importantly, within this 'clash' it is national groups, and not religious 'Empires', that dominate the context of investigations. Nationally contextualised research projects understand 'the West' through the local national scale producing 'the Western nation' versus Islamic national groups, mirroring Huntington's 'religious civilisation' focus at a different geopolitical scale. Studies conform to methodological nationalism (Wimmer and Glick Schiller, 2002) being conducted within nations investigating how national media mobilise public opinion in the name of national interest. The mobilisation of opinion aims to ensure the security of the nation-state, as a secular, territorially defined, cultural and political form, through warning of the perceived negative impacts of 'religion' for the 'secular state'. Increasingly, in contemporary debates the threat of religion is generally equated to the threat of Islam. Whilst the nation is mobilised in its own defence, Islam itself is investigated as a national discourse, becoming an investigation of Islam through Bangladeshi youth (Eade, 1998), or Pakistani women (Dwyer, 1999, 1999a, 2000), or Lebanese 'ethnic crime' (Collins *et al.*, 2000). This national geography of investigation reinforces the strength of underlying discourses of national belonging in discussions of identity, helping to structure debates by drawing national identities into convergence with religious identities without challenging the essentialised national religious stereotypes that result. Said recognised the importance of national discourses to the structures of Orientalism noting that it is through the constructed myths of the Orient that Islam has been given 'the authority of a nation' (1978: 307). It is hoped that this chapter will step into the debate and help draw important distinctions between the nation and religion in the construction of, and subsequent investigation of, religious minorities.

This discussion of Islam in the media begins with a national group of Iranian origin, and is based on research conducted with the children of Iranian migrants, the second generation, from different religious backgrounds in Sydney, London and Vancouver.[2] This research does not assume that to study Iran is to investigate Islam. Rather, Iran is chosen in this case as the container of diversity against which the assumptions of a homogenously Muslim Iran need to be set. The national category of Iran was chosen, not because it allows an investigation of the realities of Islam, but because the assumption of a wholly Islamic Iran is not a valid starting point. Migrants from Iran and their children living in the three cities under investigation do not represent a discrete 'community'. As Sreberny notes in her work with people of Iranian background in Britain, "To ask 'Where is the Iranian community in London?' is to assume that one exists" (2000: 183). In fact, Iranians in the diaspora represent multiple possible communities based on complex interactions between national, ethnic, religious and linguistic identities (amongst other possible trajectories of communal identity). The choice of investigating Iranian representations within the three national contexts

---

2   The research for this paper was completed as a part of PhD research into the future directions of multiculturalism in Australia, Britain and Canada conducted through the University of Sydney. The research investigated the way the children of Baha'i and Muslim Iranian migrants negotiated their identities, particularly focussing on the intersections of national and religious identities within the context of multicultural policy and representations of Iran and Iranians in the mainstream media. The research was conducted between 2000 and 2003 in Sydney, London and Vancouver.

allows a clearer investigation of the elision of significant 'national Others' from the map of Iran in the Western media. This is done whilst at the same time investigating the conflation of Muslim identities with the constructed (Arab/Middle Eastern/Oriental) Iranian identity to produce an essentialised and monolithic Muslim Iranian Other. The focus on the national geopolitical context, rather than through the exclusive lens of religion, makes sense in the light of the way that media representations of Iran have become increasingly emblematic of wider international Islam in recent times. Even throughout the dominant media coverage of the recent US-led incursions in Iraq and Afghanistan, Iran has remained the focus of US ire, through its constructed position in the 'Axis of Evil', as a 'state sponsor of terror', and a 'nuclear threat', and hence has remained consistently visible in media representations.

The Media and Meaning

The media plays an important role in defining communal forms through the selective deployment of representations of people and places (Herman and Chomsky, 1988; Hall, 1997; van Djik, 1987). In particular, visual representations are central in the construction of essential stereotypes associated with different groups of people. This ocular centrality in human-environment relations, particularly in the Western intellectual tradition (Langford, 2005), demands the attention of geographers. Gillian Rose (2001) asserts that one aspect of media representations that has been inadequately dealt with in academic discussions is the impact of photographs in the construction of meaning. Recent work on affective and representational geographies has challenged limitations of discussions to the visual, pointing to the importance of the other senses in building a comprehensive understanding of relations to place (see Porteous, 1985; Smith, 1997; Jazeel, 2005; Dunbar-Hall and Gibson, 2004; Connell and Gibson, 2003, 2004; Gibson and Connell, 2005). Yet, the role of visual representations of people and places in understanding issues of identity and belonging remains under-researched.

Despite the contemporary recognition of the photographic image as a mediated representation of reality (Barthes, 1972; Hall, 1997; Rose, 2001), the photographic image in journalism remains imbued with the power of objective evidence (Griffin, 2004). Photographs in the print media are used to provide evidence for the written stories of journalists (Geraghty, 2000) with the inclusion of images in articles producing a testament to the 'witnessing' of events. In this sense, photographs are used as supporting evidence for the claims of a 'professional norm of objectivity' in journalism (Richardson, 2004: 45) imbuing photographs in newspapers with 'factual' depth. In this context photographs and their associated captions help to 'anchor' (Barthes, 1977) meaning, to make the meaning of an article more stable (Geraghty, 2000). The claims to objectivity in reporting have been shown to be fallacious with a 'value-free' or 'unbiased' journalism tending to reproduce dominant power relations where 'balance' equates to 'white (male) values' (Santos, in Richardson, 2004: 44). This implication of objectivity in the nascent power relations of the media environment tends towards the continuation of "an imbalance between the representation of the already privileged on the one hand, and the already underprivileged on the other"

(Fowler, in Richardson, 2004: 45). Whilst there are wide ranging critiques of the perils of the concentration of media ownership and journalistic bias on content that influence these truth claims in journalism in a wider context (Zelizer *et al.*, 2002; Tiffen, 2000; Hardt, 2000), the power of photographs to convey 'the truth' remains relatively unchallenged (Hardt, 2004).

The constructed nature of photographs as truth claims has been widely discussed in theories of representation. These claims to the reproduction of reality in the image have been questioned across the threefold reality of the visual image; the image production, the actual claims of the image itself, and consumption of the image (Rose, 2001). Gillian Rose, in her extensive survey of visual methodologies states, "all visual representations are made in one way or another, and the circumstances of their production may contribute towards the effect they have" (2001: 17). In production of an image, objectivity is interrupted by questions over who took the image, why did they chose a particular composition, and, in the case of journalism, who selected the image for publication and why. In a related sense, it is also necessary to ask why any particular photograph was taken at all (as opposed to any other). The questions over these selective criteria of the production of photographs imply a decision-making process embedded in networks of power relations. In the case of the media's use of photographs, these decisions are subject to the relations of power, directly by the owners and operators of media corporations (McChesney, 2003), and less directly by the networks of elite politicians and owners of capital within which media owners circulate (Murdoch, in Richardson, 2004). The image itself is made up of components or elements influenced by the different technologies in use (e.g. whether the image is in black and white or colour) or influenced by particular social practices (e.g. is the photo to be sold for commercial use, or is it a tourist photograph?). Of great importance to an image's own effects is its 'compositionality', the arrangement of the elements within the frame of the image, and what this tells us about the image's 'way of seeing' (Rose, 2001: 24). Finally, the truth claims of an image are interrupted by the contingency inherent in the consumption of the image. Representations have the potential to tell as many stories as there are people who come in contact with them. Constructivists such as Stuart Hall (1997), claim that there is a space of interpretation between the image and the viewer where meaning is constructed. Meaning is produced from media representations through the distinctive readings of individual viewers, whose own context rules their understanding, interpretation and negotiation of the representation. The image means nothing until it is read, a wholly context-driven and contingent process. Hall notes that the 'preferred meaning' (Hall, 1997)[3] of the image is interrupted by the audience through the contingent act of consumption of the representation.

The social identities of the consumers of media representations are intimately tied to the construction of meaning. As will be discussed in this chapter for the case of the children of Iranian migrants in Sydney, London and Vancouver from Muslim and Baha'i backgrounds, the ongoing negotiation of individual and group identities is influenced by the representations of Iran and Iranians in the press. The choice of what

---

3   Preferred meaning in this sense is the intention that results from the decision processes of image production (i.e. selection, composition, editing, publication, distribution, etc.).

identity an individual takes is not made in a value-free social environment. Decisions over self-identity are contingent upon the available social space for their expression. That is, decisions over the negotiation of identity are made by *and* for the individual, as agency over self-representation is set within wider networks of understanding the Other. The media is one such structurating force, which through representation, attempts to convey particular meanings to society at large (Hall, 1997). It is against these structures that the individual seeks to claim agency (Giddens, 1986). Negotiation of, and contestation over, individual identity by the children of Iranian migrants needs to be therefore predicated on a discussion of media representations of Iran and Iranians so we may understand the context against which these negotiations are set. Through investigation of the media we can analyse the social framework that is both constituted by, and constitutive of, the practices of media agenda-setting set within national geopolitical and sociocultural contexts (Louw, 2001).

Iranian 'Muslims' in the media

Whilst there has been a great deal of recent research on Islam in the media, to date there has been little direct research on the form of media representations of Iranians.[4] The representations of Iranians in the media centre on particular media frames that essentialise Iran and Iranians. Photographs and illustrations that accompany articles about Iran often construct an inscrutable Muslim threat (Richardson, 2004; Poole, 2002; Hippler, 1995; Hippler and Lueg, 1995). Figure 3.1 presents an image taken from an article on the rise of the internet in Iran, featured in the Internet Technology (IT) section of *The Guardian*'s London edition. This image captures some examples of standard themes used in representations of Iran. The article itself begins with an illustration of a woman in purdah sitting at a computer. She is rendered anonymous through her wearing of the *chador*, stripped of agency; a point neatly juxtaposed in this image against her use of the computer and by extension the internet. It is worth noting here that the full-face covering in the illustration, whilst typical of Islamic dress codes upheld in some majority Muslim nations, is not the standard accepted form in Iran where the *hijab* covers the hair and leaves the face uncovered. Illustrations such as this in the print media are not subject to the same evidential truth claims as photographs. However, this representation alludes to the same themes found in many photographs in news articles about Iran; themes of repression, anonymity, and the wider role of women in an Iranian society under the rule of Islam. As a case in point, this same article continues to include an easily recognisable full colour photograph of an anonymous woman walking in front of a large mural of the Ayatollah Khomeini in Tehran. This second image, like the first illustration, dominates the page. Yet,

---

4   One notable exception is a recent study by Elli Lester Roushanzamir (2004) who investigates representations of Iran in the mainstream media looking at the form of representations of Iranian women in the print media in the US. This work parallels the research in this study in the Canadian, Australian and British contexts highlighting the importance of considering how visual representations of Iran and Iranian women in particular construct a monolithic Islamic Iran. See also Naficy (1993), Sreberny (2000), and Keshishian (2000) on relationships between diasporic Iranians and the media.

unlike the illustration, the photograph does not deal directly with the theme of the article, the availability of the Internet in Iran, but instead draws on wider issues of gender in Islam. Such a use of imaging women, often out of context, is typical of the way a media frame has been built up around Iran (Roushanzamir, 2004).

Murals of Ayatollah Ruhollah Khomeini, mainly in Tehran, are commonly featured in photographs accompanying articles about Iran. The visual representations of the Ayatollah signify the panoptic gaze of the theocratic state and by extension the ubiquitous nature of the institutional (male) repression of the (female) populous. The ubiquity of representations of anonymous veiled women in articles concerning Iran in the Western mainstream media serves to gender Iran as female (Roushanzamir, 2004) and subject to the colonisation of the masculine Islamic religious apparatus. In this context, the media conforms to wider geopolitical discourses of the liberation of the Middle East from these unnatural structures of oppression. The assumption of this discourse of decolonisation is that Islam is not a natural part of society, but an antisocial foreign body that once removed would leave 'society' to find its natural democratic values.[5]

Figure 3.1: Illustration of woman in the *chador*
Source: © Emma Dodd.

---

5   This discursive construction of the separateness of Islam to societies in the Middle East was clearly seen in the US rhetoric in the lead up to the Afghan and Iraq conflicts, where Donald Rumsfeld and George Bush (and subsequently by Tony Blair in Britain and John Howard in Australia) continually emphasised the ease with which religion could be removed from the structures of power for the benefit of 'the people'. The inadequacy of this discourse is further typified by the change in the rhetoric once US forces were 'on the ground' as the process of decolonisation of Islam particularly in the case of Iraq, has become not merely more difficult, but ultimately unachievable. Indeed, the irony can not be avoided when the results of the recent historic 'democratic' elections in Iraq have successfully installed a religious government where before a secular regime held power.

Figure 3.2 from *The Sydney Morning Herald* shows the use of the signifying anonymous Muslim female completely out of context, accompanying an article on the imminent arrival of International Atomic Energy Agency (IAEA) inspectors in Tehran. The women, identified only as "students", are unified by the signifying *hijab*, which constructs a metaphorical extension that these are the faces of all Iranian women, and in turn that all Iranian women are Muslim. The accompanying caption reinforces the preferred meaning, producing the women as anonymous and homogenised, universally subject to the repression of the *mullah*s who control Iran behind a "veil of secrecy". It is the caption which anchors the meaning of the image, bringing the two discursive worlds of text and image together to structure the intention of the photograph. These images, common throughout the sample,[6] represent the apparently natural conflation of Iranian and Muslim through the use of visual texts constructing a monolithic Islamic Iran that structures popular understandings of Iranians. This construction of distinctive Iranian media frames dominates visual representations in the press, often contradicting the more liberal tone of the accompanying written text allowing the visual representation to convey meaning beyond the expressed focus of the news article.

Despite the implied topic of the article in Figure 2, as set out in the text and through the headlines, the restriction of the image to a recurrent and predictable theme, that of Muslim Iranian women repressed by the ever-present religious state apparatus, attempts to inform 'us', the readers, that even if Iran is complying with IAEA inspections, 'they' (i.e. women) are still subject to the oppression of the *mullahs*. This visual discourse of representation complies with the general Western political view of Iran as a 'problem state', with the imagery in the press conforming to Herman and Chomsky's (1988) critique of a consenting media involved in the perpetuation of compliant journalism that takes the form of nationalist propaganda (see also Lang and Lang, 2000).[7] The visual symbols of Otherness commonly used in the press during the sample construct metaphorical connections to the deviancy of Iran and the theocratic Iranian state that are often beyond the scope of the article to inform. Thus these constructions create visual allusions that "make a statement implicitly that the paper may well balk at making explicitly, while simultaneously seeming to provide 'evidence' to support that statement" (Huxford, 2001: 67). By pursuing the visual media frame of the Iranian woman repressed by the Islamic state the metaphorical construction becomes confused with reality, "the representation of reality becomes reality itself" (Huxford, 2001: 67).

---

6   The newspapers in this study were systematically sampled from 1st January, 2000 – 31st December, 2001, with subsequent inclusion of random samples from January 2002 to June 2004. Newspapers sampled in this analysis included a mix of tabloids and broadsheets including: in Sydney, The Sydney Morning Herald, The Daily Telegraph and The Australian; in London, The Sun, The Times, The Guardian, and The Mirror; in Vancouver, the Globe and Mail, The Province, and the Vancouver Sun.

7   The self-censorship of the media and the setting of agendas for visual representations has been noted in other settings within the 'Orient' (Griffin, 2004).

Figure 3.2: **"Students" walking in front of mural of Ayatollah Khomeini (*Sydney Morning Herald*, Nov. 12, 2003: 12, with permission)**

Although the visual images under investigation were taken from newspapers of three cities in three different nations, there was a convergence in terms of the imagery used to represent Iran and Iranians. All of the newspapers, both tabloids and broadsheets, in each of the three cities were guilty of deploying simplistic images of Iranian women in the chador standing in front of representations of the structures of repression of the Islamic theocracy in Iran. Even when these anonymous women were absent from representations the wider structures of repression remained apparent. Figure 3.3 pictures a hand feeding worry beads through its fingers in front of a poster of the late Ayatollah Khomeini. This image was printed in both the *Vancouver Sun* and in *The Australian* during the February 2000 election that took place in Iran.[8] This image feeds into the existing conflation of Iran as composed of conservative Muslims and Iranians that practice Islam through religious action, as discretely referenced by the image of a hand fingering beads, and as in other representations, set against the oversight of the stoic *mullah*. While Figure 3.3 pictures an election site, religious oversight or influence on the election process itself is clearly implicated. Whilst there are ongoing issues as to the electoral restrictions placed by the religious judiciary in Iran, it is significant to note how images in the media denigrate the democratic process in place in Iran as sullied by religious intervention. The use of such images, particularly those sourced through agencies such as *Reuters*, contribute to the production of similar representations of Iran and Iranians between the cities considered in this research. In this sense, whilst there were contextual differences in the coverage of Iran in each of the three cities, what remains of importance to this analysis is the significance of the convergence of representations, sometimes facilitated by the modes of media production, and always structured within a discourse of (Iranian) Islam as deviant and repressive.

Figure 3.3: Images of the February 2000 election. Reprinted with kind permission of Reuters and News Limited

---

8   This image was also used out of context, sourced from file, in an historical piece centred on Shah Reza Pahlavi (*Financial Review*, Nov. 28, 2003: Review p4) illustrating the ongoing relevance of file material.

Between and within the three cities of Sydney, London and Vancouver there were differences in newspaper reporting (Zeliter *et al.*, 2002), not least of which between the tabloid press and the broadsheets. While the tabloids are recognised for their sensationalist journalism, the broadsheets are generally viewed as operating with more journalistic integrity and less (if any) bias (Zeliter, *et al.*, 2002). Whilst the overtly racist reporting of the past may no longer be socially and politically acceptable in the media, more subtle constructions of negativity are common (Parekh, *et al.*, 2000). As noted by Richardson, the conservative tabloid press is not alone in constructing a negative portrayal of issues surrounding 'migrants', and in particular 'Muslim migrants'. The broadsheets sampled in this analysis exhibited an 'inferential racism' (Hall, 1981) that normalises difference whilst explicitly denying more overt racism. The more 'reasonable' approach to the 'natural' differences between groups in the broadsheets protects this upmarket reporting from racist critiques (Richardson, 2004).

Finally it is noteworthy that the reporting of Iran has produced a neo-Orientalist (Sardar, in Poole, 2002: 32) construction of a homogenously Islamic Iran that appears to transcend historical variation. This contemporary Islamic reality is constructed despite the realities of the reporting of 'cosmopolitan' Iran prior to the 1978-1979 revolution. Throughout the 1980s images of Iran progressively merged with images of Islam in general (Brasted, 2001). This constructed an unquestioned Islamic reality that was not present prior to 1979. The undoing of the 'Westoxification' of Iran, announced by the Ayatollah Khomeini on his return from exile in Paris in 1979, marked the beginning of the change in reporting from the predominantly secular Pahlavi state to the current quintessentially Islamic nation. Over time Iran has become a coherent national fragment of neo-Orientalist discourse, in that its constructed Islamic homogeneity comes to be emblematic of the schism between 'the West' and 'the (Islamic) Orient'. In conformity with Halliday's (2003) 'myth of confrontation' Iran has been constructed as the national standard-bearer of the contemporary 'Clash of Civilisations' (Huntington, 2003).

Deconstructing Visual Discourses of Iran/Islam

The media has the power to influence the way people see themselves and others through the particular representations they convey (Hall, 1981; van Dijk, 1987). As noted by Mahtani (2001), "it is important to ask how media representations of minorities affect the construction of identities". She quotes Henry's work on the criminalisation of race in the print media in Toronto, mentioning "that it is imperative to research media-minority relations because the media play a crucial role in the creation of social identities" (Henry, in Mahtani, 2001: 2). The second generation from an Iranian background, like all individuals in society, respond to representations of themselves and others within a complex contextual field of cultural processes. For the children of the 'Iranian diaspora', the media creates a dilemma in terms of expressions of identity as they are impacted by the specific images and texts used to represent Iran and Iranians. This constructed identity causes individuals to compromise and negotiate their own identities as they respond, either directly or indirectly, to the power of media representations to define 'what an Iranian is?'. The media construct expectations amongst the non-Iranian mainstream, and also, to an extent, amongst other 'migrants', of 'what an Iranian is?', and 'what Iran is like?', such that the decision to express one's identity as Iranian is considered within the context of what the Other thinks (or is assumed to think) constitutes an 'Iranian'. Whilst media representations inform the construction of meaning by wider non-Iranian audiences, they also, as a result, set up a reflexive schema within which 'Iranians' construct meaning from representations, which subsequently inform how they construct a self-image to (re)present to others (be they 'Iranian' or not).

For the individual, meaning is constructed from visual images in a way that goes beyond the narrative organisation of text and the image in a particular story. Meaning is negotiated within "the ideological formations of the society that produces it" (Geraghty, 2000: 367). Visual representations form a narrative with the text in a story, linking the particular story with stories that have gone before. Thus, photographs play a mimetic role where the connotations, or 'body of attitudes' that surround the image (Barthes, 1977), bring the individual story into a wider discourse of understanding in a complex and contingent manner such that the meaning of any image shifts relative to its consumption. The children of Iranian migrants 'decode' (Hall, 1980) representations of Iran and Iranians within wider discourses of racism as represented by the media and interpreted by the individual. In this way representations are removed from their immediate context and placed within the connotative field of meanings that surround the stories in the media and shape the "wider realms of social ideology" (Hall, 1997: 38-9). As Parekh, *et al.* note,

> Any one news story is interpreted by the reader or viewer within the context of a larger narrative, acting as a kind of filter or template. If the larger narrative is racist … then the story is more likely to be interpreted in a racist or majority-biased way, regardless of the conscious intentions of reporters, journalists and headline-writers (2000: 169).

Yet newspaper articles are not merely subject to larger racist narratives, they are also constitutive of these discourses, informing the reader and reconfirming to the reader subtle (and sometimes not so subtle) signifiers of the relations of power that mark groups as subordinate.

Interrupting the Preferred Meaning: Iranian Realities

Against the preferred meanings of a history of repression of women set against the ubiquity of the structures of male religious control as identified in the newspaper representations of Iran and Iranians, a more informed historical reality can be set. Far from being a homogenous Persian Islamic nation-state, Iran is home to a wide variety of ethnicities, religions and linguistic backgrounds. In reality, the Persian population of Iran make up only approximately half of the more than 60 million people (Shaffer, 2002).[9] The rest are ethnically divided into several major and minor groups. Azeris,

---

9   There has been no systematic collection of statistical data concerning ethnic and linguistic diversity by the Iranian state. Mojab and Hassanpour (1996) quote two sources from

or Azerbaijani Turks, make up approximately 24 per cent of the population, Kurds another 9 per cent, followed by Baluchis (3 per cent), Arabs (2.5 per cent), and Turkmen (1.5 per cent) (Mojab and Hassanpour, 1996). Further ethnic distinctions include the Assyrian, Armenian and Jewish peoples of Iran who are tied to the diasporic migrations of their earlier history. Tehran, according to Shaffer, is itself dominated by non-Persians (particularly Azeris and Kurds) creating a multi-ethnic centre of what is assumed to be a homogenous demographic landscape (Shaffer, 2002).

The demographic map of Iran becomes more variegated when religious differences are taken into account. There are groups adhering to a variety of established religious faiths including populations of Christian, Jewish and Zoroastrian faiths, Baha'is and Shi'i and Sunni Muslims. It also bears noting that communities constructed on religious affiliation are themselves unsettled and stratified by varying degrees of practice, a point that will be elaborated upon subsequently for the 'Muslim Iranian' communities in the diaspora. These religions cross the boundaries of ethnicity and linguistic divisions in multifarious ways to produce a complex map of different communities in Iran (Mojab and Hassanpour, 1996).

In considering the diaspora, the revolution of 1978-1979 marks the onset of large scale contemporary Iranian emigration. Since 1980, the presence of immigrants of Iranian birth in countries such as the United States, Sweden, the Netherlands, Britain, Canada and Australia increased significantly. The large increase in immigration of Iranians following 1980 is reflective of both the initial persecution of the elites and political minority groups within the Shi'a and the continuous persecution of religious minorities coupled with the uncertainties of the Iran-Iraq war (1980-1988). The number of Iranian-born people in Sydney, Vancouver and London according to Census figures is between 10 000 and 20 000 for each city, although when the children of migrants born outside of Iran are included these figures for the 'community' of Iranian background appear quite conservative (Sreberny, 2000). Within the context of minority ethnic and religious persecution it should come as no surprise that religious, ethnic and linguistic minorities are over represented in the diaspora. There are distinct groups of Baha'is, Assyrian and Armenian Christians, Zoroastrians, Jews, Kurds and Arabs, most in greater concentrations than are represented in Iran. This discussion of diversity indicates that it is more accurate to refer to the existence of multiple Iranian communities in Sydney, Vancouver and London.

In this research, discussions were undertaken with individuals of Muslim background and of Baha'i background in order to reflect upon the religious diversity that unsettles the dominance of national discourses of belonging. Individuals from the second generation were interviewed and also took part in an ethnographic photography exercise designed to produce a counter narrative to the essentialised representations of Iranians in the newspaper media.

---

the 1950s based on 'population according to language' figures from the 1956 Census and the data from the Geographical Dictionary of Iran compiled and published by the Iranian military in the early 1950s. Underreporting and over-reporting of figures has routinely been used to prop up political agendas (Shaffer, 2002; Keddie, 1995).

A Cultural Muslim Community

Many of those who emigrated from post-revolutionary Iran were part of the mobile educated middle class who had formerly been part of an increasingly affluent urban elite in Tehran. Those who came from a Muslim background included many non-practicing, or 'secular' Muslims. Their children, the second generation, grew up in a diasporic environment that emulated the pre-revolutionary middle-class Iran, replete with progressive attitudes to secularism and education that were fostered by the urban Iranian middle class. Many individuals of Muslim background express a relatively benign relationship to Islam that can be thought of as 'cultural Islam' where their everyday secular and cosmopolitan social actions remain imbued with 'Muslim values' through the tight association of Iranian identity with Islam. Rather than turn their back altogether on Islam, which implies, through its popular intertwining with Iranian identity, a denial of Iranian-ness, individuals maintained a core sense of Islam as a benign part of their Iranian selves. I describe the relationship as benign not in the sense that there exists no conscious thought about their feelings of Muslim identity, but more in the sense that Islam is a fact of life that guides rather than rules the actions of the individual.[10]

The popularly perceived dominance of Shi'i Islam in Iran has served to produce an image of Islam as the 'national religion', a perception that was entrenched through the rise of the Islamic theocracy following the revolution. Despite the majority of Iranian Muslims in the diaspora fleeing the strictures of religious conservatism, the centrality of Shi'i Islam to national identity in its present form serves to legitimate the *natural* congruence of Islam and Iranian identity. For the second generation in particular, who have had little or no contact with Iran, the perceptions of congruency of Islam and Iran are (at least partially) driven by mainstream media representations.

Muslim ascription is not uniform across the second generation of Muslim and Iranian background. As can be expected, in all three cities considered, some individuals can be thought of as cultural Muslims, whilst some have wholly secularised their lives, successfully alienating their Iranian identity from its Islamic base. Others are active practising Muslims mediating their social relations more thoroughly through religious interpretation. Far and away the largest group within those of Muslim background in the three cities were individuals who thought of themselves as Muslim in a more utilitarian or pragmatic manner that is more liberal and manifests itself in many social contexts as Islamic values, rather than Islamic practises. For these cultural Muslims Islam is often seen as less a religion than a moral code embedded within Iranian identity.

---

10   In Iran, and particularly Tehran, the tension between the religious and the cultural sense of Islam is played out through a variety of fields of action from the private individual, all the way to the leaders of government. The reform movement reflects this tension between the conservative religious infrastructure that seeks to produce society according to strict Islamic rules of conduct, and the progressive Islamic movement that views religion as more benign in society allowing the flexibility for individual interpretation in order to embody individual freedom of choice. Even beyond this conservative/progressive dichotomy many of those of a more secular disposition in Iranian society have become more and more vocal in opposition to what they see as the slow pace of reform.

I don't say it's a ritualistic thing. I don't pray five times a day. I don't fast during *Ramadan*. In a sense that I react to things, because I've been brought up in a certain way and told certain things are correct and I can make my own way in life.

Ali, 25, (Muslim, London).

Figure 3.4:   Ninth day of *Moharram* in the Cricklewood (Iraqi)[11] Mosque in London (photograph from Fereshteh)[12]

---

11   In this case the parents of one respondent moved between Iraqi Arab and Iranian Persian religious communities.

12   As part of this research, respondents took part in a photoethnographic analysis whereby they used disposable cameras to document their life and the things important to them in the everyday. As a precondition to taking part in this aspect of the research respondents

I don't see Islam as a religion … I don't drink, but it's not because I follow Islam at all. I wouldn't call myself Muslim … If something makes sense then I (keep it). Now some of the laws and regulations, either I interpret them wrong or I just completely don't agree with them.

Kaveh, 24 (Muslim, London).

For most respondents, their cosmopolitan lifestyles, as aspirational middle-upper class educated elites, were not necessarily antithetical to their feelings of being Muslim. Their individual ideas of Islam were negotiated as a cultural identity that exists as a part of their individuality, in much the same way as they consider themselves Iranian. Given this process the inconsistencies of a conservative interpretation of Islam were partially avoided. As one respondent noted,

Figure 3.5:   Dancing at a *Norooz* (New Year) party in a club in London (photograph by Ali). During *Moharram* and *Norooz* some respondents moved easily between parties and the mosque

The New Years was at 5pm on the 20th. And I went … for the coming of the Year, around 5pm, I went to (my friends) house because she has family and everything there … And we exchanged gifts and said happy New Years and stuff. And we had the traditional. And then after that I went home and changed and went to the party, which was just the younger people … It was just us having fun dancing and drinking and stuff.

Farzaneh, 20 (Muslim, Vancouver).

---

were informed of, and consented to, the potential use of images they produced in research publications. The photographs used in this article are subject to this consent.

This flexibility over the interpretation of Islam (see Figures 3.4 and 3.5) has allowed the respondents to, on the one hand distance themselves from the contemporary theocracy in Iran, and on the other, to avoid alienating Islam altogether from the imagined Iranian nation and national identity. Islam remains a cogent part of their Iranian identity as a set of core (national) values that inform everyday cultural and secular interactions.

For many of these Iranian 'cultural Muslims' the popular misunderstanding of the complexity of their lives as Muslims was manifest through the inadequacy of media representations of Iran and Iranians. Constructed notions of Iranians as 'fundamentalist Muslims' and Iran as a homogenous conservative nation in the media structured their own explanations of what Iran was really like. It was against this represented context, of Iran as homogenously subject to the power of the conservative Islamic state, that the second generation framed their identities. For many, the key to discussing their identity with me was to first respond to this context and show the inadequacies of media-driven dominant discourses of understanding what an Iranian is like, opening the account to more complex and contingent explanation. Some cultural Muslims, who have undertaken trips to Iran, particularly in the period of 'reform' instituted by former president Khatami in the late 1990s, were keen to highlight these differences. As Farzaneh noted following her most recent trip,

> In Iran you can drink as much as you want, if, you know, you know where to get hold of it, if you've got the money. And you can do whatever you want with the opposite sex. ... There are a lot of parties there, and it was good ... you were there because you want to be with the people who are there. It's a private society there, so you know who is there.

Farzaneh, 20 (Muslim, London).

For others their own perceptions of Iran were so intimately tied to the essential nature of representations in the media that on their return they were surprised by the complexity of Iranian society.

> In one of the big parks in Tehran, there was like a rollerblade rink. Like an outdoor one. And out of the loudspeakers they were pumping out really loud sort of techno music. And I was sort of like (surprised), in a public park, you know, that they would just do that.

Jahanshah, 22 (Muslim, Sydney).

For these individuals who had taken part in 'the return' their views of Iran, developed from afar through the complex interaction of media representations with the stories of the homeland conveyed by family and friends, were unsettled and given depth by the act of return.[13] Whilst some were surprised on their first visit to Iran that Islamic control was not uncontested, others expressed little surprise, reflecting their interruption of the preferred meaning of mainstream media representations.

---

13   Recent developments in Iran saw a softening of the conditions of exile for some in the diaspora. Significantly, Baha'is, whose position as Islamic apostates has remained unchanged, continue to be excluded from the act of return.

Racism and the 'Muslim Iranian'

The degree to which Iranians and Iran are (mis)represented in the press and demonised by politicians is linked to the appearance of significant events in the international arena that both directly and indirectly involve Iranians. The '9/11' terrorist attacks sent reverberations around the world fuelling an anti-Islamic sentiment in Western nations reported in and reproduced by the media, that has in turn, aroused more open racism against migrants and others identified as Muslim.

> Like a week after September the eleventh, every time we went to school and open(ed) the newspapers there was all this negative stuff about Islam, and that was bad for me, being a religious person. I don't think the media reacted good to it at all. And the government sort of backed the media up in a way. Doing it together, and so the peoples' reaction would go towards it as well 'cause it was all over the media. And I think it just destroyed their own pictures as well of the Muslims, and I didn't like that.

> Masoumeh, 17 (Muslim, London).

> Nader: We had this terrible terrorist label, and now it seems to have come back on us again,[14] so I don't know what's going to happen next year...

> Question: Where's that come from?

> Nader: It's, you know, Mr Bush and his Axis of Evil. It seems to be coming back and I don't know what's going to happen, but it doesn't look good, 'cause they seem to have made a decision they are going to go for it [the War in Iraq].

> Nader, 24 (Muslim, London).

For those of Iranian background in Sydney, Vancouver and London it may be simple to assume that the individual's experience of racism has increased accordingly. However, there is a more complex relationship to racism linked on one level to the question of visibility.

For most of the respondents both Baha'i and 'Muslims', when asked about their own experiences of racism, particularly following the '9/11' attacks, they expressed an awareness of people who had suffered racist incidents, from slurs to assaults. However, what was most interesting was that many of these individuals did not see themselves as subject to the rise in anti-Islamic sentiments.

> Mohammad: Probably now, when there's more anti-Muslim sentiment, they are going to face more ... people are going to come and they are more accustomed to their own culture ... that's going to cause them to have a harder time.

---

14   For Iranians in London, the 1980 Iranian Embassy siege has had a significant historical impact on perceptions of Iranian migrants in London. During the sample period commemorations and celebrations for the 20th anniversary of the successful Special Air Service (SAS) operation were widely reported.

Question: In the last two years, have you personally found any difference in the way people perceive you?

Mohammad: In the last two years ... I haven't found any examples.

Mohammad, 23 (Muslim, Sydney).

Question: Has the wider public's attitude towards Iran and the people from Iran changed since the terrorist attacks on September 11th, 2001?

Azadeh: Yeah, the people I've come in contact with.

Question: In what sense?

Azadeh: They look more down on the Middle East than they normally would.

Question: Have you experienced racism due to these attitudes?

Azadeh: I haven't.

Question: You haven't, but you've heard of other people?

Azadeh: Yeah. Not Persian people, but yeah ... friends.

Azadeh, 20 (Baha'i, Vancouver).

On one level these responses can be understood as recognition that as either non-Muslims (e.g., Baha'is), or as cultural Muslims, or secular Iranians, they should not be conflated with, or mistaken for, 'Muslims' (that is, fundamentalist Muslims). Those of Muslim background cast themselves as 'non-Muslim' despite the core national Muslim values that intersect in their complex identities. This opens up the question of the perception of Otherness, where the second generation problematise the popular conflation of Iranian with Muslim in response to the rise in racist incidents. Whilst the first generation may be subject to racism due to their 'difference', the second generation have more flexibility to deny the relevance of racist acts through their positionality beyond migrancy (at least compared to 'new migrants'). Hence, some second generation individuals strategically minimise their difference to the white centre, and maximise their difference to new arrivals and the older first generation (see Noble and Tabar, 2002). Despite possibly being mistaken by the press and by 'white' community members as a 'Muslim' because of their Iranian background, the reality of the second generation's self-awareness seems to have allowed many to see the rise in racist attitudes as something that does not, and should not, happen to them. A feeling of disengagement arose in discussions about racism that again indicated a degree of agency over their interstitial position in identity relations.[15]

---

15   One important consideration here is the influence of a white male interviewer on these discussions. Despite explicit discussion of my own problematising of racist discourses, the fact remains that my positionality implicates me within relations of unequal power as a representative of the dominant white centre of national identity. Whether and to what extent this had a bearing on discussions of racism remains unclear.

This was particularly the case for the Baha'is in all three cities who saw themselves as less implicated in national discourses of identity,[16] and in particular as less 'Iranian' than their 'Muslim' counterparts.

Azadeh: I would say definitely, that … people feel scared and they generalise the whole population.

Question: Do you feel subject to that generalisation in any way?

Azadeh: No.

Azadeh, 20 (Baha'i, Vancouver).

When faced with racism, 'non-Muslims' of Iranian background, whether Baha'is or cultural Muslims, feel at least some agency over how they respond to racist acts. Their agency is manifested by their actively interrupting the preferred meaning of racist acts and reconfiguring the meaning through their reading.

For practising Muslims, the increase in racist incidents had a different implication. Here the popular conflation in the media of Iranian with Muslim does find its concrete footing. These respondents tended to submit to the dominance of media stereotyping, conforming to the unmediated preferred meaning that reproduces them as 'Muslim' Iranians in accordance with a popularly supported representation implicating them in wider racial/religious stereotyping. The visibility of second generation practising Muslims as 'Iranians', 'Arabs', or 'of Middle Eastern appearance' is signified by their skin colour, their language, their religion, and most apparently, through their attire. This was particularly the case for those practising Muslims that were female. For these individuals their visibility as Muslims, through the signifier of the 'veil', and, by extension, their association with the veil's iconic visibility in the media, marked them as open for public attack by racist individuals (see Dwyer, 1999a; 2000). In contrast to 'non-Muslims', practising Muslims of Iranian background tended to feel the full weight of racism, thereby confirming a societal congruency with the preferred meaning of media representations of Iran that essentialise 'Iranians' necessarily as

---

16 For Baha'is, as minority 'Iranians' both within Iran and in the diaspora their sense of national belonging is mediated against the knowledge of their liminal relationship to national identity. The Baha'i Faith problematises relationships to national identity and the nation-state. According to one of the key texts, the Baha'i Faith "insists upon the subordination of national impulses and interests to the imperative claims of a unified world" (Effendi, 1938/1955: 42). This eschatological relationship of practising Baha'is to the nation-state places the nation as both a vessel for contemporary action and a source of distraction from the search for global unity. For the Baha'is, the desire for global unity in diversity demands disengagement with national identity as a relic of the past that must be discarded as we move into the next global epoch. At the same time, Baha'is recognise the importance of action in the present and the current geopolitical and sociocultural dominance of national forms. Under these conditions it was found that Baha'is from Iranian background were more likely to see national belonging in an instrumental manner (see Waters, 2002; Ip, Inglis and Wu, 1997) as having a pragmatic 'use value', deploying national identity in a flexible manner where value is found in the conferred rights of citizenship rather than the affective ties to belonging.

'Muslims'. The media representations of anonymous dehumanised female Muslims, signified by the presence of the *hijab*, but also reinforced by their anonymity in visual media representations, constructs a target for anti-Islamic racism in cities such as Sydney, Vancouver and London.

> Question: Has this had any implications for you at a personal level?
>
> Masoumeh: The September the eleventh event did. I had a lot of problems with that, wearing a scarf and everything. And I've had a few friends in college that would get together and talk about it. ...
>
> Question: In a bad way?
>
> Masoumeh: Well, you had a lot of problems as in a sense, if you're Muslims you're linked to it anyhow, I don't know how. ... I had a lot of friends that had so many [stares] down the street walking around and they had so many problems.
>
> Question: Friends who wear a scarf?
>
> Masoumeh: Yes.
>
> Masoumeh, 17 (Muslim, London).

As the previous dialogue indicates, instead of being able to express agency over inclusion in the 'Muslim Iranian' stereotype, a path more open to Baha'is and cultural Muslims, possibilities for agency and resistance play themselves out in different ways. In one concrete example of a response to racism, Masoumeh in London described her school peer group as the 'scarfies', referencing the fact that they were seen as different by virtue of their religious clothing (see Figure 3.6). Here the respondent expresses the right to reclaim power over the construction of difference by appropriating the sometimes pejorative term for female Islamic dress, the scarf, or the headscarf, and using it as a term of self-recognition. When discussing the friends seen in Figure 3.6, Masoumeh indicated that they were Sunni Muslims none of whom were of Iranian background.

> These are my scarfie friends ... None of them are Shi'as. I'm the only Shi'a in the College. ... I think, back in Iran it would have been (a problem) but over here it's just ... I think they're more united as Muslims.
>
> Masoumeh, 17 (Muslim, London).

The young women's act of appropriation of the pejorative as their own has become a sense of communal resistance that in turn overcomes possible differences between them. Constructing a Muslim community in Masoumeh's school environment by conforming to the preferred meaning of Islamic representations does not represent in this case a passive, or disempowered response to racism. Rather, these young women have taken advantage of their subjection to essentialised Muslim stereotypes as a point of commonality that overcomes the other modes of difference between them, be they along religious, national, intellectual, or any other grounds. This does not, however, deny racist acts. Rather it recognises the various patterns of response to racism that range from the reappropriation of the terms of racism to an outright denial of its application.

**Figure 3.6:   London female respondent with her school friends, 'the scarfies'
(photograph from Masoumeh)**

For other respondents, their relative visibility marked them as legitimately 'non-Muslim', where their appearance did not outwardly match the constructed images of Iranians in the media, saving them from being targeted by racists.

> In a way, during the whole September eleven thing I was lucky, because I look to others like I'm Indian. Had the Indians blown up, been implicated, then I'm sure I would have got a lot of racist remarks, you know. But I didn't feel that. But you know, my father and my sister and other family members, they did … Yeah, they were harassed.

Parvaneh, 24 (Muslim, Sydney).

Question: Have you experienced racism due to these attitudes?

Niloufar: No. Me, I don't look Persian either, so I get it pretty easy.

Question: And that's important, the way you look?

Niloufar: Well, people. A lot of people pre-judge. So they can say because you look Persian, or whatever, you're a terrorist. And I think I have it easy because I look European.

Niloufar, 22 (Baha'i, Vancouver).

Question: Have you experienced racism due to these attitudes?

Samira: I haven't, no. Simply because of the way I look, I think. Because a lot of people when they go 'Where are you from?', they never guess Iran. ... They usually go 'Italian, Spanish'. You know they usually go along those lines. And I'm like, 'try Middle Eastern'. And I don't wear a scarf either, so people don't know that I'm Muslim. And so I haven't no. But I know people who have.

                                              Samira, 21 (Muslim, Sydney).

Racism for the second generation thus differed greatly along lines of both self-recognised religious affiliation, as well as the implied religiosity that visible markers afford those who perform racist acts. The form of racist acts, and the sense of involvement in these acts related directly to the construction of a conflated Muslim Iranian in the media and to the centrality of the *hijab* as a visible signifier.

The second generation of Muslim background, whether practicing, or cultural Muslims, were more likely to construct meaning from representations of Iran through recourse to further national stereotyping. For those of Muslim background these re-presentations of Iran rarely hinged on the question of diversity within the nation. Instead, the discussions continue to be mired within a discourse of essentialised national identity. Iran was re-presented to me as a nation under the mantle of reform, or through the imagining of the nation as Persia, the glorious forebear to the contemporary dysfunctional nation of Iran we see represented in the media. In a reflection of the dominance of national belonging within discourses of community, even when the performance of representations of Iran was interrupted by 'Muslim' individuals, they continued to elide the national landscape of religious and ethnic minority voices, despite the fact that significant communal demarcations can be drawn along these lines in the diaspora. In contrast, for Baha'is of Iranian background, their experience as minorities at the periphery of 'Iranian' identity both in Iran and in the diaspora, accords national belonging, and hence Iranian-ness, as portrayed in the media, much less importance. The recognition of their religion as a minority both here and there, coupled with their theological questioning of the permanence of nation-states as geopolitical entities, leads them to a complex understanding of their position beyond the essentialised constructs of the Iranian national community.

Complex Geographies of the Visual

The media is one of the disjunctural fields of influence (following Appadurai, 1990) that acts upon, and is the context through which individuals negotiate 'communal' identities. It is in the media that the discursive interaction between national identities and Others are played out (Billig, 1995). It is here that questions about inclusion and exclusion within the nation find their popular voice (Hage, 1998). As Billig notes in the concluding remarks to *Banal Nationalism*, "the newspaper addresses 'us', its readers, as if 'we' are all nationals" and in this way we are reminded "of 'them' and foreignness" (1995: 175). If a place has multiple meanings, as Massey (1993) has astutely noted, then the media are key players in attempts to fix the meaning of places. Whilst the other senses do play a role in mediating representation of affective national geographies (eg, through national anthems), this chapter has investigated the importance of visual representations. The newspaper media in particular relies on the ocular centricity of Western epistemologies and the privileging of the visual in the construction of fixed national geographies. Hence we can think of the print media as one of the contexts that influences, fixes, and at the same time opens up the possible questioning of the hegemony of national identities in popular (and academic) discourses of belonging.

Media representations of individuals as nationals or migrants, as criminals or victims, or nations and communities as deviant or utopian, are intimately implicated in the processes of production and reproduction of images of community. It is through the media that some of the expression of dominant 'national' power relations makes itself apparent. The Others against which the nation is defined are constituted through the media producing a 'fictive ethnicity' (Balibar, in Jakubowicz *et al.*, 1994: 32). As a mouthpiece for dominant views, the mainstream media in particular creates communities in its image through the specific processes of representation, both textual and visual. In the three cities explored in this research, the selective use of text and, more specifically for this analysis, image, constructs a communal image of 'Iranians' and other 'national migrant' communities.

Much of the work on media representations of Islam focuses on the way the wider community constructs essentialised meanings *about* migrant groups (Pinn, 2000; Hippler, 2000; Poole 2000, 2002; Richardson, 2001, 2004). However, we must remember that the migrant communities themselves interact with the performance of the mainstream media to construct communal and individual meanings that define their place in society. This is even more important for the children of migrants caught between dominant national stereotypes. The divergence between the stereotypes portrayed in the media and the reality of life in Iranian diasporic communities impacts the ways the children of Iranian migrants construct or imagine their communities *here* and the homeland *there*. In particular, the context against which the children of Iranian migrants discuss their complex identity negotiations is dominated by visual representations of Iran and Iranians.

Visibility in the media has been linked to the normalising of practises of exclusion (Parekh *et al.*, 2000; Richardson, 2004). Whether individuals are perceived as 'Muslim' depends on more than their Iranian background. It is intimately tied to the form of media representations of Iranians (and other national groups) as Muslims. If these individuals look like the photographs featured in newspapers, whether of a veiled woman or an 'Arab-looking' man, they are more likely to be the subject of racist acts. Further, if they are practicing Muslims, and thereby perceive themselves as conforming to a popular conflation of Islam with Iran, then they may feel more subject to racism. The more individuals of the second generation perceive that they look like the photographs in the media, the more they understand that they are threatened by wider discourses of racism as they manifest themselves in 'real life'. For those who are included in the conflation of Iran and Islam in the wider media but do not consider themselves as Muslims, whether they are Baha'i or cultural Muslims or wholly secular, racism against 'Muslims' may not appear directly associated to them. These individuals are aware of the stereotypes portrayed in the media that underwrite wider perceptions of who is a Muslim, and they problematise these representations, denying them as representative of their complex identities.

Neither Muslims, nor Iranians necessarily form the object of 'anti-Muslim' racist acts. However, those who *look* Muslim, or who conform to the visual expression of Iranian identity as uniformly Muslim, may subsequently become the target of religious intolerance. Photographs used in the press construct categorisations of the threat to 'white' mainstream national identity and belonging in Australia, Canada and Britain. Whether they are women who wear the *hijab*, or men who look 'Arab' or 'Middle Eastern', these commonly deployed visual stereotypes become the containers in which individuals are placed (or place themselves). The congruence of individuals with deployed images in the media, visual representations that speak beyond factual reporting towards a subjective bias against Islam, subjects them to the disproportionate weight of racist acts. To think of this as a Muslim issue or as an Iranian issue is only partial. Rather, the fictive ethnicity constructed in the media points to a racist issue that crosses the boundaries of scale and form.

References

Appadurai, A. (1990) 'Disjuncture and Difference in the Global Cultural Economy'. *Theory, Culture & Society*, **7** (2), 295-310.

Barthes, R. (1972) *Mythologies*, London: Cape.

Barthes, R. (1977) *Image – Music – Text*, Heath, S. (trans.), London: Fontana.

Bell, P. (1992) *Multicultural Australia in the Media*, Canberra: Australian Government Publishing Service.

Billig, M. (1995) *Banal Nationalism*, London: Sage.

Brasted, H. V. (2001) 'Contested Representations in Historical Perspective: Images of Islam and the Australian Press: 1950-2000', in Saeed, A. and Akbazadeh, S. (eds.), *Muslim Communities in Australia*, Sydney: UNSW Press.

Collins, J. *et al.* (2000) *Kebabs, Kids, Cops and Crime: youth ethnicity and crime*, Sydney: Pluto Press.

Connell, J., Gibson, C. (2003) *Sound Tracks: Popular Music, Identity and Place*, New York: Routledge.

Connell, J., Gibson, C. (2004) 'World Music: Deterritorialising Place and Identity', *Progress in Human Geography*, **28** (3), 342-361.

Dunbar-Hall, P., Gibson, C. (2004) *Deadly Sounds, Deadly Places: Contemporary Aboriginal Music in Australia*, Sydney: UNSW Press.

Dwyer, C. (1999) 'Contradictions of Community: questions of identity for young British Muslim Women', *Environment and Planning A*, **31**, 53-68.

Dwyer, C. (1999a) 'Veiled Meanings: young British Muslim Women and the negotiation of differences', *Gender, Place and Culture*, **6** (1), 5-26.

Dwyer, C. (2000) 'Negotiating Diasporic Identities: Young British South Asian Muslim Women', *Women's Studies International Forum*, **23** (4), 475-486.

Eade, J. (1998) 'The Search for Wholeness: The construction of National and Islamic Identities among British Bangladeshis', in Kershen, A. (ed.), *A Question of Identity*, Aldershot: Ashgate.

Effendi, S. (1938/1955) *The World Order of Baha'u'llah*, Wilmette, Illinois: Baha'i Publishing Trust.

El-Farra, N. (1996) 'Arabs and the Media', *Journal of Media Psychology*, **1** (2), http://www.calstatela.edu/faculty/sfischo/, accessed: July, 2004.

Geraghty, C. (2000) 'Representation and Popular Culture: Semiotics and the Construction of Meaning', in Curran, J. and Gurevitch, M. (eds), *Mass Media and Society* London: Arnold.

Gibson, C., Connell, J. (2005) *Music and Tourism: On the Road Again*, Clevedon: Channel View Publications.

Giddens, A. (1986) *The Constitution of Society: Outline of the theory of structuration*, Berkeley, California: University of California Press.

Glass, C. (1996) 'A Prejudice as American as Apple Pie', *New Statesman*, **127** (4412), 9-10.

Griffin, M. (2004) 'Picturing America's 'War on Terrorism' in Afghanistan and Iraq: Photographic motifs as news frames', *Journalism*, **5** (4), 381-402.

Hafez, K. (ed.) (2000) *Islam and the West in the Mass Media: Fragmented images in a globalizing world*, Cresskill, New Jersey: Hampton Press Inc.

Hafez, K. (2000a) 'Imbalances of Middle East Coverage: A Quantitative Analysis of the German Press', in Hafez, K. (ed.), *Islam and the West in the Mass Media: Fragmented images in a globalizing world*, Cresskill, New Jersey: Hampton Press Inc.

Hage, G. (1998) *White Nation: Fantasies of white supremacy in a multicultural society*, Sydney: Pluto Press.

Hall, S. (1980) 'Encoding/decoding', in Hall, S. (ed.), *Culture, Media, Language: Working Papers in Cultural Studies,* London: Hutchinson.

Hall, S. (1981) 'The Whites of their Eyes: Racist Ideologies and the Media', in Bridges, G. and Brunt R. (eds), *Silver Linings: Some Strategies for the Eighties*, London: Lawrence and Wishart.

Hall, S. (1997) 'The Work of Representation', in Hall, S. (ed.), *Representation: Cultural Representations and Signifying Practises*, London: Sage.

Halliday, F. (2003) *Islam and the Myth of Confrontation: Religion and Politics in the Middle East*, London: I. B. Tauris.

Hardt, H. (2000) 'Conflicts of Interest: Newsworkers, Media, and Patronage Journalism', in Tumbler, H. (ed.), *Media Power, Professionals and Policies*, London: Routledge.

Hardt, H. (2004) 'Introduction: Photojournalism: Professional Work and Cultural Expression', *Journalism*, **5** (4), 379-380.

Herman, E. S., Chomsky, N. (1988) *Manufacturing Consent: The Political Economy of the Mass Media*, New York: Pantheon.

Hippler, J. (1995) 'The Islamic Threat and Western Foreign Policy', in Hippler, J. & Lueg, A. (eds), *The Next Threat: Western Perceptions of Islam*, London: Pluto Press.

Hippler, J. (2000) 'Foreign Policy, the Media, and the Western Perception of the Middle East', in Hafez, K. (ed.), *Islam and the West in the Mass Media: Fragmented*

Images in a Globalizing World, Cresskill, New Jersey: Hampton Press.

Hippler, J., Lueg, A. (1995) *The Next Threat: Western Perceptions of Islam*, London: Pluto Press.

Huntington, S. P. (1993) 'Clash of Civilizations?', *Foreign Affairs*, **72** (3), 22-49.

Huxford, J. (2001) 'Beyond the Referential: Uses of symbolism in the press', *Journalism*, **2** (1), 45-71.

Ip, D., Inglis, C., Wu, C. (1997) 'Concepts of citizenship and identity among recent Asian immigrants in Australia', *Asian and Pacific Migration Journal*, **6**, 363-384.

Jakubowicz, A., Goodall, H., Martin, J., Mitchell, T., Randall, L., Seneviratne, K. (1994) *Racism, Ethnicity and the Media*, Sydney: Allen & Unwin.

Jazeel, T. (2005) 'The World is Sound?: Geography, Musicology and British-Asian Soundscapes', *Area*, **37** (3), 233-241.

Keddie, N. (1995) *Iran and the Muslim World: Resistance and Revolution*, New York: New York University Press.

Keshishian, F. (2000) 'Acculturation, Communication, and the U.S. Mass Media: The Experience of an Iranian Immigrant', *The Howard Journal of Communications*, **11**, 93-106.

Lang, K., Lang, G. E. (2000) 'How Americans View the World: Media Images and Public Knowledge', in Tumbler, H. (ed.), *Media Power, Professionals and Policies*, London: Routledge.

Langford, M. (2005) 'Becoming-Bodies in Iranian Cinema(s): Melodrama in Majidi, M., *Baran' Imagining Iran: A Symposium on Iranian Cinema*, University of New South Wales, November 18, 2005.

Lueg, A. (1995) 'The Perception of Islam in Western Debate', in Hippler J. and Lueg, A. (eds), *The Next Threat: Western Perceptions of Islam*, London: Pluto Press.

Macmaster, N., Lewis, T. (1998), 'Orientalism: from unveiling to hyperveiling', *Journal of European Studies*, **28** (1-2), 121-136.

Mahtani, M. (2001) *Representing Minorities: Canadian Media and Minority Identities*, Commissioned by the Department of Canadian Heritage for the Ethnocultural, Racial, Religious and Linguistic Diversity and Identity Seminar, Halifax, Nova Scotia, November 1-2, 2001.

Massey, D. (1993) 'Questions of Locality', *Geography*, **78** (2), 142-149.

McChesney, R. (2003) 'Corporate Media, Global Capitalism', in Cottle, S. (ed.), *Media Organization and Production*, London: Sage.

Mojab, S., Hassanpour, A. (1996) 'The Politics of Nationality and Ethnic Diversity', in Rahnema, S. & Behdad, S. (eds), *Iran After the Revolution: Crisis of an Islamic State*, London: I. B. Tauris & Co.

Naficy, H. (1993) *The Making of Exile Cultures: Iranian Television in Los Angeles*, Minneapolis: University of Minnesota Press.

Noble, G, Tabar, P. (2002) 'On Being Lebanese-Australian: Hybridity, Essentialsim, Strategy, in Hage, G. (ed.) *Arab Australians Today*, Melbourne: Melbourne University Press.

Parekh, B., *et al.* (2000) *The Future of Multi-Ethnic Britain*, London: Profile Books.

Pinn, I. (2000) 'Right-Wing Movements, Islam, and the Media: The Influence of the Media on Ethnic-Religious Integration in Europe', in Hafez, K. (ed.), *Islam and the West in the Mass Media: Fragmented Images in a Globalizing World*,

Cresskill, New Jersey: Hampton Press.

Poole, E. (2000) 'Framing Islam: An Analysis of Newspaper Coverage of Islam in the British Press', in Hafez, K. (ed.), *Islam and the West in the Mass Media: Fragmented Images in a Globalizing World*, Cresskill, New Jersey: Hampton Press.

Poole, E. (2002) *Reporting Islam: Media Representations of British Muslims*, London: I. B. Taurus.

Porteous, J. D. (1985) 'Smellscape', *Progress in Human Geography*, **9** (3), 356-378.

Richardson, J. E. (2001) 'British Muslims in the Broadsheet Press: a challenge to cultural hegemony', *Journalism Studies*, **2** (2), 221-242.

Richardson, J. E. (2004) *(Mis)Representing Islam: The Racism and Rhetoric of British Broadsheet Newspapers*, Amsterdam: John Benjamins Publishing Company.

Rose, G. (2001) *Visual Methodologies: An Introduction to the Interpretation of Visual Materials,* London: Sage.

Roushanzamir, E. L. (2004) 'Chimera Veil of "Iranian Woman" and Processes of U.S. Textual Commodification: How U.S. Print Media Represent Iran', *Journal of Communication Inquiry*, **28** (1), 9-28.

Runnymede Trust (1997) *Islamaphobia: A Challenge for Us All*, London: Runnymede Trust.

Said, E. (1978) *Orientalism*, London: Routledge.

Said, E. (1997) *Covering Islam: How the Media and the Experts Determine How We See the Rest of the World*, London: Vintage.

Shaffer, B. (2002) *Borders and Brethren: Iran and the Challenge of Azerbaijani Identity*, Cambridge, Massachusetts: MIT Press.

Smith, S. J. (1997) 'Beyond Geography's Visible Worlds: A Cultural Politics of Music', *Progress in Human Geography*, **21** (4), 502-529.

Sreberny, A. (2000) 'Media and Diasporic Consciousness: An Exploration Among Iranians in London', in Cottle, S. (ed.), *Ethnic Minorities and the Media: Changing Cultural Boundaries*, Maidenhead: Open University Press.

Tiffen, R. (2000) 'Conflicts in the News: Publicity Interests, Public Images and Political Impacts', in Tumbler, H. (ed.), *Media Power, Professionals and Policies*, London: Routledge.

Van Dijk, T. (1987) *Communicating Racism: Ethnic Prejudice in Thought and Talk*, Newbury Park, California: Sage Publications.

Waters, J. (2002) 'Flexible Families? "Astronaut" Households and the Experiences of Lone Mothers in Vancouver, British Columbia', *Social and Cultural Geography*, **3**, 117-134.

Wilkins, K., Downing, J. (2002) 'Mediating Terrorism: Text and Protest in Interpretations of *The Siege*', *Critical Studies in Mass Communications*, **19** (4), 419-437.

Wimmer, A., Glick Schiller, N. (2002) 'Methodological Nationalism and Beyond: Nation-state building, migration and the social sciences', *Global Networks*, **2** (4), 301-334.

Zeliter, B., Park, D. Gudelunas, D. (2002) 'How Bias Shapes the News: Challenging *The New York Times'* Status as a newspaper of record on the Middle East', *Journalism*, **3** (3), 283-307.

Chapter 4

'The Other within the Same': Some Aspects of Scottish-Pakistani Identity in Suburban Glasgow

Sadiq Mir

Introduction

In a British context, Scotland is a nation rarely associated with a burgeoning non-white minority-ethnic population. Popular perceptions of Scotland's non-white population instead remain predicated upon visions of sporadic, embryonic communities rendered insignificant by their much more extensive counterparts south of the border in England. However while non-whites account for only 2 per cent of Scotland's overall population; their numbers are mushrooming, having increased by 60 per cent between the census years of 1991 and 2001. The vast majority of non-whites, estimated at 102,000 during the last census, is nevertheless heavily localised in Scotland's four principle cities of Edinburgh, Dundee, Aberdeen and Glasgow, of which the latter contains by far the significant majority. The dynamic nature and growing, localised significance of Scotland's non-white communities is best illustrated by the Pakistanis, the most numerous of all Scotland's non-white groups, and whose numbers grew by 66 per cent over the same intercensal period.

With over half of Scotland's 32,000 Pakistanis residing in the Glasgow area, this West coast city represents a fascinating example of how Scottish-Pakistani identities are not only becoming imprinted on Scotland's broader cultural landscape, but how they are also having novel effects on the prevailing social geography of the city. These effects are exemplified in this chapter with reference to the suburbanisation of Glasgow's Pakistani community, where it is argued that the diverging, professionalizing, and evidently 'hybrid' identities of Scottish-born Pakistanis are a crucial contemporary driver of the community's dispersal to the affluent suburbs. These empirical findings, obtained through semi-structured interviews and focus group discussions with members of Glasgow's Pakistani community in 2002 and 2003, instruct disciplinary calls for a more sustained, sensitive and inclusive line of geographical inquiry that: first, gives more consideration to the experiences of non-whites living *outwith* traditional inner city 'epicentres' of ethnic segregation; secondly, recognises the transformative geographical potential of British-born members of non-white ethnic groups; and, thirdly, is committed to the recovery of narratives of prosperity, success and upward mobility, which have until now been lost under hegemonic visions of Pakistani economic and social marginality, suspicion, threat and the lawlessness of Pakistani youth. While the experiences of young Pakistanis in England's northern 'textile towns' are a stark reminder of ways in which some young British-Pakistanis are excluded from both the well-paid jobs of the post-industrial urban economy and the green lawns of suburbia, this chapter nevertheless offers a timely and relevant reminder of the alternative and much more successful side of the British-Pakistani experience.

'New' Identities/'New' Geographies: Young Pakistanis and Suburbanisation in Glasgow

> Although it is possible to predict the likely behaviour of the present generation, the social and economic goals of second generation Asians are wholly unpredictable, and it is they who will ultimately affect the behaviour of this distinctive and important group within Glasgow's urban system.

> (Kearsley and Srivistava, 1974: 124)

Thirty years ago Glasgow's Pakistani population was almost exclusively contained within pockets of sandstone tenements[1] in selected areas of the inner city (Kearsley and Srivistava, 1974). Nowadays, however, a 'new', accelerating and very specific pattern of dispersal is evident, characterised by the movement of Glasgow-Pakistanis to relatively prosperous suburban areas on the fringes of the city. In the suburban council districts of East Dunbartonshire[2] (to the North of the city) and East Renfrewshire[3] (to the South), there are now 508 and 1,765 Pakistanis representing 0.47 per cent and 1.98 per cent of each district's respective populations. The scale of this dispersal is more appreciable when we remember that the number of Pakistanis living within the Glasgow City district itself (*not* including these suburban areas) stands at 15,314, of which the vast majority still remains in the tenemental areas of Govanhill, Pollokshields and Woodside to the centre of Glasgow (Figure 4.1). Therefore, while the community is still nucleated in a few, inner-urban neighbourhoods, the growth of the suburban Pakistani population is such that it cannot be glossed over within modern day discussions of Glasgow-Pakistani settlement.

These accelerating levels of Glasgow-Pakistani suburbanisation mask a landmark moment in the community's development. The Pakistani population is strikingly youthful (Figure 4.2) and the experiences, thoughts, desires and overall life strategies of these young Pakistanis are deviating from those of their elders. The cultural trends and characteristics of these Pakistanis are bringing about changes to established patterns of Glaswegian social geographies in relation to

---

1   The term 'tenement' refers to a style of traditional Glaswegian house type, usually made from local sandstone. Similar in many ways to traditional 'flatted' or apartment-style housing on the outside, internally they consist of several families living off one communal staircase (known locally as a 'close').

2   Containing the settlements of Bearsden, Milngavie, Bishopbriggs, Lenzie and Kirkintilloch.

3   Of which Giffnock, Clarkston and Newton Means are the main settlements.

the distribution of the city's Pakistani inhabitants. The first or migrant generation tried much harder to replicate traditional lifestyles upon their arrival in Britain; this we can gather from their relative (and academically well documented) isolation from mainstream social, economic and cultural arenas (Anwar, 1979; Dahya, 1973; Khan, 1979). The maintenance/replication of traditional codes and structures is nonetheless diminishing amongst young Pakistanis for whom things 'Scottish' hold greater resonance. Thriving ethnic centres, which traditionally offer a territorial base for the maintenance of distinctive ways of life as well as a space for the mobilisation of co-ethnic political activity (Solomos and Back, 1995), are thus less of a necessity to these young Glasgow-Pakistanis who are more able to cope without the amenities and close co-ethnic social ties these areas have nurtured through decades of historical Pakistani settlement. Increasingly, young Pakistanis are swapping these core areas for the perceived practicalities of suburbia (which include space, good schools, and seclusion) as well as many of the positive codes, values and associations that suburban living entails. In these instances the identities of younger Pakistanis are more in line with what we may call a *white*, middle-class Scottish suburbanite identity (as opposed to a distinctly 'Pakistani' identity). Either way, it is time to finally take heed of Kearsley and Srivistava's (1974) earlier foresight (above) and register how second and third generation Pakistanis are impacting current geographical trends in the city, and how they shall ultimately determine the future development of the community.

Figure 4.1: Row of tenements in Govanhill, a traditional area of Pakistani settlement in Glasgow

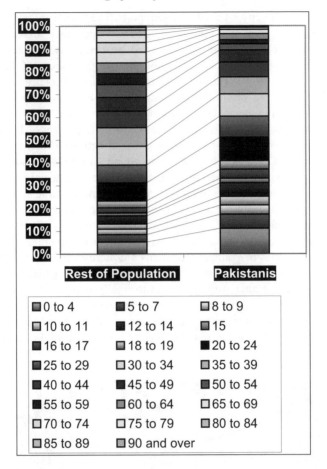

Figure 4.2: Glasgow's Pakistani population by age

This does not mean, however, that Glasgow-Pakistani suburbanisation is reducible to discussions of young, hybrid Pakistani identity alone. Suburban Pakistani communities are the outcome of much more than recent dispersals of culturally 'hybrid', professionalizing young Pakistanis. Reducing the suburbanisation process to this group alone would render invisible the initial wave of first generation suburban colonisers who formed the bedrock of these ethno-suburban communities, and who, through instigating further migrations of Pakistanis to the urban periphery, usually of children and other family members, continue to play a pivotal role in their expansion. Moreover, the relationship between these first generation Pakistanis and orthodox, 'mainstream' (white?) constructions of suburbia is less pronounced than it is with the younger group. Older Pakistanis are, for example, generally more detached from the various informal, indigenously centred networks of support, friendship and leisure typically accrued in the Glasgow suburbs, preferring instead to stick to co-ethnic spheres of activity.

Age nevertheless represents only one of a dense network of fracture points within Glasgow-Pakistani identity. Class, gender and the historical (geographical) origin of one's family all impose themselves on the systems of meaning Pakistanis use to structure their lives. Glasgow-Pakistani identity is thus a necessarily tricky and at times contradictory presence. This is demonstrated in this chapter with reference to the Pakistani community of Bearsden, an affluent suburban dormitory settlement[4] to the Northwest of Glasgow. It is agued that, in this particular instance, the suburb cannot be thought of as a site of *unrestricted* cultural intermixing, but rather as a location in which more stubborn identities are articulated as individuals frequently strive to maintain some sense of 'who they are'. Beginning with an illustration of how the identities of Bearsden-Pakistanis sometimes correlate with a middle-class *Scottish* suburbanite identity (as homeowners, house-proud and sending their children to good schools), especially where the young, mostly professional suburban Pakistanis are concerned, this chapter then proceeds to show how these 'typically' suburban values are nevertheless often juxtaposed with (sometimes) tenacious attempts at retaining a more obvious 'Pakistani' identity, from the learning and practice of religion; the use of 'mother' tongue; to a host of more 'mundane' life practices.

The themes visited and specific arguments proposed in this chapter also attach themselves to intrinsic academic and political debates concerning the nature of non-white and British-Pakistani representation within the discipline of geography and British society at large. The first of these relates to the dominance of the inner city within geographical enquiries into issues of 'race' and ethnicity in Britain. The signs from Glasgow are that, some forty years after the pinnacle of non-white migration to the U.K, Britain's minority-ethnic communities are developing in such a way that geographers must show more sensitivity to the experiences of these groups within 'other' areas besides the inner city. Given its concern with Pakistani suburbanisation, this chapter thus sides with the nascent literature exposing the over-dominance of the 'inner city' within geographical perspectives on 'race' and ethnicity in Britain (see below). Furthermore, the chapter's engagement with narratives of Pakistani 'success' and 'integration' counters – or at the very least ruptures – extant narratives of the British-Pakistani experience in which the (social, economic and cultural) marginality and 'exotic' nature of these communities is given primacy. Recent popular, academic and political statements on British-Pakistanis are more often than not pasted-up within discussions of self-segregation, rioting and terrorist threat; the latter two most often thrown at later generation Pakistanis in particular. The intention is not so much to disprove these associations but, instead, to show that more nuanced realities exist. It is in relation to these academic and political concerns that this chapter begins.

---

4   Dormitory settlements are best described as those locations, usually on the edge of the city, where a large proportion of the adult working population commute into the city or surrounding urban hinterland to work. Their defining characteristics are arguably their affluence, the daily 'rat race' occurring twice daily at rush hour times, and, subsequently, their 'no-one at home' appearance during the working week.

'Race' and Ethnicity in the City

Phil Cohen (1993: 7) laments the 'spatialisation of race' in which popular understandings of Britain's inner cities have become fixed around 'blackness' and the marginal experiences of various non-white groups. Identical criticisms may also be levelled at the geographical literature on 'race' and ethnicity in Britain. As well as being overwhelmingly based within (often deprived) urban centres, geographical insights have been driven by a conventional and incomplete wisdom that only non-white groups and non-white individuals 'have' ethnicity (Bonnett, 1996; Jackson, 1998). The spaces of British geographical inquiry into issues of 'race' and ethnicity are thus little more than the inner reaches of its main towns and cities.

While some may not consider this to be a point of much contention (the vast majority of Britain's non-white communities *do* inhabit these areas, after all), of more concern is the way that these inner city spaces are 'racialised' (Solomos, 1993); that is, imbued with and bound by an amalgam of harmful 'racial' meanings. It is those geographers concerned primarily with the statistical measurement and spatial mapping of British minority-ethnic communities who are mostly responsible for this 'fixing' of the inner city as a pathological terrain. 'Spatial sociology', the term given to this intellectual tradition by Jackson (1987), was the first-established paradigm within contemporary British geographical theorisations of 'race' and ethnicity (Bonnett, 1997), and, spurred on by the inclusion of the 'Ethnic identity' question within successive British censuses,[5] remains arguably the most productive canon of work within the subfield today (see Peach, 1999; 2002). My criticism centres on the intense skepticism spatial sociologists have fuelled towards non-white inner city populations. Segregation remains *the* buzzword as they continue to see co-ethnic clustering as some kind of urban disease threatening the fate of British towns and cities. They see it as their job to measure this epidemic and establish whether the situation is improving (as would be indicated by a reduction in non-white concentrations) or getting worse (by growing concentrations of non-whites). Their conclusions usually rest on the former, even if these assumptions (as is quite often the case) are later challenged (e.g. Phillips, 2004; Simpson, 2004).

However over the last quarter of a century discussions of ethnic segregation have at times been re-packaged under an even more radical and sinister guise. I am referring here to those sometimes frantic attempts at determining whether 'ghettos' exist in the UK. The problem here is that ghettos continue to be stylised as the antithesis of social development, echoing the earlier North American spatial sociological tradition which was so meticulous in its presentation of the US ghetto in all its 'glory' (for example, Duncan and Duncan, 1955; Teauber and Teauber, 1964; Rainwater, 1970).[6] In the UK this 'ghetto panic' took form in a series of journal exchanges debating the correct scale to use when measuring minority-ethnic

---

5   The 1991 Office of National Statistics Census was the first to include a question asking respondents to specify their ethnicity. This was in contrast to previous censuses in which respondents' countries of birth were used to infer ethnicity.

6   Indeed, the title of Morril's (1965) publication *The Negro Ghetto: Problems and Alternatives* acts as a useful synopsis of this earlier work.

segregation (Jones and McEvoy, 1978, 1979a, 1979b; Lee, 1978; Peach, 1979a, 1979b), and culminated in Peach's (1996) aptly named analysis of 1991 census data: 'Does Britain have ghettos?'. Bequeathing the ghetto ontological primacy, these studies depart from more liberal, post-positivist analyses of ghettos in which, rather than being something which exists *per se*, they are posited as 'nothing more' than ideological and symbolic constructions emanating from various systems of racism (Keith and Cross, 1993; Keith, 1993).

White Suburbia?

Geographical narratives of the 'black inner city' are reinforced by a related view of British suburbia as a cradle of 'whiteness'. Rarely have the suburbs been the location for research into non-white groups. Some efforts have nonetheless been made to challenge this black/suburban duality. In undoubtedly the most seminal of these, Watt (1998), inspired by Bonnett's (1997) earlier deconstruction of previously unproblematic and uncontested white identities, argues that such criticisms should extend into a disruption of white *places*. With this in mind he is clear on how his own study into the leisure pursuits of minority-ethnic youths in England's Home Counties achieves this:

> As we have seen, if whiteness needs to be problematised, as Bonnett (1997) argues, so do those suburban and rural areas of the country which are noted for their whiteness, and perhaps none more so than the Home Counties of the South East, the beating heart of 'Middle England'.

(Watt, 1997: 688)

Crucial therefore to Watt's (1997) arguments are two dominant, mutually reinforcing popular imageries of the Home Counties area, each of which is formed around a melding of Englishness, whiteness and being middle-class. The first relates to the Home Counties as a *white space*, and Watt relies here not only on Cohen (1993: 34), who remarked that 'as everyone knows, [it] is where the real English live', but also on Urry (1995: 205) who sees the Home Counties as 'a racial landscape, one which is presumed to be white'. The second set of images constructs the South East as a *placeless space* – a middle-class 'non-place' where high levels of social and physical mobility mute individual attachment to particular places, stifling senses of community and neighbourliness. The area is thus: '[A] spatially extended zone of formless urban development, the product of a service economy, of high levels of home and car ownership and of much prosperity, personal mobility and privatism' (Watt, 1997: 689).

Placeless space or white space, contends Watt, contribute to the unchallenged and taken-for-granted images that 'marginalise and render invisible the presence of minority-ethnic groups living in the region' (Watt, 1997: 689). Given his empirical concerns, Watt is thus able to salvage complexity in a landscape otherwise racially sterile (white); thus leading to his call for fuller recognition to be given to the variety of ways in which space is racialized, both by majority *as well as* by minority groups.

Following Watt's lead, the British suburb is another place requiring opening up in terms of minority-ethnic experience. Sibley, for example, talks of the purified British suburb in which there is a 'concern with order, conformity and social homogeneity' (Sibley, 1995: 38-39). Despite the general indifference shown towards 'Others' (fuelled by their desire to lead relatively anonymous, private lives), '[suburbanites] do occasionally turn against outsiders, particular when antagonism is fuelled by moral panics' (Sibley, 1995: 39). Boundaries – both real and imagined – thus exclude the impure, transgressive and deviant (those who have been deemed, quite literally, 'out of place').[7] While Sibley, as a prominent British human geographer, here uncovers some of the practical and ideological systems perpetuating 'white' suburbia, the same critical insights must also be turned inward to recognise how the *practice of geography itself* reinforces suburbia's whiteness. This brings one back to the spatialisation of 'race' within the geographical imagination. While research on non-white communities is synonymous with the inner city, suburbia, on the other hand, is rarely the setting for such work. Therefore, to disrupt this duality geographers and social scientists more generally, must be prepared to locate the 'other' within the 'same': non-whites in suburbia.

Of the few geographical engagements with 'race' and ethnicity in a British suburban setting, Naylor and Ryan's (2002) historical account of the building (and later extension) of the London Fasl Mosque[8] provides the most explicit rejection of any attempts to impose homogenous, ethno-religious narratives upon British suburbia. Reflecting on the amalgam of contested meanings inflicted upon the mosque, Naylor and Ryan identify how the 'exotic' mosque was deemed out of place by many among the white, middle-class, quasi-Christian and majority suburban social order. Underpinning this rejection, the authors argue, was the anti-mosque campaign's commitment to the preservation of suburbia as a repository of 'true Englishness'. Naylor and Ryan, however, are highly critical of attempts like this to bound suburbia as a site of 'pure' English identity. This would, after all, signal ignorance towards the multicultural history of suburbia: 'The history and geography of suburbia in Britain is inexorably bound up with the historical and geographical processes of colonialism, migration and settlement, by which different faith groups and minority-ethnic groups have come to reside there' (Naylor and Ryan, 2002: 56).

Since the history of British suburban development is inescapably multi-ethnic, the authors see any attempts at 'fixing' British suburbia around a unitary 'white' identity as ill-founded. However some questions may be asked of Naylor and Ryan's approach. First of all, by forwarding such a unitary history of British suburbia – one that is based upon the (apparent) ubiquity of multi-ethnic input – the authors are guilty of homogenising the historical development of British

---

7   Mike Davis (1990) had already made similar observations within a North American context. Davis portrayed the Los Angeles suburb as a fortress-like site of gated communities, combating the apparent threat of the urban poor who, so often, were non-white.

8   Planned, built and opened in the 1920s in the suburban borough of Wandsworth, the Fasl Mosque was London's first ever purpose built mosque.

suburbia. Certainly not all suburbs have the same historic multi-ethnic richness as Wandsworth. Secondly, some doubt surrounds the suitability of their empirical focus to the broader, intellectual agenda they are pursuing in which they look to counter 'common representations of Muslims, Sikhs and Hindus (and other minority-ethnic groups) as somehow 'belonging' only in 'inner-cities' and not in suburban or rural Britain' (Naylor and Ryan, 2002: 56). While they are intent on demonstrating Muslim 'belonging' to British suburbia they are arguably more successful in writing them further *out* of suburban narratives since, through their review of the mosque's contested history, they are really only confirming that minority-ethnic attempts at leaving indelible religious footprints on suburban space are vigorously contested.[9] How this particular empirical vignette demonstrates Muslim *belonging* to suburbia therefore remains unclear. This does not, however, detract from the overall worth of the authors' thematic and conceptual concerns and their call for the retrieval of suburban multiethnicity.

On Suburban Narratives of Pakistani 'Normality'...

Clearly, then, there is a need to register the 'everyday' and 'mundane' aspects of the minority-ethnic/suburban nexus. For Pakistanis especially, such representations would indicate a considerable turnaround given the nature of prevailing (academic, popular and political) opinion relating to them. Academically, studies of Pakistani communities have tended to focus on the dramatic, conflictual and exotic aspects of the British-Pakistani diaspora such as racism (Hopkins, 2004), rioting (Drummer and McEvoy, 2004), and other 'mysterious' aspects of Pakistani/Muslim life such as consanguineous (intra-familial) marriage (Shaw, 2001). Well-trodden imageries like these are just as prevalent from a public and policy perspective where they arguably reach more extreme depths. Over the last four years British-Pakistanis have come under intense public scrutiny in response to events both global and local in origin. In the summer of 2001 there were street confrontations and riots involving Asian youths in the former Northern English mill towns of Oldham, Bradford and Burnley, followed shortly after by '9-11' and its fallout. Since that tumultuous year, the integrity, morality and allegiance of British-Pakistanis have become lightning rods for increased public suspicion which, in some instances, has translated into far-right political activity and attacks on Pakistani homes, workplaces and places of worship and ignited further by the '7/7' transport bombings: 'Race attacks rise after bombs', (*Guardian* newspaper, August 1st 2005). Levels of suspicion were only magnified by the publication of two policy-orientated reports into the mill town disturbances. 'Self-segregation' became the watchword for both the Ouseley Report (2001) and Home Office Report entitled *Building Cohesive Communities* (Denham, 2001), with both blaming the violence on the desire of Asians to limit themselves to co-ethnic social spheres, whether it be in relation to housing, education or place of work. These papers, and the surrounding social distrust of Muslims and Pakistanis, prompted Ash

---

9   Indeed, as we see later on, there is a similar example of ongoing suburban conflict in Bearsden, in which Pakistani plans to build a religious and cultural education centre are being vigorously opposed by 'locals'.

Amin (2003: 460), a prominent non-white British human geographer, to make the following appraisal of current British/Muslim relations: 'We – immigrants, asylum seekers, Muslims – once again are becoming the objects of the nation's gaze, lumped together as undesirable strangers'. However as Kundnani (2001) explains, it is second and later generation Pakistani Muslims, especially young males, who have fared particularly badly at the hands of public opinion:

> Like most inner-city race riots in Britain since the 1970s, those in Oldham, Burnley and Bradford involved young men, and their street defiance too has led to their wholesale vilification in public opinion. The media gathered snippets of fact and fiction to demonize them as drug dealers or addicts, petty criminals, school dropouts, car cruisers, perpetrators of gratuitous attacks on elderly whites, beyond the control of their community, disloyal subjects, [and] Islamic militants.

(Kundnani, 2001: 108)

Such widespread disaffection with young (predominantly) male Muslims is ultimately in danger of rendering invisible the positive inroads made into British society by a large and growing proportion of this group. Many young Glasgow-Pakistanis' achievements in both 'formal' labour market occupations, especially the growing band who are joining the professional and managerial classes) and self-employment (in both 'new' and 'old' areas of Pakistani enterprise (see Mir, 2005), certainly propel them into this category, so the inclusion of such young voices within this chapter restores complexity to these otherwise stereotypical views of young British-Pakistanis and Muslims.

Hybrid Suburban-Pakistani Identities

Providing 'people's source of meaning and experience' (Castells, 1997: 6) identity informs us what we can; cannot; should; and should not, do. It also determines how we see others, acting further as source of division, friendship, war, and camaraderie. Black, brown, white; gay, straight, bisexual; Muslim, Christian; male, female: there can, then, be little doubt that identity matters. However, for all its significance, identity remains a messy and complex subject. Rather than a solid, natural set of references with which one can say for certain 'who one is', identity is, instead, highly contingent and contextual, given meaning by the particularities of the milieu in which it is performed. In this way, Peach (1999: 284) makes the following appraisal of his own (apparently) white, male, Welsh and middle-class (academic) identity: 'I can be Welsh in England, British in Germany, European in Thailand, [and] white in Africa'.

Such ideas have been at the forefront of academic debates on identity for some time now, fuelling scepticism of models of identity as fixed and monolithic. Identity formation is instead being cast as a continual process while the resultant identities themselves are merely points of connection, 'points of temporary attachment to the subject positions which discursive practices construct for us' (Hall, 1996: 5). Ferguson (1993), for example, talks of 'mobile subjectivities' in her assessment of the (post)modern subject: 'I have chosen the term *mobile* rather than *multiple* to avoid the implication of movement from one to another stable resting place' (Ferguson, 1993: 158; author's emphasis). Thus, while identities *do* crystallize they do so only for brief, sometimes fleeting, moments.

Given this denunciation of identity as a natural, 'God-given' division of humanity, it is relatively unsurprising that hybridity and discussions of hybrid cultural forms have come to fore within the armoury of cultural theorists intent on mapping more emancipatory forms of cultural representation (e.g. Anzaldua, 1987). Signalling *multiple* belonging(s), residence and/or loyalty, hybridity recognises the amalgam of (sometimes contradictory) cultural reference points that merge during identity construction which, ultimately, place subjects 'between' cultural domains.

Using these ideas, this section proposes that hybridity is a useful starting point within theorisations of Scottish-Pakistani identity within suburbia. Above all, hybridity is sensitive to how, despite being 'Pakistani', many of the values these individuals place on suburbia and suburban living correlate to a (albeit stereotypical) vision of middle-class *Scottish* suburbanite identity in that the reasons these respondents gave for their relocations to Bearsden called upon *generic* constructions of suburbia (with no direct reference to 'ethnicity' or their ethnic origin being made).

> Arif: We came here (Bearsden) for our kids really. Like any parents we wanted to provide the best for the children and our youngest was about to start school… we heard that this (suburbia) was the best platform for them.

> (Male, aged 62)

> Qasim: I remember coming up here before we bought the house…we were just looking at the time. It was so different, even then…there was so much space which was something we weren't used to, but that was good – it was something we liked…the children could play without getting into trouble and you weren't always worried about where they were or who they were with.

> (Male, aged 49)

> Uzma: We liked the privacy you get with these types of houses and gardens…you can just get on with your lives and bring up the kids, while if you want to mix with other people you can do that too. It's basically the best of both worlds when before it was just buildings and people…I think that you can only take that for so much.

> (Female, 58)

Arif, Qasim, Uzma, Umar and Mohammed[10] each moved (along with their respective spouses and children) to suburbia from established areas of Pakistani settlement. Arif explained his relocation in terms of the improved schooling available in Bearsden, where local state-run primary and secondary schools are among the best in Glasgow and the public (private fee-paying) schools of the West End are in

---

10   Pseudonyms are used throughout this chapter to ensure the anonymity of the respondents.

easy reach. With its greenbelts, parklands and proximity to the countryside, Qasim and Uzma, on the other hand, saw Bearsden as possessing aesthetic qualities that were particularly conducive to family life, especially when younger children were concerned.

Then, on top of the practicality of suburbia, were issues of class, status, achievement and exclusivity. Ownership of a Bearsden home implies success and engenders respect. It reflects determination, ambition and, as Umar (Male, aged 60) touched upon, a lifetime's hard work. When cataloguing his previous forms of employment and the arduous tasks and long work hours that went with them, most recently as a Post Office operator, Umar remarked with some pride that he had "worked hard" for his home before going on to elaborate on how the home was a testament to both his commitment to work *and* his dedication to providing what he saw as a pleasant, safe environment for his family. Being a suburban homeowner therefore inferred success on two fronts. Firstly, there is the implication of being a successful family member (as a father and husband) in that, through his driven attitude towards work, he has been able to provide his wife and children with a home in Bearsden. Secondly, there is the related implication of financial and career success in that he was able to meet the high financial costs of suburban living in the first instance. Mohammed (male, aged 45), on the other hand, was more forthcoming on the relationship between Bearsden and personal/family status. He said that he would "be lying" if he did not acknowledge the exclusivity of Bearsden as one of its key attractions; this before proceeding to claim that this would also be true of the majority of other Bearsden residents, *irrespective* of ethnic background.

However it is among the professionalizing later generations that the inter-relationship between class, identity and suburbanisation is especially valorised. Partly due to the first generation's 'hothouse' approach towards their children's education,[11] young Pakistanis are showing a remarkable orientation towards university and college education as nearly one-in-five Pakistanis aged 16 or over are currently in full time education, compared to a figure of one-in-ten for Glasgow's white population. These tertiary educated Pakistanis are consequently pursuing careers in the professions and specialist service industries. It is not uncommon to find young Pakistani doctors, solicitors, dentists, social workers and accountants. Newfound skills in fields such as business, management and marketing are also being applied within non-traditional areas of entrepreneurialism. There are examples of trailblazing business success in the information technology, financial and property services, and also in high value retailing where computer and mobile phone businesses are especially common. These careers bring with them a new dimension to Pakistani identity. There is now a self-aware and elite band of young Pakistani professionals looking for opportunities to confirm their newfound bourgeois status. One respondent reflected on how this

---

11   Pakistani parents are learning here from their own experiences in the labour market where they typically had to negotiate insecure forms of employment with low skill requirements, or be at the mercy of the Glaswegian public in small retail, take-away and other food businesses. The migrant generation therefore press educational attainment onto their children in the belief that this will lead them into what they perceive as more rewarding forms of employment in the professions or management.

group is motivated by their perceived role as the "new ambassadors" of Britain's Asian population. They are happy to be lauded as success stories since they feel that this disproves indigenous fears of Asian self-segregation and cultural insularisation. For these young Pakistanis, the purchase of a suburban house is therefore a means to an end. It is a concrete manifestation not only of one's affluence, but also of one's desire and ability to lead integrated, 'mainstreams' lives.

> Nadeem: Most people think the same way [here in Bearsden]…they have the same mentality because they work hard, often doing the same type of jobs. We get on better here as a result…They say that [suburbanites] like to be anonymous, keeping themselves to themselves, but I wouldn't say this was true here…we are more of a community.

> (male, aged 34)

For Nadeem, class-consciousness penetrates Bearsden residents, creating common bonds and affiliations beyond those that come from simply 'sharing the same place'. Importantly, these bonds are such that they straddle ethnicity, thus providing a conduit for cultural hybridisation. This was clear from the ways in which, since his relocation from the core, Nadeem has become involved in a suburban network of social and leisure connections made up entirely of white people. Nadeem and Saima (his wife) often host neighbours during evening meals at their house, for example, and this is reciprocated at other times. They also regularly take part in a variety of (mainly) social events organised through their local health and fitness club, which they are members of. It was through one of these (a pre-natal class) that Saima met one of her closest friends.

Nonetheless, discussing these 'everyday' suburban networks leads towards an important cleavage point within otherwise middle-class, Scottish-Pakistani identities. Differences in occupational status (as either a 'professional' *or* a business owner/entrepreneur) are reflected in the varying depths to which suburban Pakistanis become immersed in these networks. The professional class is definitely more outwardly orientated compared to their more insular counterparts amongst the business community. As a doctor, Nadeem's involvement in these networks was typical of the professional class, whose social ties mimicked those from the workplace in that they stipulated relatively scant interaction with co-ethnics. This was in stark contrast to the more introverted business class who largely remained loyal to the 'tried and trusted' co-ethnic networks of interaction based on familiarity through shared ethnic origin. Again this mirrored work-related connections where it is not uncommon to find Pakistani businesses based almost entirely on co-ethnic input; from property source (leaseholder, vendor) through suppliers, employees and, finally, to the clients themselves (although, and as touched upon earlier, the enterprises of young Pakistanis in trailblazing businesses are increasingly geared towards multi-ethnic as well as non ethnic-specific markets). This overlap between the intra- and extra-workplace relationships of the business class is explained by the fact that many Pakistani business contacts and relationships *evolve from* pre-existing co-ethnic ties and connections, and vice versa. This class distinction – or deviation – was particularly tangible to Tahir, a retired physicist who, along with his wife and children, holds the notable distinction of being the first Pakistani to settle in Bearsden.

> Tahir: I have not experienced any racism at all [in Bearsden]. I came here as a professional – I was treated as a professional…not as a coloured person…I did not have any great deal of communication with the rest of [the] Pakistanis in the city when I came here to Bearsden. But [this is] because I am not in the business community, you see…I was an outsider with them, so I didn't have very much communication or contact with [the] Pakistani community in Glasgow…Most of my friends were local people either from my office or my neighbours.

(male, aged 58)

In his eyes Tahir's professional status distinguished him from the 'beating heart' of the Glasgow-Pakistani community, equated here with the business class. Additionally, it constituted a source of similarity with fellow (white) suburbanites, having the final say on how he was perceived by this group (as a professional instead of a 'coloured' person). Ethnicity is therefore playing blind to issues of class and status here as Tahir and his family continue to embed themselves further within the suburban social fabric. The imagined boundaries between Tahir and the 'rest' of the Pakistani population are nevertheless exacerbated by real, material boundaries. The physical separation between core and suburbia means that geography drives a further wedge between the two. Indeed, such were the infrequency of Tahir's trips to the core, and such was his lack of connections with the community there, he has begun to question the existence of any remaining continuity between himself and the undiluted, bastions of 'true' Pakistani identity; the business class (even referring to himself as an "outsider").

Stubborn Identities

For all this talk of dynamic, flowing and hybrid identities, some commentators have also reminded us of the need to recognise how groups and individuals consciously try to slow-down or resist processes of interculturation and cultural syncretism. These ideas were central to Valins' (1999) study of ultra-orthodox Jews in Manchester (England) in which he illustrated how this proud community attempts to stabilise, institutionalise and bind 'their' identities and demarcate 'their' space in the face of threats and challenges to their distinctive, ultra-orthodox way of life (in the form of inter-marriage, decreasing overall populations and racism). Such 'stubborn' identities (borrowing from a later paper by Valins, 2003) were also observed by Pratt (1999) in relation to the behaviour of Filipino domestic workers in the homes of their rich employees in the US. Through a range of covert anti-subversive tactics (such as cooking and decorating to their own tastes) Pratt elucidates how some of these transnational migrants were able to salvage elements of their 'own' authentic identity while at work within otherwise repressive settings. As well as illustrating how people may consciously impose boundaries around 'their' identities and, subsequently, how we must be careful not to overvalue hybridity, these examples also demonstrate how, rather than being negative and reactionary,[12] such attempts at cultural 'purity' may nonetheless be just as emancipatory as the very processes of hybridisation they are resisting. As Pratt herself states: 'marking boundaries, insisting on the materiality and persistence of differences, may be as politically productive as blurring them in the notions of mobility, hybridity and thirdspace' (Pratt, 1999: 164).

These sentiments also apply to Scottish-Pakistani identity in suburbia. Bearsden is far from a seamless melting pot of homogenous, middle-class *Scottish* identities. There are, instead, many 'sticking points' as efforts are made to retain traditional elements of religion and culture and although such retentions are by no means specific to suburbia their intensity is. Respondents stated that *extra* effort was required in maintaining their ethno-religious distinctiveness as high levels of concentration and close geographical proximity did not naturally solidify their cultural autonomy as happens in core areas of settlement. Ultimately, the most tenacious of these attempts centred upon religion and on a commitment to both the beliefs and practices of Islam. Being a Muslim is an important point of structuration within the lives of suburban Pakistanis, providing them with a way of remaining 'true to one's roots' when their identities are so obviously juxtaposed with, and polarized by, the 'whiteness' of suburbia. However, so too is an array of distinctive ethno-cultural practices used by Pakistanis in order to maintain a clear sense of who they – as 'Pakistanis' – are. Either way however, these attempts at bounding Pakistani identity are both most well defined and most intense in situations of adult (usually parental) guidance to children. The *inter-generationality* of Pakistani identity is therefore of utmost concern to suburban Pakistanis. To get a better handle on these ideas we first need to consider the following interview excerpt in which Kalda and Fahad reveal some of the emotions they typically experience when returning (for whatever reason) to core areas of Pakistani settlement:

Kalda: Yeah I do feel different; it's a nice change in a way...being among all these Pakistanis kind of reminds me where I came from.

(female, aged 28)

Fahad: Living in suburbia doesn't mean I have turned my back on the [Pakistani] community, but sometimes I feel this way when I'm in places like Allison Street [in Govanhill]...I sometimes feel bad that the children don't really experience this type of place, this would give them a better sense of who they are.

(male, aged 41)

Kalda and Fahad shed some light here on the identity dilemmas faced by suburban Pakistanis. They feel disenfranchised from the inner city repositories of Pakistani cultural

---

12 A relevant example concerning the British Muslim community relates to the aftermath of the Salman Rushdie affair, in which the post-colonial author became accused of making blasphemous statements towards Islam in his 1989 publication *The Satanic Verses*. What arguably emerged was a more defined, cohesive and defensive British Muslim (imagined) community, which had positioned itself staunchly against 'The West' and threatening Western discourse.

identity, leading them into modest expressions of sadness and even guilt. However it is here in these dilemmas that religion becomes especially important. Islam posits an imagined community in which geographical differences are overwritten by an adherence to the universal codes and strictures of Islam. One's separation from the 'heart' of the community is therefore less of an issue if one is fully committed to Islam. Nevertheless, so too is religion an important mode of self-assertion, letting Pakistanis 'carve out' identities in the face of hegemonic (suburban) cultural narratives. While older Pakistanis are safe in the knowledge that their own identities are secured, they are less confident about their children, whose suburban upbringings may stifle the very religious identities their parents are looking to secure.

Kalda: I would say that in terms of religion, parents here [in suburbia] try that wee bit harder. I mean we really encourage the religious education of our children – more so than in any other area in Glasgow I think. You have to remember that the same influences do not exist here as they do in other areas…Islam is not all around you like in other places.

(female, aged 28)

Fahad: I am proud of my roots, but I wonder where my children's priorities will lie tomorrow…I just have this thing that a lot of the Pakistani community has; that I am Muslim before I am Scottish…

(male, aged 41)

Sadiq: And you plan on conveying this to your children?

Fahad: Well, when you say 'convey' – I am not conveying anything. What I am doing is… I am merely making sure my children are brought up as Muslims.

(male, aged 41)

Stressing the importance of Islam to children is a method of 'coping' in socially uncertain times, bringing coherence and stability to a cultural identity in danger of fragmentation. These observations are not new within a British context, however. Jacobson (1997) found religion to be *the* source of identity in the lives of young British-Pakistanis, much more important than 'ethnicity', a much looser attachment to one's country of origin and 'things Pakistani', and 'not much more than loyalty to disparate customs from a distant place' (Jacobsen, 1997: 240). Jacobson states that young Pakistanis turn to religion since 'Islam's teachings are a source of precise and coherent guidance which enables them to rise above the uncertainties of existing in a world which they perceive as comprising two cultures' (Jacobsen, 1997: 254). These observations thus clarify the importance of religion to suburban Pakistanis, who, arguably, have to contend with *even more* extreme instances of cultural juxtaposition as their minority status is magnified by the surrounding 'whiteness' of suburbia.

It would, however, be wholly inaccurate to say that ethnicity plays no role in suburban identity construction. A plethora of disparate references to Pakistani and 'Asian' heritage are used *alongside* religion to further solidify identity, perhaps the most obvious example being the widespread use of *Urdu* as the 'mother' tongue. Parents led by example in this respect, using it as much as they could in the home so that children would follow suit. It was also not uncommon to find strictly monolingual households where Urdu was mandatory at all times. The importance of language is reflected in the weekly language classes for Pakistani children, which have been established in Bearsden for some time now. There are also expectations that these classes will eventually attain Scottish Qualifications Board (SQB) status so that the children will gain formal qualifications upon their completion. While these classes are currently run from the classroom of a local secondary school there are plans to develop a purpose-built cultural education centre in Bearsden for this and other purposes. Since the beginning, however, these plans have been vigorously contested with approximately 650 individual objections raised in relation to the first proposal put forward in 1998; some of these coming from individuals living as far as twenty miles away. One respondent I spoke to, a co-chairperson of the *Bearsden Asian Association*, the principle lobbyists in the development, voiced ill-feeling towards the nature of some objections which he claimed were based upon misplaced judgements and stereotypes. One source of anxiety he found particularly difficult involved the claims of some local residents that suburban tranquillity would be interrupted by 'blaring' prayer calls at inappropriate times in the morning, this even though the facility was not intended as a site of religion worship.

Several respondents said that ethnicity was both most relevant and most strongly retained by Pakistanis whose family origins lay in rural, as opposed to urban, regions of Pakistan. Adeel (male, aged 36) spoke about this distinction at some length, detailing how his parent's 'stuck in their way' attitude led to major conflict and disagreement between them. Upon hearing of their son's decision to marry a Scottish woman, Adeel's parents, who are originally from a small farming community in the Jallandhar district of the Punjab, accused their son of turning his back on his 'true' culture by rejecting their proposals of an arranged marriage, and also of a 'makeweight' arrangement in the shape of his marrying a co-ethnic bride of his choice. This, Adeel insisted, boiled down to their staunchly traditional, rural values.

Yet the binding qualities of ethnicity, its elements, and their overall usefulness to attempts at slowing down or resisting processes of cultural hybridisation are not always so clear-cut. Above all, there seems to be a lessening of those (imagined) affiliations with Pakistan (the place) and, indeed, Pakistanis (the people: one's self-distinction 'as' Pakistani). Saima, for example, preferred 'Asian' over 'Pakistani' as a signifier of her ethnic origin:

> Saima: I use the term 'Asian' as I am of Pakistani origin but I don't feel the same divisions that the first generation do between Indian, Bangladeshi and Pakistani. To me, I am Asian. I would call myself Scottish-Asian because I was born in Scotland, but very much my identity is an Asian identity because there is a lot of similarity between the culture in Indian Punjab and Pakistani Punjab where my parents come from.

(female, aged 35)

Any announcement of the demise of ethnicity as a source of identity would, of course, be widely inaccurate since 'Asian' still constitutes a term, albeit less specific, of ethnic reference. Yet Saima's views on ethnicity were by no means atypical of the younger generation, with several saying that they were 'Asian' (or Scottish-Asian) before they were 'Pakistani' (although Islam remained the clearest signifier of identity). Saima's sense of 'being Asian' was propelled by her recognition of the shared origins and histories of many Pakistanis and Indians; something she felt the first generation showed less sensitivity to.

Conclusions

It is fair to say that Britain's non-white communities have fared badly at the hands of extant academic commentaries. Their rigid, epistemological commitment to the quantitative analysis of inner city populations means that the store of existing knowledge of these communities is excessively narrow and incomplete. As it stands, we are thus well versed on the patterns of residential concentration and segregation endemic to these communities, if little else. For British Pakistani communities this situation is nevertheless especially problematic. An explosion of interest in the 'conflictual' and 'exotic' aspects of the British-Pakistani experience has joined these already problematic academic representations of insular, self-segregated groups inhabiting Britain's decaying inner cities. Furthermore, such narratives of marginality are compounded by emerging popular verdicts on British-Pakistani communities over the last five years with these frequently developed in response to events both local and global in origin. Taken together, such generalised, stereotypical understandings of marginality, scepticism and distrust ultimately suffocate the more nuanced realities of British-Pakistani settlement in which 'normality' and 'success' often feature. With reference to Glasgow's Pakistani community, and the demographical, attitudinal and cultural shifts therein, this chapter highlighted one such dimension of the British-Pakistani experience so far understated: the outward dispersal (suburbanisation) of Pakistanis to prosperous settlements on the urban periphery. It noted how young Pakistanis are fuelling the suburbanisation process via their association with, and articulation of, (upper) middle-class, 'professional' identities. Nevertheless, whilst not wanting to fold this particular account into another generalised narrative of a British-Pakistani community, it should be recognised that such evidently hybridised identities run in tandem with often-determined attempts to retain elements of 'Pakistani' identity, with these attempts usually forged around the universal doctrines and intended intergenerationality of Islam. Such complexities must be projected onto, and reflected in, future research directions on British-Pakistanis and other non-white communities which can no longer focus entirely on the migrant generations. Some forty years after the height of New Commonwealth migration to the UK it is now necessary to give full consideration to the social consequences experienced by the younger generations. One implication of this, as far as human geography is concerned, is that further attempts must be made to 'open up' and challenge the supposed 'racial' neutrality and 'whiteness' of British suburbia where accounts of uniform suburban ethnic relations are no longer valid (Mir, 2005; Naylor and Ryan, 1999: Watt, 1998).

References

Amin, A. (2003) Unruly strangers? the 2001 urban riots in Britain, *International Journal of Urban and Regional Research*, 27 (2), 460-463.

Anwar, M. (1979) *The Myth of Return: Pakistanis in Britain,* London: Heinemann.

Anzaldua, G. (1987) *Borderlands/La Frontera: the New Mestiza*, San Francisco: Spinsters/ Aunt Lute.

Bonnett, A. (1996) Anti-racism and the critique of 'White' identities, *New Community*, 22, 97-110.

Bonnett, A. (1997) Geography, 'race' and whiteness: invisible traditions and current challenges, *Area*, 29, 193-199.

Castells, M. (1997) *The Power of Identity*, Oxford: Blackwell.

Cohen, P. (1993) *Home Rules: Some Reflections on Racism and Nationalism in Everyday Life*, London: University of East London.

Cross, M. and Keith, M. (1993) *Racism, the City and the State*, London: Routledge.

Dahya, B. (1973) Pakistanis in Britain: transients or settlers?, *Race*, 14 (3), 241-277.

Davis, M. (1990) *City of Quartz*, London: Vintage.

Denham, J. (2001) *Building Cohesive Communities: A Report of the Ministerial Group on Public Order and Community Cohesion*, London: HMSO.

Drummer, T. and McEvoy D. (2004) 'Ethnic segregation and community incoherence: the Bradford (UK) riot of July 7 2001', paper given at the Association of American Geographers (AAG) annual meeting, Philadelphia, 2004.

Duncan, O. and Duncan B. (1955) A methodological analysis of segregation indexes, *American Sociological Review*, 20, 210-217.

Ferguson, K. (1993) *The Man Question: Visions of Subjectivity in Feminist Theory*, Berkeley, University of California Press.

Hall, S. (1996) 'Introduction', in S. Hall and P. Du Gay (eds), *Questions of Cultural Identity*, London: Sage.

Hopkins, P. (2004) Young Muslim men in Scotland: inclusions and exclusions, *Children's Geographies*, 2 (2), 257-272.

Jackson, P. (1998) Constructions of 'Whiteness' in the geographical imagination, *Area*, 30 (2), 99-106.

Jackson, P. (1987) *Race and Racism: Essays in Social Geography*, London: Allen and Unwin.

Jacobson, J. (1997) Religion and ethnicity: dual and alternative sources of identity among British Pakistani teenagers, *Ethnic and Racial Studies*, 20 (2), 238-256.

Jones, T. and McEvoy, D. (1978) Race and space in cloud-cuckoo land, *Area*, 10 (3), 162-166.

Jones, T. and McEvoy, D. (1979a) Race and space, *Area*, 11 (1), 84-85.

Jones, T. and McEvoy, D. (1979b) More on race and space, *Area*, 11 (3), 222-223.

Kearsley, G. and Srivistava, S. (1974) The spatial evolution of Glasgow's Asian community, *Scottish Geographical Magazine*, 90 (2), 110-124.

Keith, M. (1993) *Race, Riots and Policing: Lore and Disorder in a Multi-Racist Society*, London: UCL.

Khan, V. S. (1979) 'Migration and social stress: Mirpuris in Bradford', in Khan, V.S. (ed.) *Minority Families in Britain: Support and Stress*, London: MacMillan, 37-57.

Kundnani, A. (2001) In a foreign land: the new popular racism, *Race and Class*, 43 (2), 41-60.

Lee, T. (1978) Race, space and scale, *Area*, 10 (6), 365-367.

Mir, S. (2005) 'From Villages 477 and 482 to Suburbia: The Suburbanisation of Glasgow's Pakistani Community', unpublished PhD thesis, University of Glasgow.

Morill, C. (1965) The Negro ghetto: problems and alternatives, *Geographical Review*, 55 (3), 339-361.

Naylor, S. and Ryan, J.R. (2002) The Mosque in the suburbs: negotiating religion and ethnicity in South London, *Social and Cultural Geography*, 3 (1), 39-60.

Ouseley, H. (2001) *Community Pride not Prejudice: Making Diversity Work in Bradford*, Bradford: Bradford Vision.

Peach, C. (1979a) Race and space, *Area*, 11 (1), 82-84.

Peach, C. (1979b) More on race and space, *Area*, 11 (1), 82-84

Peach, C. (1996) Does Britain have ghettos?, *Transactions of the Institute of British Geographers*, 21, 216-235.

Peach, C. (1999) Social geography, *Progress in Human Geography*, 23 (2), 282-288.

Peach, C. (2002) Social geography: new religions and ethnoburbs – contrasts with cultural geography, *Progress in Human Geography*,? 252-260.

Phillips, D. (2004) 'British-Asian housing opportunities: narratives of change', Paper given at Department of Urban Studies seminar, University of Glasgow, May 7, 2004.

Pratt, G. (1999) 'Geographies of identity and difference: marking boundaries', in D. Massey, J. Allen and P. Sarre (eds), *Human Geography Today*, Cambridge: Polity Press.

Rainwater, L. (1970) *Behind Ghetto Walls: Black Families in a Federal Slum*, Chicago: Aldine.

Shaw, A. (2001) Kinship, cultural preference and immigration: consanguineous marriage among British Pakistanis, *The Journal of the Royal Anthropological Institute*, 7 (2), 315-334.

Sibley, D. (1995) *Geographies of Exclusion*, London: Routledge.

Simpson, L. (2004) Statistics of racial segregation: measures, evidence and policy, *Urban Studies*, 41 (3), 661-681.

Solomos, J. (1993) 'Constructions of Black criminality in perspective: racialisation and criminalisation in perspective', in D. Cook and B. Hudson (eds) *Racism and Criminology*, London: Sage.

Solomos, J. and Back, L (1995), *Race, Politics and Social Change*, London: Routledge.

Taeuber, K. and Taeuber, A. (1964) The Negro as an immigrant group, *American*

Journal of Sociology, 69, 374-382, reprinted in C. Peach (ed.), (1975), *Urban Social Segregation*, London: Longman.

Urry, J. (1995) 'A middle-class countryside, in social change and the middle classes', in T. Butler (ed.), cited in P. Watt (1998), *Going Out of Town: 'Race' and Place in the South East of England, Environment and Planning D: Society and Space*, 16 687-703.

Valins, O. (1999) 'Identity, Space and Boundaries: Ultra-Orthodox Judaism in Contemporary Britain', unpublished PhD thesis, University of Glasgow: Scotland.

Valins, O. (2003) Stubborn identities and the construction of socio-spatial boundaries: Ultra-Orthodox Jews living in contemporary Britain, *Transactions of the Institute of British Geographers*, 28 (2), 158-174.

Watt, P. (1998), Going out of town: 'race' and place in the south east of England, *Environment and Planning D: Society and Space*, 16, 687-703.

Chapter 5

Migration and the Construction of Muslim Women's Identity in Northern Ireland

Gabriele Marranci

We are not our veils, we are not stupid; we are not passive; we are not Paki, Arabs, and Bangladeshi and so on. We are Muslim: Muslim women in Northern Ireland.

(Pakistani woman)

Introduction

While many studies have focused on Muslim women, both new migrant and second generation Muslims living in western countries, one European region has been overlooked: Northern Ireland. This chapter focuses on the processes through which Muslim women in Northern Ireland, and in particular its capital, Belfast, construct their identity. Before discussing my specific ethnographic case, I provide the reader with my interpretation of the concept of identity as well as a brief description of the Muslim community in Northern Ireland. This is followed by a discussion of the experiences of Muslim women in Northern Ireland and their attitudes towards Islam being part of their identities. It is important to emphasize that when I mention Muslim women, I am referring exclusively to Muslim migrant women and those born of migrant parents.

This chapter is based upon my three years of ethnographic research in Northern Ireland (between 2000 and 2003). The methods I employed included participant observation of the Belfast Muslim community, in addition to unstructured and semi-structured interviews with seventy-six Muslim women in Northern Ireland, some of which were conducted as group discussions on particular topics. While some interviews were tape-recorded, the majority were shorthanded since the tape recorder was often perceived as intrusive by many of my female respondents. Notwithstanding being a male anthropologist, I did not encounter problems in interviewing Muslim women as I had initially expected. In fact, my access to influential 'gatekeepers' in the community in addition to the use of group discussions facilitated the development of trust between researcher and respondents.

The Northern Irish Muslim Community

The absence of previous studies on Muslim *ummah* or community of believers in Northern Ireland has made it difficult to determine its local history. Indeed, prior to September 11, 2001 the community attracted little if any attention from mass media and local authorities. As such I was not surprised to discover that people in Northern Ireland considered Muslims to be recent immigrants. Contrary to this popular perception, Muslims in Northern Ireland are part of a well-established community with an interesting local history. Yet it is a history without archives and documentation thus, similar to other histories of 'religious' minorities, it is forged by personal memories.

Muslims initially arrived in Ireland around 1780 as members of the East India Company. At the beginning of the nineteenth century, the majority settled in the cosmopolitan city of Cork whilst one new arrival married an Irish woman from Belfast and moved there. In 1920, at a time when Muslim presence was increasing, the Government of Ireland Act established Northern Ireland as a separate political unit. This Act caused the relationship between Dublin and London to deteriorate and in the 1930s; Valera's Fianna Fáil (FF) government initiated a trade war. Many Muslims, concerned about the political situation in the region, decided to move to England where they had relatives or friends. However, in Ballymena, some Indian Muslims had developed businesses and decided to remain. These Muslim immigrants did not try to organize an *ummah* by building mosques or setting up prayer rooms since they saw their migration to Northern Ireland as temporary, with the intention of returning to England. For this reason, many Muslims kept strong linkages with family members living in English cities. However, these contacts actually further stimulated immigration to Northern Ireland instead of a return to England because of the economic opportunities available there. Economic opportunity continues to act as a pull factor for immigrant groups to Northern Ireland, as seen with the recent growth of the Bangladeshi community. During the 1950s, Muslims originating from the Middle East joined Indian and Pakistani Muslims, who predominated at the time. For the most part, these Arabs were students of the Queen's University of Belfast. Upon their arrival, they were unaware of the tensions that were growing in Northern Ireland. In 1953, Muslims from several different countries prayed together in a private flat to celebrate the *id-al-fitr* (the end of Ramadan). *Id-al-fitr* is not only a religious rite marking the end of Ramadan, but also a symbol of unity and an emotional experience. For Muslims in Northern Ireland during that time, this event was particularly an emotional experience. In fact, according to the people that took part in the ceremony in Northern Ireland, this was the first time that Muslims of diverse backgrounds prayed communally in order to celebrate an Islamic rite. This event can be linked to the political and sectarian tensions which were rising within the region. The tensions resulted in the so-called 'border campaign' by the Irish Republican Army (IRA) and, a few years later, in violent terrorist activities between the paramilitary factions. Given this context, it is noteworthy that Muslims in Northern Ireland, for the first time, felt the need to develop a community that would provide them with a unique status so as to differentiate themselves from the Northern Irish Roman Catholics and Protestants. This has facilitated a new sense of re-discovery of unity – what I could call the 'emotion of the *ummah*' – engendering the need for an Islamic place in Northern Ireland.

By the 1960s, the weekly congregational prayers (*salat al-jummah*) and sermon held on Fridays were being performed in the same private flat that housed the milestone event a decade earlier. Congregation membership increased considerably over time, so much so that by 1972 the 'Islamic Society of Northern Ireland' (ISNI) was set up to coordinate activities including, among others, the collection of funds to build a mosque. Prior to acquiring a mosque, the members of ISNI had to hold their meetings in the Student Union building of Queen's University. Finally, in 1979 they bought a flat in South Belfast and turned it into a mosque and Islamic Centre. The people attending the Friday *jummah* increased to such a level that the prayer room in the flat was unable to accommodate the worshippers and the need for a larger place of worship became evident. In 1985, collected funds and a donation from Dublin Islamic Centre enabled the purchase of a semi-detached house at Wellington Park, close to the South Belfast flat, which became, and still is, the home of the Belfast Islamic Centre (BIC). The only symbol to distinguish this house from the surrounding houses is a green-white insignia reading 'The Belfast Islamic Centre', written both in English and Arabic. For the local Muslim population, the Islamic Cultural Centre and its mosque became a symbol of unity for the Northern Irish *ummah*. Whether Shi'a, Sunni, Arab, Pakistani, Indonesian, Malaysian, Moroccan, Algerian, Indian, or Afghan, all Muslims shared the mosque and social-political community space regardless of their origin.

Until recently, Muslims in Northern Ireland have avoided being involved in the sectarian religious divisions marking Northern Irish society (see Marranci, 2003a, 2003b, 2004). Hence, they have formed trans-community relationships with both Nationalists and Unionists. Since Muslims in Northern Ireland are aware of the cultural, social and political tensions characterizing this society, they have made efforts to adopt a low profile by de-emphasizing symbolic elements such as the use of Arabic or foreign languages in favour of the adoption of English as the official language of the community.

Among the difficulties I encountered during my fieldwork, the one that proved to be the most challenging was the generation of an accurate estimate of the number of Muslims living in the region. According to the Belfast Islamic Centre, the number of Muslims currently residing in Northern Ireland is estimated at 4,000 (2,000 of which were registered with the mosque during the time of my field research). Surprisingly, this statistic was inconsistent with the number given to me by the Northern Irish Statistics and Research Agency. This agency recorded only 997 Muslims living in Northern Ireland, which is an estimation since the 1991 Census did not collect data on religious affiliation. According to the 2001 Census, which for the first time included a non-compulsory question concerning religious affiliations, there were 1,943 Muslims in Northern Ireland; consequently, they represent the largest non-Christian religious community in the region. Although the majority of the Muslim population is concentrated in Belfast (727 according to the census), Muslims are found in many other Northern Irish cities and towns, including Castlereagh (where they number 159), Craigavon (149), North Down (132), Newtownabbey (103) Ballymena (67) and Derry (60).

From Emotion to Identity

There is no other subject in social science that has attracted as much attention as human identity. In fact, the question 'who am I ?' is one of the most challenging we ask ourselves. The majority of studies on identity have approached the topic from an 'outsider's' perspective (see Marranci, 2006). In other words, scholars have studied what individuals do in everyday life, when interaction occurs and, consequentially, how individuals use each other's identities in an instrumental way. In this case identity becomes a social instrument and what we think of the other becomes *the real* other. Furthermore, in such a context identity becomes a matter of differentiation that facilitates the process of interpreting people's actions as delineating boundaries. It appears that this understanding of identity is logically flawed (Bateson, 2002). Although differentiation marks identity in the social world, should we assume, as many social scientists do, that the individual experiences his or her identity as social differentiation?

After sifting through the various theories of identity and self that emphasize the unique role of culture in identity formation, I have observed that an alternate interpretation can be brought to the fore. By interpreting, as Milton suggested (Milton, 2002 and Milton *et al.* 2005), culture as an ecological part of nature, I believe that the environment has an impact on human beings. According to certain recent anthropological studies (Ingold, 1992, 1993 and Milton, 2002, 2005), emotions are central to the way in which we perceive our surrounding environment. However, recent neuroscientific studies (see Damasio, 2000) have challenged the common notion of emotions as subjective feelings, by suggesting that emotions are merely bodily responses which are perceived to provoke feelings. Based upon these conflicting interpretations, Milton *et al.* (2005) have proposed that emotions are ecological rather than social phenomena, though social interaction surely contributes to emotions. If this is the case, as I believe it is, then what we call 'self' and 'identity' are not the products of social interaction (although social interaction can provoke changes in them). Thus, this novel notion contradicts the claim of the majority of social science theories. Damasio (2000) provides a convincing argument of how we come to form our autobiographical self. I accept Damasio's point of view and I am in agreement that identity is a 'delicately shaped machinery of our imagination [which] stakes the probabilities of selection toward the same, historically continuous self' (Damasio, 2000: 225).

I have explained (Marranci 2006) that identity is a process which allows human beings to make sense of their autobiographical self and express it through symbols which communicate, at an inner level, feelings which would otherwise be incommunicable. I have suggested that it is *what we feel to be* that determines our identity. This implies that identity statements such as 'I am Muslim' are, therefore, the symbolic communication of one's emotional commitment through which individuals experience their autobiographical self. To illustrate my point, let us consider a fictitious Muslim women named Salima to consider a fictitious Muslimwoman named Salima who wears a headscarf and states "I am Muslim". Salima is no different from other human beings, thus she engages in the process that I interpret as the formation of human identity. In other words, Salima has an autobiographical self which she makes sense of through the delicately shaped machinery of her imagination that enables her to communicate the symbolic expression "I am Muslim". Finally, Salima is what she feels to be, regardless of what others, engaged in countless public discourses around the use of cultural markers, might perceive her to be. As such, the statement "I am Muslim" implies that Salima feels herself to be Muslim.

This illustrative example highlights the existence of a circuit which is initiated by environmental stimuli that produce emotions (the body's reaction to stimuli). These emotions are perceived by Salima as feelings, in turn affecting her autobiographical self that is experienced (or made sense of) through the delicately shaped machinery of her imagination which she refers to as her Muslim identity. Of course, her identity is now affected by the feelings she experiences, in other words by what I have described is a circuit of causalities based on information both internal and external to the individual with this circuit aiming to maintain equilibrium at different levels. Indeed, physiological as well as psychoanalytic studies tell us that equilibrium between self and identity is essential to a healthy life. Very simply put, I can say that what we call personal identity is a circuit connecting the autobiographical-self to the environment. Yet the needed equilibrium can be disrupted by changes in the environment which can ultimately challenge the sophisticated circuit that composes our identity.

Bateson (2002) has explained how 'positive gain' (i.e. progressive escalations), which he refers to as schismogenesis, can disrupt any circuit form. As such, the relationship between the autobiographical self and the process of identity formation, which allows human beings to make sense of it, can be subjected to schismogenetic events. In this situation, I argue (Marranci 2006) that people try to find their equilibrium by self-correcting their identity through 'acts of identity'. Such acts are expressed through rhetorically symbolic forms which attempt to change the surrounding environment so as to perceive challenges as less threatening.

In the following section, I explain how Muslim women in Northern Ireland have developed specific acts of identity through Islamic rhetoric which suit the Northern Irish political, social and cultural environment.

The Experience of Migration

Over the last twenty years, social scientists have demonstrated an increasing interest in the study of diaspora and migration. Despite this fact, such studies have often overlooked the specific role played by gender in these phenomena. Coincidentally Freedman and Tarr (2000) have observed that,

> Studies about immigration and post-colonial society in France tend to ignore or marginalize the gendered nature of their subject. If recently some attention has been paid to children of Muslim immigrant parents in Europe, the same could not be said in the case of Muslim immigrant women.

(Freedman and Tarr 2000: 1)

Recently, the experience of migrant women has started to be reported in ethnographic studies. Nonetheless, Bretell (2000: 119) rightly observed that '[W]omen were generally ignored in the study of migration until quite recently. If women were considered at all, then it was as dependents and passive followers of the initiating male migrant'.

Bretell (2000: 109) noted that anthropologists 'have been at the forefront in theorizing about the significance of gender in migration'. Additionally, he highlights a number of anthropological studies which have focused on women's migration experience.[1] However, none of these works has discussed Muslim women's migration experience in western countries. One of the most recent publications that address this topic is by Bujis (1993). This book contains three essays concerning Muslim women immigrants (see Abdulrahim 1993 and Bhachu 1993). The contributing authors focus in particular on the relationship their respondents developed with their host societies. For instance, Abdularahim (1993) suggests that some Muslim migrant women have used their religious and ethnic traditions to mark clear boundaries between their Muslim identities and their host society. These scholars tend to present the experience of migration as traumatic to which Muslim migrant women react through a conservative cultural process. However, Bhachu has suggested that cultural practices which western people consider oppressive and archaic, such as the dowry, arranged marriages, and strong family networks, may have liberating effects on immigrant women since they can empower them within their families (Bhachu 1993: 99-118.). Shaw (1988) expressed a similar idea in her study of the Pakistani community in Oxford,

> Some women see their roles in Britain quite explicitly in terms of maintaining and transmitting cultural and religious values and protecting their families from western influences. A major theme in this book is that it is largely women who are responsible for the distinctive structure and social life of the community today; it is in this that their power lies.

(Shaw, 1988: 5)

In contrast, other authors have paid attention to the role that surrounding environments have on Muslim migrant women.[2] Salih (2000) conducted fieldwork among Moroccan women in Emilia-Romagna, Italy, where she observed that Muslim migrant women were not passive in their migration process but rather interacted with different identities. In fact, Salih found that Muslim migrant women go beyond the conservative attitude of pre-existing traditions. Rather, Salih has discovered that her respondents, 'contextually negotiate boundaries of inclusion and exclusion and self and Other, according to the diverse and sometimes intersecting hegemonic discourses that they may be facing in different places and phases of their lives'(Salih, 2000 : 323).

It is evident in Salih's (2000) study how Islam itself is part of a negotiation process instead of a conservative, defensive attitude towards the host society. She recognizes Islam as an important factor in this process :'[W]hile some women identify with a global Muslim community, the *umma,* and refuse contact with non-practicing Muslims, other women redefine or locally challenge religious meanings and combine different cultural and religious repertoires' (Salih, 2000 : 333).

Migration to Northern Ireland

According to the 2001 Northern Irish Census, approximately 600 Muslim women live in the region. This is an underestimate of the number of Muslims living in Northern Ireland, since many decide not to answer the Census question related to religious affiliation (Marranci 2003). The majority of Muslim women are part of the first generation of migrants who migrated to Northern Ireland mainly for two reasons: following their husbands or completing their studies. South Asians, and Pakistanis in particular, comprise the largest ethnic group within the Northern Irish Muslim community (about 70 per cent), although the two local universities (Queen's University of Belfast, and Ulster University) have attracted some Arab students who have decided to settle in the region and form about 20 per cent of the Muslim population. Nonetheless, the majority of Muslim women are of Pakistani and Bangladeshi descent (80 per cent).

Some of the women migrated to Northern Ireland from other parts of the UK while others arrived from Bangladesh and Pakistan without any prior experience of living in a western country. Nonetheless, both groups had to adapt to the particular social, political and cultural environment of Northern Ireland, a context which has undoubtedly improved since the beginning of the peace process initiated by the 1998 Good Friday Agreement. Yet for the first wave of Muslim migrant women to Northern Ireland in the late 1970s, this new place seemed dangerous and threatening and this sentiment is captured in the experiences I collected from the first Muslim women living in Belfast.

Rashida followed her husband, a heart surgeon, to Belfast. Since the beginning of their residence in Belfast, she missed her home in Karachi. Everything was different, from the smell of the place to the taste of the food. Rashida and her husband lived in one of the Protestant areas, which she thought to be particularly threatening since British soldiers regularly patrolled the area. Rashida recalled how she started to understand the sectarianism among Northern Irish Christians as something similar to the sectarianism between Sunni and Shi'a Muslims in Pakistan. Despite the violent environment, she told me, 'There were bombs and killings, but of course, this was something affecting the Christian communities. I felt protected by my religion and, at that time, by my dark skin. It was clear that I was a foreigner and because of my headscarf, a non-Christian one' (Rashida, interview).

At the time there were very few Muslims in Northern Ireland, thus isolation was a central issue that arose. In order to cope with isolation, some Muslim women tried to build relationships and friendships with Northern Irish women of both Catholic and Protestant traditions. Notwithstanding their efforts and the Northern Irish hospitality, cultural differences and religious misunderstandings affected many of these relationships and only a few became long-term friendships. One of the interviewees explained why she found it so difficult to develop cross-cultural relationships in Northern Ireland:

> It was very hard! Too many differences. Even when you build a relationship, in many cases there are some kinds of problems that are very difficult to overcome: first of all they drink lots of alcohol. Here it is part of the culture. They did not think that inviting a

Muslim woman to a pub was quite similar to offending her. Then, when I was wearing my *hijab* they thought that it was my husband that wanted it. They did not believe me when I told them that I want to wear the *hijab*.

(Salima, Iraqi woman, aged 52)

The problems that these women faced were not only limited to isolation and lack of understanding with the autochthones, but also lack of basic Muslim services, such as shops and *halal* butchers. Even cooking the simplest dish became a struggle, as a respondent emphasized, 'we were eating fish only, and I had to change all the traditional dishes, trying to cook something palatable for my family'. The threatening environment, the lack of relationship with the local communities, and the limited number of Muslims living in the region, forced many Muslim women to see their homes as the safest place in which to spend their days. Although unemployment among Muslims in Northern Ireland tends to be lower than in other parts of the United Kingdom, even today, only about 30 percent of Muslim women are employed, with the second generation being comprised mainly of students. Indeed, the majority of Muslim women in Northern Ireland define themselves as 'housewives' or 'full-time mothers'.

As El-Solh and Mabro (1994: 16-18) have pointed out Muslim women have very different opinions on family and kinship relationships than many western women (see also Shaw 1988). What a western woman might perceive as a hindrance to her freedom could be perceived by a Muslim woman as personal fulfillment: her family, her house, her husband, her parents and her childcare (Arebi 1991). Muslim women in Northern Ireland consider themselves the pillar of their family unit. This belief is heightened by the context within which they live, including the following factors: a difficult political environment, the unfamiliar and incomprehensible divisions between one sectarian neighbourhood and another, the various and difficult to master Northern Irish accents, and the deep differences in customs and ethical traditions. These external factors increasingly reinforced their Islamic identity; thus they came to see themselves as not just women but *Muslim* women:

I prefer to stay at home. I do not like to walk alone or take the bus here. It's so different from Libya. You don't know anybody. And I would have to make too many compromises to work here. I have the responsibility of my children and my husband, and we can cope with what my husband earns. I feel that in this way I might be a good Muslim woman.

(Fatima, Libyan woman, aged 40)

Nonetheless, in some instances the home becomes a challenging space for Muslim women migrants. This is the case for women migrants that have come to reside in Northern Ireland through arranged marriages, a common practice for the Bangladeshi and Pakistani members of the Muslim community. These new brides, who no longer receive the support of their family, must depend on their husband's family. Thus the lack of traditional support that a young bride usually receives impacts her life as a Muslim woman migrant. In some instances, the new bride discovers upon her arrival that her husband does not match the description she was given by the person who arranged her marriage: such descriptors may include hardworking, kind, religious and a dedicated family man. In other circumstances women who migrate due to an arranged marriage, while hoping for socio-economic improvement in their lives, may be subjected to marital abuse and isolation, as one of respondents mentioned,

> Some women are even severely beaten by their husbands. There are a lot of problems, in particular among the Pakistanis. They [women] do not have any support ... the family is what they have here. What should they do? You know ... many women in Northern Ireland suffer domestic violence and this is affecting the Muslim families as well!

(Malika, Pakistani woman, aged 54)

As indicated earlier, during the 1980s the Muslim community increased significantly. This increase was the result of Muslim women joining their husbands or their families living in Northern Ireland. The establishment of the Craigavon Mosque, and later of the BIC, gave the migrant women their first opportunity to meet and share their experiences. These migrants started women's circles and organized social activities, which became central to the life of their community, in particular in the teaching of Islam to second generations. While the Muslim women's circles focused on several issues, the most important was to provide support to Muslim women suffering from domestic violence. The women that participated in the circles felt empowered by the study of the Qur'an and the Sunna. Indeed, these women believed that the study of sacred texts would allow them to support their arguments more strongly than those of men, who often do not have the time, or the will, to study Islam:

> They [Muslim women in Northern Ireland] have many problems because they don't know the Sunna and Qur'an very well. They think that domestic violence is part of their lives, part of the marriage. When they arrive in Northern Ireland, they discover that Northern Irish women also suffer domestic violence ... this doesn't help them [men] to think that domestic violence is wrong. Islam is clear about violence within the family. Islam empowers the Muslim women within the family, not only because of the protection that it gives to them, but also because of the economic power that women can achieve. I want to say ... Islam is good for women.

(Nora, Pakistani woman, aged 54)

Concurrently, the Muslim women living in Craigavon thought that being organized in a visible association would facilitate their relationship with the host society without compromising their personal Islamic values. Consequently, Muslim men in the community became concerned when the women's organization achieved success and their strong voices were heard. In order to subvert their efforts, Muslim men forced the women in Craigavon to stop their organizing. Despite this outcome, their experience has influenced women's groups in other cities. For instance, an officially registered organization, the Al-Nisa Women's Group was formed in Belfast. This group was established by Mrs. Khan and Pakistani women in 1998, the same year of the Good Friday Agreement. During one of my conversations with Mrs.

Khan she explained why they decided to form this organization, which would have an important impact on the integration of Muslim women within Northern Ireland,

> Twenty-seven years ago there were few Muslims in Northern Ireland and even fewer women. Moreover, no women were involved in the activities of the mosque. They did not have any influence. Even though they were very active - more than men I have to say - we did not have any woman on the [mosque's] committee. So we needed to do something to educate Muslim women in an Islamic way. Well, three years ago we organized Al-Nisa thanks to the funds that the government and NICEM had provided. We are now a charity organization with our charity number. Of course, men were not very happy about this organization and our independence and freedom, even though all our activities and actions were completely Islamic!

(Mrs Khan, President of Al-Nisa)

The divide between the Muslim migrant women and some male members of the local mosque was thus provoked by their different interpretations of what the term 'Islamic' means.

The Construction of an Active Muslim Identity: The Experience of Muslim Women in Northern Ireland

Muslim migrant women have actively tried to fight the isolation they were subjected to as a result of the particular Northern Irish political environment and the strong patriarchal structure of the Pakistani and Bangladeshi Muslim communities. The women's efforts to become an active part of Northern Irish society had led to increased tension with local mosque leaders. The fact that the Al-Nisa women's group was ostracized by the BIC highlights the difficulty of integrating Muslim women into the male majority. As a result of their irreconcilable differences, the collaboration between the Al-Nisa Women's Group and the BIC broke down in the summer of 2002. Although the relationship between the two groups was never smooth, the tension reached its climax during a special General Meeting of the BIC during which the Al-Nisa Women's Group found itself at the centre of a heated discussion. The qualifier 'heated' is indeed appropriate, for during the meeting, a young Muslim man attempted to set fire to a controversial annual report issued by the Al-Nisa Women's Group's. This hostile action was instigated by the transcript of a speech given by the president of the Al-Nisa Women's Group at a conference on the topic of women in Northern Ireland. The controversy surrounded the following statement: 'As women, let us not forget that other equally strong elements make up our identities. Some of us are disabled, old, young, *lesbian or bisexual*, rich, poor and so on'.

Clearly the reference to women's sexual orientation was seen as inappropriate and unacceptable by the Muslim men of the BIC. However, the statement made by the president of the Al-Nisa Women's Group was misinterpreted as it referred to Northern Irish women in general, and not specifically to Muslim women. This disagreement emphasizes the fact that members of the Al-Nisa Women's Group had developed an identity that took into consideration the emotional environment of the mainstream society, while the Muslim men's identity did not. The outcome of the BIC General Meeting included banning the Al-Nisa Women's Group from using the BIC logo and requiring the group to leave the BIC premises. Despite being shunned by the BIC, the Al-Nisa Women's Group did not disappear, as was the case of the Muslim women's group in Craigavon. In fact the group was offered a meeting space and office in the Women's Aid organization in Belfast which addressed the needs of refugees. This generous donation resulted from its trans-community support network that had developed over the years.

While both Muslim migrant women and Muslim migrant men claim to have 'Islamic' identities, the formation of their respective identities originates from two different processes thus reflecting the different ways in which Muslim men and Muslim women came to experience Northern Irish society and their shared Muslim community. In order to understand how Muslim migrant women have successfully integrated into Northern Irish society while maintaining their sense of Muslim identity, it is necessary to study the dynamics through which this process occurred. According to Ganguly (1997), immigrant women's memory plays an important role in this process:

> The recollections of the past serve as the active ideological terrain on which people represent themselves to themselves. The past acquires a more marked salience with subjects for whom categories of the present have been made unusually unstable or unpredictable as a consequence of the displacement enforced by postcolonial and migrant circumstances.

> (Ganguly 1997: 29-30)

Earlier I explained how identity formation is a process that allows us to make sense of our autobiographical selves which in turn is expressed through symbols that communicate personal feelings. We have also seen that schismogenetic processes can affect the relationship between the environment and the autobiographical self. Muslim migrant women in Northern Ireland have experienced two schismogenetic processes: first, a difficult integration within Northern Irish society and, secondly, an uneasy relationship with male members of the Muslim community. In order to overcome these destabilizing obstacles, Muslim migrant women in Northern Ireland have developed a particular Islamic rhetoric. For these women, Islam represents more than just a religion; Islam becomes the framework through which they make sense of their current situation, in addition to a hegemonic (Gramsci 1971: 324) lens through which they filter their environment. In other words, Islam becomes their 'act of identity'. In contrast, Islam to Muslim migrant men in Northern Ireland represents a conservative frame which they see as structuring and preserving their distinctly asserted identity.

As such, by employing Islam as an 'act of identity' instead of a 'boundary marker', Muslim women have been able to overcome their obstacles. Despite being exposed to the Northern Irish conflict and the patriarchal system of their community, Muslim migrant women have been able to foster a sense of being part of Northern Irish society without feeling challenged by its western values and Christian sectarian environment. The emphasis on religion that the women were exposed to in Northern Ireland inspired them to rethink Islam as into being an empowering force.

For the Muslim women, the decision to organize an independent association affiliated with the Northern Irish government, and to focus on women's issues affecting the multicultural communities of Northern Ireland, affirmed their active Islamic identity. Thus this Muslim organization can be considered a 'community of emotions'. Maffesoli (1996) and Hetherington (1996) have argued that people form communities in order to share emotions and identify empathetically. Although this process requires identification, Maffesoli (1996: 98) has argued that personal identities find their expression in the community through mutual transformation,

> ... this bond is without the rigidity of the forms of organization with which we are familiar; it refers more to a certain ambience, a state of mind ... It is a case of a kind of collective unconscious (non-conscious) which acts as a matrix for varied group experience, situations, actions or wanderings.

(Maffesoli, 1996: 98)

The Muslim women's active study of the Qur'an and the Sunna gave them the opportunity to reflect on their past lives in their homeland and their present experiences in the Northern Irish environment. By emphasizing the universal message of Islam, the process of self-reflection reinforced their belief that they are able to express themselves both as Muslims and women living in and part of Northern Ireland. In fact, to be part of Northern Ireland, (hence being Muslim women *of* Northern Ireland) has deconstructed the second schimogenetic process: the patriarchal structure of the local Muslim community, which had attempted to deny the Muslim women of their identity. Thus to the women, becoming part *of* Northern Irish society has allowed them to alienate the patriarchal power that the Muslim community may have exerted upon them.

Conclusion

In this chapter, I have discussed how Muslim migrant women of Northern Ireland have formed their Muslim identity in relation to their environment. After describing the Muslim community of the region, I suggested that in order to understand identity it is necessary to consider human emotions and the function they play in making sense of our environment. Indeed, my findings indicate that emotions have played a very important role in the formation of Muslim women's identity. This identity was forged by the feelings of instability and insecurity that marked their first experiences in Northern Ireland, and facilitated their control by patriarchal male members of their Muslim community.

However the formation of Muslim women's circles and organizations challenged the schismogenetic processes at hand. Organisations, such as the Al-Nisa Women's Group, helped Muslim migrant women reconceptualize their religion into an innovative act of identity rather than a conservative element in their lives. These women's organizations became, to use Mafessolian (1996) terminology, 'communities of emotion', in which the Muslim migrant women share feelings about their past as well as their challenging present. Many of the Muslim women that migrated to Northern Ireland lost the support of their family members. Given this occurence, the 'community of emotion' helps the migrant women overcome their feelings of isolation and displacement. Thus, instigated by schimogenetic processes, the women rethought their past and present through Islam. This act of identity allowed the women to feel part of Northern Irish society without compromising their beliefs.

Notes

1. Among the works quoted, the most relevant to this study are: Brettell and Callier-Boisvert (1997: 149-203); Goode and Schneider (1994); Hondagneu-Sotelo (1992: 393-415), Morokavisic (1983: 13-31); and Simon (1986: d).
2. See Clifford (1994); Freedman and Tarr (2000); Lacoste-Dujardin (2000: 57-68), Saint-Blancat (1998: 107-115); Hussain and O'Bien (2000: 7-12); Peels (2000: 77-89).

References

Arebi, S. (1991) Gender anthropology in the Middle East: the politics of Muslim women's Misrepresentation, *The American Journal of Islamic Social Studies*, 8 (1), 99-109.

Bateson, G. (2002) *Mind and Nature*, Brodway: Hampton Press.

Bhachu, P. (1993) Identities constructed and reconstructed: representations of Asian women in Britain, in G. Buijis (ed.), *Migrant Women: Crossing Boundaries and Changing Identity,* Oxford: Berg, 99-118.

Brettell, C. B. and Hollifield, J. (eds) (2000) *Migration Theory: Talking Across Disciplines,* London: Routledge.

Buijs, G. (ed.) (1993) *Migrant Women: Crossing Boundaries and Changing Identity,* Oxford and Providence: Berg.

Clifford, J. (1994) Diasporas, *Cultural Anthropology*, 9 (3): 302-338.

Damasio, A. R. (2000) *The Feeling of What Happens*: *Body, Emotion and the Making of Consciousness*, London: Vintage.

El Guindi, F. (1999) *Veil: Modesty, Privacy and Resistance*, Oxford: Berg.

El-Solh, C. and J. Mabro (ed.) (1994) *Muslim Women's Choice, Religious Belief and Social Reality*, Oxford: Berg.

Freedman J. and C. Tarr (eds) (2000) *Women, Immigration and Identities in France*, Oxford, New York: Berg.

Ganguly, K. (1997) Migrant identities: personal memory and the construction of the selfhood, *Cultural Studies*, 6 (1): 27-50.

Gramsci, A. (1971) *Selection from the Prison Notebooks*, New York: International Publisher.

Hetherington, K. (1998) *Expressions of Identity: Space, Performance, Politics,*

London: Sage.

Hussein, F (ed.) (1984) *Muslim Women,* London and Sydney: Croom Helm.

Ingold, T. (1992) 'Culture and the Perception of the Environment', in E. Croll and D. Parkin (eds), *Bush Base: Forest Farm,* London: Routledge.

Khaf, M. (1999) *Western Representation of the Muslim Woman. From Termagant to Odalisque,* Austin, Texas: University of Texas Press.

Lewis, P. (1994) *Islamic Britain: Religion, Politics and Identity Among British Muslims,* London: I.B. Tauris.

Lutz, H. (1991) *Migrant Women of 'Islamic Background': Images and Self-Images,* Amsterdam: Stichting.

Maffesoli, M. (1996) *The Time of the Tribes,* London: Sage.

Marranci, G. (2003a) *The Adhan among the Bells: Studying Muslim Identity in Northern Ireland,* PhD Thesis, Belfast: The Queen's University of Belfast.

Marranci, G. (2003b) "We Speak English" Language and Identity Processes in Northern Ireland's Muslim Community, *Ethnologist,* 25 (2): 59-77.

Marranci, G. (2004) 'South Asian Muslims in Northern Ireland: Their Islamic Identity, and the Aftermath of 11th of September', in A. Tahir (ed.), *Muslims in Britain; Community Under Pressure,* London: Zed Books.

Marranci, G. (2006) *Jihad Beyond Islam,* New York and London: Berg.

Mozzo-Counil, F. (1994) *Femmes Maghrébines en France,* Lyon: Chronique Sociale.

Milton, K. (2002) *Loving Nature,* London: Routledge.

Milton, K. and Svasek, M. (eds) (2005) *Mixed Emotions: Anthropological Studies of Feelings,* London, New York: Berg.

Polese, C. and P. Elis (2002) 'A comparative study of Somali women refugees in the United Kingdom and Italy', paper presented at *Global Refugees: The Sociology of Exile. Displacement and 'Belonging',* Staffordshire University; 17-19 April 2002.

Roald, S. A. (2001) *Women in Islam*: *The Western Experience,* London and New York: Routledge.

Salih, R. (2000) 'Shifting boundaries of self and other', *The European Journal of Women's Studies,* 7 (?): 321-335.

Shaw, A. (1998) *A Pakistani Community in Britain,* Oxford: Blackwell.

Siddiqi, M. Z. (1961) *Hadith Literature,* Cambridge: The Islamic Texts Society.

Chapter 6

Reconstructing 'Muslimness': New Bodies in Urban Indonesia

Sonja van Wichelen

Introduction

In the past three decades the process of 'Islamization' in Indonesia has conjured up new images and discourses of Muslim bodies. During this period various Islamic groups have gained influence in political decision-making and have taken up issues pertaining to gender and sexuality in public discourse to achieve or solidify political presence. In the socio-political landscape of post-Suharto Indonesia, the presence of Islamic symbols and representations of 'Muslimness' have become more visible and, especially, more gendered. These changes have given rise to public debates centring on the topics of marriage, veiling, female circumcision, polygamy, and women's roles.

This chapter discusses the production of Muslim bodies in post-Suharto Indonesia by reading mass-mediated but historically situated images of and debates on the veil and polygamy. Different socio-political periods in Indonesian history have allocated different meanings to the praxis of veiling and polygamy. I intend to relocate and refocus these debates in a time when the consumption of global information flows and the re-imagining of the nation-state give specific meaning to the politics of identity produced in these debates.

To give a historical context to the topics, the chapter starts out by discussing the process and practice of 'Islamization' in Indonesia. In the subsequent section, I discuss the increasing visibility of veiled women in public spaces and mediatized landscapes of urban centres. Two dominant images of veiled bodies are explicated. The first adheres to a consumerist discourse prevailing in the middle and upper classes and the second image adheres to a politicized discourse appearing in the lower middle class stratum. Following this, I turn to discuss the debate on polygamy that exploded as a result of the polygamy promoting 'events' of the polygamous entrepreneur Puspo Wardoyo. Here I illustrate that while the representations of veiling reaffirm 'Muslimness' rather than femininity, the act of being polygamous seems to reaffirm masculinity rather than a mode of Muslim identity.

In comparing the discourse on veiling to that of polygamy I argue that both contribute to constituting a notion of 'Muslimness' that is grounded in class as well as gender. Two modes of 'Muslimness' can be distinguished: while the one normalizes its stigmatized identity by commodifying 'Muslimness' in order to promote sameness, the other reinforces the same stigmatizations by politicizing 'Muslimness' in order to promote difference. This chapter concludes by asserting that these public contestations make visible the different factions of the Muslim middle class in urban Indonesia today. The new Islamic visibilities, moreover, illustrate how the heritage of New Order power structures continue to exert social influence on the one hand, while new Islamist power structures are consolidated on the other.

'Indonesian Islam' and Islamization

Indonesia is the largest Muslim-majority nation in the world. While a great part of the Muslim population is considered to be nominal Muslims (*abangan*) the other is regarded as being devout Muslims (*santri*)[1] The *santri* population can be divided into the modernists and the traditionalists who found their homes in the respective mass organizations *Muhammadiyah* and *Nahdlatul Ulama*. The modernist mass organization aimed to reform Indonesian Islam through the central doctrines of mainstream Sunni Islam. They opposed cultural appropriations or hybridizations of culture with Islamic thought. This was the case for instance in Java where Hindu-Buddhist (for the urban upper class) or Animist (for the rural lower class) elements intersected Islamic belief. The *Muhammadiyah* aimed to purify Indonesian Islam by strictly adhering to the Al Qur'an and the Sunnah. Their reformist agenda is most visible in their network of modern schools called *madrasah* where a modern education system is being combined with religious teachings. In contrast, the traditionalist *Nahdlatul Ulama* holds on to traditional and local adaptations of Islam. The organization also has its bases in education, namely the Islamic boarding schools called *pesantren* that are scattered throughout rural Indonesia. In the past 30 years, the *Nahdlatul Ulama* has often been associated with its influential chairman (and former president) Abdurrahman Wahid, who managed to internally restructure the conservative mainstream. Under the strong influence of Wahid and other key figures, the *Nahdlatul Ulama* had become a modern and forward-looking organization that regards women's rights, for instance, as an important issue (Barton and Feillard 1999).

During the independence struggle from Dutch colonial rule after World War II, Islamic movements took pains to exert influence in the political formation of the nation-state that included the aim to implement the Islamic law (*shariah*) as the

---

1   The terms *abangan* and *santri* are terms coined by the anthropologist Clifford Geertz (1976) in his famous work on the religion of Java where he classified Javanese society into three groups, the *abangan*, *santri* and *priyayi*. The *abangan* comprise of nominal Muslims that 'follow a lifestyle reflecting religious beliefs and practices popular during the Old Javanese, Hindu, and Buddhist periods, albeit with some adaptation to Islamic and Western cultures that arrived later' (Federspiel 1995: 1). The *santri* on the other hand identify themselves foremost as Muslims (as opposed to Javanese), and they adhere to the five pillars of classical *Sunni* Islam. The third group, the *priyayi*, primarily refers to civil servants of bureaucratic parts in society. Recent scholarship, however, has critiqued this distinction by stating that religiosity in Indonesia is much more complex and refined than portrayed by Geertz classification (Fakih 2002). Nevertheless, no scholarly work can dismiss Geertz' divisions as much work has been built around his concepts.

state's main political system. The new national leaders, Sukarno, Hatta, and Syahrir, however, implemented the *pancasila* state ideology that separated religion from the state.[2] Although Islamic parties were among the parties within the government, political Islam did not acquire considerable power in political decision-making. Sukarno's successor, Suharto, practiced an even stronger politics against political Islam. For the sake of economic development and the fear of Islamic extremism, President Suharto limited the influence of Islamic groups in his administration. Thus, as long as the creeds remain outside of politics, the secular Indonesian state guaranteed tolerance for monotheistic religions through the guiding ideology of *pancasila*. However, as with many Muslim societies, boundaries of secularism are seen clearly when turning to family or marriage law which adheres to the authority of religious courts.

The 1970s and 1980s witnessed a period of 'Islamization', also known as the 'Islamic turn', *santrinisation* or the 'greening process', the latter referring to the colours of Islamic political parties. This process is highly complex and cannot be seen as a unified pattern of a so-called 'Islamic revival', which implies a return to something that was lost (Heryanto 1999). Islamists or conservative *santri* do make an appeal to a purer Islam. However, instead of referring to an actual Indonesian past, an 'invented tradition' (Hobsbawn 1983) emerged of an idealized, mythic, and homogeneous Islamic history which was disposed of Javanese elements.[3]

The influence of the Iranian revolution in 1979, the influx of Islamic literature from the Middle East, and the new veiling of women at universities in urban centres contributed foremost to this process of Islamization. At best, this period can be described as adapting protest against the anti-Islamic attitude of the Suharto regime and 'Islamization' continued through the 1990s. In the meantime, however, under persisting pressure, Suharto decided to support a newly established Association for Indonesian Muslim Intellectuals (Ikatan Cendekiawan Muslim Indonesia or ICMI), in an effort to contain and 'colonize' Islam into his politics. Many Muslim intellectuals, especially from the modernist *Muhammadiyah*, joined this association leaving other Islamic groups weakly positioned against the Suharto administration. This new direction, of incorporating Islam into state politics, introduced the New Order's populist rhetoric of proclaiming religiosity on the road to prosperity. While disempowering political Islam, it further enhanced Suharto's developmentalist ideology that focused primarily on economic development and political stability while ignoring political pleas for freedom or human rights.

At the same time, however, the establishment of the ICMI had the effect of constituting Muslim identity for the urban middle class (Hasbullah, 2000). Rather than being seen as 'backward' or 'extremist', Islam was now represented by key figures that symbolized technological progress, modernity and cosmopolitanism.

---

2   *Panca* (five) *sila* (principle) is the state philosophy announced by Sukarno at the onset of the new nation-state was based on five interrelated principles: belief in one supreme God; just and civilized humanitarianism; nationalism as expressed in the unity of Indonesia; popular sovereignty arrived at through deliberation and representation or consultative democracy; and social justice for all Indonesian people.

3   See Hobsbawn (1983) for his account of the term 'invented tradition'.

This new attitude resulted in the flourishing of a Muslim cultural politics which at that time, namely in the 1990s, only extended to the upper middle classes of urban centres in Indonesia. This was most visible in the Islamization of popular music or lifestyle cultures where Islam was increasingly associated with modern beauty and wealth.

The process and practice of Islamization both disorganized and reconfigured the categorization of Indonesian Muslims into modernists and traditionalists (Fox, 2004: 9). These two new categories can be identified as the Islamists and the Muslim liberal left.[4] The Islamists comprise the *Tarbiyah* movement and the militant *Mujaheddin*.[5] The *Tarbiyah* movement consists of campus-based networks that aim to educate and give religious guidance to Indonesians eager to engage in personal transformation as Muslims. Since 1998 groups such as the Indonesian Muslim Students Action Front (KAMMI) and the allied Prosperous Justice Party (PKS) have emerged out of the *Tarbiyah* movement. Both KAMMI and PKS can be seen as symbolizing a new generation of young Muslims who promote 'an uncompromising purification of Islamic belief and strict adherence to religious morals, while simultaneously pushing for political modernization' (Miichi 2003: 22). Their followers were recruited from campuses all over Indonesia and consist of many young women and men from the well-educated urban middle class. In the 2004 election, the PKS picked up more votes in Jakarta than any other party, indicating the increasing popularity of this party.

In the social imagination of urban Indonesia, groups such as KAMMI or the PKS are often erroneously associated with militant *Mujaheddin* groups. Although both *Tarbiyah* groups, like *Mujaheddin* groups, have called for the implementation of the *shariah* law, the latter, however, do not shy away from force or violence. Unlike the PKS or the KAMMI, militant *Mujaheddin* groups – such as *Jemaah Islamiyah*, *Laskar Jihad,* or the *Front Pembela Islam* – have a strong anti-western, anti-democratic and anti-modern attitude which, in combination with their belief in Zionist conspiracies, has triggered numerous conflicts in the public arena.

In spite of the fact that the *Mujaheddin* groups share similar ideologies and operate with similar violent methods, important differences can be pointed out. Some, like *Laskar Jihad*, exert strong institutional power in various regions, in this case in the Moluccas. Others, such as *Jemaah Islamiyah*, are reputed to operate actively in religious boarding schools (*pesantren*) and to be working transnationally with terrorist networks. A third distinction is that some groups, such as the *Front Pembela Islam*, consist mostly of poverty stricken urban youth who draw a lot of media

---

4   The term Islamism has been used in academic discourse to refer to a new Islamic movement that distinguishes itself from earlier Islamic revolutions in that it frees itself from traditional interpretations and successfully employ elements of modernity in its socio-political quest. As described by the sociologist Nilüfer Göle, 'in speaking of Islamism, we are differentiating between Muslim, which expresses religious identity and Islamist, which refers to a social movement through which Muslim identity is collectively re-appropriated as a basis for an alternative social and political project' (2002: 173).

5   The *tarbiyah* (education) movement is also known as the *dakwah* movement, the *mosque* movement or the campus based revival movement. For an elaboration and genealogy of the movement see Fox 2004.

attention by raiding nightclubs and gaming centres. In contrast to more organized networks, these groups should be approached as representing 'angry mobs'.[6]

A final category of contemporary 'Indonesian Islam' is the group of the Muslim liberal left. First and foremost represented by the Liberal Islam Network (Jaringan Islam Liberal or JIL), the liberal left consists of highly educated intellectuals such as *Gunawan Muhammad* and *Ulil Abshar-Abdalla*. The open forum of JIL appeals to a liberal interpretation of Islam in an effort to counter militant or 'radical' Islam. Although very visible in print and electronic media, and present in most of the current debates on religion and politics, JIL remains an intellectual forum that has difficulty in reaching a broader audience.

Summing up we can say that the contemporary Islamic landscape in Indonesia consists of modernists, traditionalists, Islamists, and the liberal left.[7] Turning to contemporary discussions on the veil and polygamy, however, illustrates how class, gender, consumerism and nation in turn affect these categories.

Veiled Bodies: Constituting Class Through Consumerist and Islamist Visibilities

In accordance with the process of Islamization, it was not until the 1980s that women started to wear the tight veil (*jilbab*). Before that, the majority of urban women wore western-style clothes while sometimes wearing a loose veil (*kerudung*) that accompanied traditional dress on special occasions. At first, the new practice of veiling occurred primarily at universities and should be seen as a subtle protest against the Suharto regime. In this period the 1982 ban on wearing the veil in all educational settings by the Suharto administration became a fiercely contested issue, which culminated in local and national protests of people pleading, successfully, for the eventual lifting of the ban.

The 1990s signaled a new phase in the process of *jilbabisasi*. Whereas in the 1970s and 1980s the phenomenon of veiling primarily took place at universities, it now expanded to the broader public sphere. Especially in the world of show business or glossy magazines, women started to cover their bodies and began to advocate modest dress and behavior. This trend intensified after the fall of Suharto when veiled women became representatives in parliament, hosts and presenters of television shows, managers in corporate offices, or the focus of Islamist protests in public space of urban centres.

Analyzing images of veiled women in the media landscape of post-authoritarian Indonesia since the fall of the Suharto regime suggests two distinct modes of veiling. The first mode suggests a consumerist discourse of the veil that prevails in the middle and upper classes, while the second mode suggests a politicized discourse

---

6   For a more precise and thorough background and analysis of 'Islamic radicalism' in contemporary Indonesia see Fox 2004, Porter 2002, Bruinessen 2002, and Santosa 1996.

7   These four groups – the nominal Muslims, the traditionalists, the Islamists, and the liberal left – are analytical categories and by no means exclusive. Many modernists for example, especially the younger generation, have joined the Islamists, while some modernists and traditionalists, have joined the liberal left.

appearing in the lower middle class stratum. The consumerist discourse appeals to the images of veiled women within the cultural tastes and lifestyle of the urban upper middle class or elite. Here trendy women's magazines such as *Amanah* and the more recent *Noor* celebrate veiling as a modern and fashionable phenomenon. In contrast to the image of the veiled woman as being 'extremist' or 'backward', this veiling discourses challenged the stigma of the veiled woman and reinforced modern images of Islamic womanhood. Occurring dominantly in mediatized spaces such as television and film, but also on billboards and in advertisements, these new images can be seen as enacting 'public performances of Islamic subjectivity' (Wong, 2003: 11).

Media celebrities or movie stars who have started to wear the veil also convey this message. Most popular is the example of Inneke Koesherawati. Having a reputation as Indonesia's 'sex bomb' in popular films of the 1990s, the 'famous' actress has now opted for a modest and religious life (-style). Anthropologist Lila Abu-Lughod describes a similar trend among movie stars in Egypt who adhere to new modes of Islamic dress: 'the 'repentant' actresses have done what an increasing number of urban Egyptian women have done: adopted the new modest Islamic dress as part of what they conceive of as their religious awakening' (1995: 64). This trend, she argues, has an enormous impact on rural and poor women in Egyptian society who start to identify with 'their' stars, believing that the admired icons have turned to the same moral principles as themselves.

On account of the popularity of these stars, veiling becomes a legitimate trend, and, in the case of Egypt, promotes urban women to return to the domestic sphere. This image in Indonesian media, however, does not entirely promote women to 'return' to the domestic domain. When analyzing women's magazines for instance, women are still expected and encouraged to have a career outside of the home. Moreover, the veiled models in these glossy magazines display little piety as they conjure up images of explicit sexuality. The anthropologist Suzanne Brenner, who identified this same trend in her analysis of the magazine *Amanah*, noted an 'apparently unproblematic blending of Muslim purity and Western sexuality in a single image [that] perfectly captures the contradictory messages and interests of the late Suharto era'; as she proclaimed, 'it is quintessentially New Order!' (Brenner, 1999: 21).

Agreeing with Brenner's observation, I would further add that the contradictory message of blending 'Muslimness' with 'western' influences can be put in the broader global framework of consumption in constituting and shaping the public sphere of Muslim communities. As Loong Wong argues in the case of Malaysia, '[i]n inducing desirable outcomes, Islam could potentially act as the carriage of a new 'protestant ethic' for urban Malay middle classes in Malaysia, enabling them to accumulate new social capital to stake out their claims within the social and political economy of the nation' (2003: 3). With respect to Indonesia, the booming of the pilgrim business (*haji*), the popularity of private gatherings for religious teachings (*majelis taklim*), the increasing participation in Islamic mysticism programs (*tasawuf*) and the demand of luxurious holiday packages that combines religious teaching with eating good food and playing golf (*pesantren eksekutif*), support this view (Hasbullah 2000). It nurtures to a more general consumerist ideology which commodifies Islamic practices – without eschewing 'western' modes of consumer appeal – in order to solidify their socio-cultural presence.

Besides the consumerist discourse of the pious but modern Muslim woman, contemporary media representations also produce a politicized discourse of veiled bodies. Increasingly, there is the image of masses of veiled women demonstrating – for instance against the Iraqi war or the ban on wearing religious dress in educational settings – who represent an entirely different discursive reality of women's bodies from the earlier commodified images. As opposed to the alluring effect of individual models or artists, these images convey the communal representation of veiled women as a form of collective action. They refer to mass protests or collective action against particular national or international issues of political importance, such as the war in Iraq or the approval of the French law prohibiting religious symbols from educational settings. Either students from the Indonesian Muslim Student Action Union (KAMMI) or (young) women from the Prosperous Justice Party (PKS) represent the majority of these women in protest. These groups can be considered part of a reinvigorated Islamist movement that has become a vital political force in urban centres of Indonesia.

Despite the stigmas attached to the veil and the overt public protests, these women proudly represent the Islamist movement with a collective identity marked on their bodies through their uniform Muslim dress. As sociologist Nilüfer Göle argues '[w]hat is common – contrary to modernist narratives and politics that have assumed the death of religion – is the shaping of Islamic agency by an assertion of religious difference, rather than its denial, [thus], [i]nstead of giving up religiosity, considered as a source of backwardness, new religious actors turn their Muslimness (similar to blackness) into an overt protest called Islamism (2003: 812). Consequently, by wearing the stigmatized veil (rather than the fashionable veil) the women in these media representations 'act up' and voice their political concerns visually. Due to its stigmatized status these veiled women obtain a form of agency in choosing – against all odds – to openly wear the veil and wear the stigma. It validates their beliefs, allocates them authority and rightfulness and can be read as accommodated protest against a situation which deprives them of a dignified identity or status (MacLeod 1992: 552).

The visual power of 'veiled women' becomes even more palpable when played out spatially. With spatial power I mean the media effects of seeing, for instance, a uniform crowd in a colossal space. Often, newspaper headings would refer to 'a sea of veils' that occupies a certain public space.[8] The 'sea of veils' exemplifies the powerful media effect of uniformity, especially in women adhering to collective representation. Rather than a symbol of personal belief or identity, as depicted in the images of the models and stars, the image of masses of veiled women becomes a potent symbol of collective identity.

---

8   For instance as one heading in a regional paper reads: 'The Senayan Arena Becomes a Sea of Veils' ('Istora Senayan jadi lautan jilbab', *Jawa Pos*, 28 September 1998). Often references are also made to a sea of *green* veils which appeals to the green banners that KAMMI members wear around their veils.

Notwithstanding empowering elements in symbolizing Islamism for the greater cause, one remains skeptical about the empowering effects in relation to gender relations. As anthropologist Aihwa Ong warns us, once Islamism turns into religious nationalism, its radical politics also (re)produce conservative sex roles (1990: 271). Moreover, as the feminist theorist Leila Ahmed rightly observes, 'the Islamist position regarding women is also problematic in that, essentially reactive in nature, it traps the issue of women with the struggle over culture - just as the initiating colonial discourse has done' (1992: 236). Although Islamists in contemporary Indonesian politics are proclaiming equality in gender relations, it remains to be seen whether they can keep this promise once political power is consolidated.

Austerity, purity or innocence plays an important role in the social imagination of the movement, which is expressed through the image of 'white' and 'clean' women in the public spaces. As explicated in their modest and simple attire, their 'clean' (free of make-up) faces and their white traditional veils, the women convey a message of austere uniformity that corresponds with their political Islamist project. The 'whiteness' or 'cleanliness' depicted by the images of these female bodies is transformed into political imagery that not only includes the practice of a clean politics (free from corruption, collusion or nepotism), but, more powerfully, also includes the strong moral connotations of 'whiteness' and 'cleanliness' that pertain to notions of austerity, purity, and innocence. As opposed to the consumerist and 'westoxified' (Abu-Lughod 1988) images of brightly coloured and 'branded' fashion in the public and mediatized sphere, this image enhances the marker of difference, of exclusivity in the margins.

As sociologist Bryan Turner argues, 'Islamism is a product [of] social frustrations of those social strata (unpaid civil servants, overworked teachers, underemployed engineers, and marginalized college teachers) whose interests have not been well served by either the secular nationalism of Nasser, Muhammad Reza Shah, Suharto or Saddam Hussein, or the neo-liberal 'open-door' policies of Anwar Saddat or Chadli Benjedid in Algeria. [...] In summary, Islamism is a product of a religious crisis of authority, the failures of authoritarian nationalist governments, and the socio-economic divisions that have been exacerbated by neo-liberal globalization' (2003: 140). Hence, in contrast to the consumerist discourse of the veil, the politicized discourse of the veil does not symbolize national stability. On the contrary, these representations signify a discontent with the current socio-political climate in Indonesia that still adheres to New Order development rhetoric which privileges the already empowered middle class and neglects 'the other middle class', namely middle-level urban workers (teachers or lower-ranked civil servants), professionals, or students without social status or power. This neglected class of people represents, as Brenner describes, 'a class of people who have been fully drawn into the state-sponsored processes of *development*, but without reaping its spoils' (Brenner, 1996: 678). The increasing visibility of 'the other middle class' in the public sphere, signals a moment of transformation where the hegemony of the wealthy middle class – which has most of the decision-making power – is being openly contested. They opt, as Lila Abu-Lughod calls it, for an 'alternative modernity' through the practice of Islamism (1998: 4). The different modes of veiling, consumerist or political, and the resulting actions attached to the different acts of veiling, are just one site of contestation within this shifting socio-political arena where the pursuit of political power seems to be played out through different Islamic visibilities.

Polygamous Bodies: Sexuality, Masculinity and the Imagination of the Nation[9]

Family Law in general and polygamy in particular have long been debated in Indonesia and in certain historical periods these political debates have resulted in legal reforms. However, as political scientist Daniel Lev argues, '[e]fforts to do away with polygamy have failed each time, primarily because of the symbolic importance of the koranic passage that allows it' (1996: 193). Although during the New Order polygamy was limited to strict conditions, the practice of polygamy was never formally prohibited or criminalized. This, as Lev further argues, had not only to do with the issue of polygamy, but relates more broadly to the status of the religious courts (Lev, 1996: 193). Many Islamic groups felt that it was not the responsibility of the state to intervene in family affairs, but that it was up to the authority of religious courts and the Islamic law to give directions regarding domestic affairs.[10]

Ignoring the positions of various Islamic groups on the topic of marriage law in general and polygamy in particular, President Suharto's government promoted the conjugal couple and nuclear family and stipulated restrictions on the practice of polygamy. These restrictions strengthened the notion that polygamy should be seen as either 'shameful' or 'backward'. This notion was challenged in post-Suharto times where, following the annulment of a law that restricted polygamy especially for civil servants, polygamy became more apparent and even promoted: artists, musicians, politicians, and entrepreneurs started to confess their polygamous marriages while books on the virtues of polygamy mushroomed in mainstream bookstores.[11]

The public discussion on polygamy did not explode, however, until a successful entrepreneur Puspo Wardoyo initiated the so-called 'Polygamy Award'. By proclaiming polygamy as a man's right and duty he set out to promote polygamy through various activities such as the founding of the Indonesian Polygamy Society, the publication of several books on leading a polygamous life, and the organization of the 'Polygamy Award' which was intended to award men who were regarded to have successful polygamous marriages. This event, which was amply trumpeted

---

9   In contrast to the term polygamy, which designates the practice of marrying more than one spouse, the correct term should be polygyny which refers to men having multiple wives. Although fully aware that the term polygamy conceals the gender differentiation that is made visible in the term polygyny, I consistently use the term polygamy out of pragmatic reasons because this is the term used in my sources and in public discourse.

10   For an elaboration on the issue of polygamy in late colonial times or during independence see Locher-Scholten 2003 and Wieringa 2002.

11   During the Megawati administration, this was most evident in the figure of the vice president Hamzah Haz. The politician from the Muslim based United Development Party (PPP) did not shy away from the press regarding his multiple marriages and 12 children. Subsequently, the minister of cooperatives, Alimarwan Hanan, acknowledged that he had two wives. President Megawati Sukarnoputri, who is the daughter of one of the nine wives of Indonesia's first president, Sukarno, has never publicly debated the issue of polygamy.

in mass media, caused enormous commotion and provoked all kinds of reactions via national television, radio and newspapers. A public debate on polygamy ensued with arguments pro-/or against the practice of polygamy. Here, the figure of Puspo Wardoyo, as a controversial personality, became a popular reference point for all discussions concerning the place of polygamy in Indonesian society today.

Whereas theological or socio-economic arguments prevailed in the more intellectual newspapers, the 'libido' argument most saliently emerged in tabloids, men's and women's magazines, and in talk shows on television or radio. Here, the act of polygamy was seen as a 'natural' consequence of men's sexual desire which, in Indonesian, is referred to as *nafsu*. The term *nafsu* should be seen in a broader definition than only libido or sexual desire. It should be placed in the Javanese tradition where *nafsu* is related to the notion of desire as a whole, as a passion relating to love, sex, money or work. When excessively present and uncontrolled, and especially when involving money, *nafsu* can become an irrational emotion that suppresses rational reasoning and that is potentially dangerous to the individual, the family and society (Brenner 1996: 150). Interlocking with *nafsu* is money or wealth. As Puspo's slogan goes: Work is *Jihad*, and many wives will bring much fortune (*rezeki*).[12] Not only is one better (morally) and will go to heaven (*surga*) when one practices polygamy, one will also gain materially from it. Although stating that every man, rich or poor, experiences the *nafsu* to be with more than one wife, Puspo Wardoyo explains that one must have enough money in order to practice polygamy. By intertwining male desire with wealth and status, polygamy becomes a status symbol that differentiates between the 'have's' and the 'have-not's', those who can afford to have multiple wives and those who cannot. As with the consumerist discourse of the *jilbab*, where the veil is commodified to produce the modern Muslim woman, it seems that a comparable trend is developing in trying to accommodate polygamy. While the veil promotes Muslim femininity, polygamy is supposed to promote Muslim masculinity. At the same time, the commodification of these veiled female bodies and polygamous male bodies produces degrees of 'Muslimness' along the lines of status and class.

As a matter of course, Puspo Wardoyo also conveys the message that polygamy is not old-fashioned; quite the reverse, it is very 'sexy' and modern. He does not oppose working women for instance, but is appalled by the fact that they remain single. This stance has recently also been voiced by single and successful women themselves, who argue that they would not rule out a polygamous marriage as an option. Some among them state that because of their careers they cannot be there all the time to serve their husband or children. A polygamous marriage would potentially be a solution for women not to leave their careers but to sustain them without accepting an unmarried life.[13] Moreover, for some it is also the only way left to 'still' get married.[14]

---

12 'Banyak Istri berarti banyak rezeki', *Suara Merdeka*, 10 June 2002.

13 'Poligami di Samping Jalan', *Koran Tempo*, 10 August 2003.

14 See for instance Reno Rahmawati (8 August 2004) 'The lengths we will go to to be wedding belles' *The Jakarta Post*.

Apart from satisfying one's own sexual desire and business – to which men have an Islamic right – Puspo Wardoyo proclaims that polygamy is also an Islamic and national duty for both men and women. In an interview Puspo gave to the glossy men's magazine *Male Emporium*, he further argued that polygamy is a solution to the problem of female overseas workers.[15] Here, reference is made to the increasing number of Indonesian women going overseas to work as domestic workers. Following the Asian economic crisis, unemployment rates increased significantly and inflation caused a rise in consumer prices of basic commodities resulting in greater poverty. This particularly affected women, prompting them to find work elsewhere.

Women play an important role in the imagination of the nation by carrying and embodying the notion of tradition (Nira Yuval-Davis, 1997: 61). Thus, overcoming the 'problem of female overseas workers' seems to call upon polygamous men to shoulder the heroic burden of saving the imagined community of a nation. Moreover, the term 'duty' - like honour, patriotism and bravery – is both nationalist and masculinist: it works as a masculine act 'that articulates very well with the demands of nationalism' (Nagel, 1998: 252). In this respect, Puspo's call to end the problem of poverty stricken women that are compelled to go overseas can be seen as a form of paternal masculinity. Here, the pro-polygamy discourse suggests that polygamous men ought to take their national responsibility for 'their women' in protecting the nation's tradition.

In general, female sexuality is more openly debated in the public sphere than men's sexuality. In the Javanese context, as Brenner argues, 'public discussion have treated women's sexuality and morality as matters for *everyone's* concern, with repercussions for the future of the entire society' (Brenner, 1999: 33) [emphasis in original]. The pro-polygamy discourse attached to the phenomenon of the 'Polygamy award', however, seems to indicate the opposite. Rather than seeing *nafsu* as potentially dangerous to the individual, the family and society, the pro-polygamy discourse suggests that acting out on your *nafsu* is actually very beneficial. Here, the spotlight is on man's sexuality (male *nafsu*) and the 'logical consequences' of that sexuality for himself, his family life, and for society at large. The emphasis on male sexuality and the prosperity it will bring to the individual/family/nation seems to reverse the cultural stigma of male *nafsu* that is linked with uncontrollable danger. The question arises as to why masculinist *nafsu* needs to be re-asserted at this particular moment in Indonesian history?

As literature on gender relations has explicated, the New Order's ideology concerning women is contradictory (Brenner, 1999; Hatley, 1999; Sen, 1998). While promoting women to become modern career women, the ideology also warned these same women not to go 'too far': women, in the long run, should not forget their offspring or should not take away men's jobs. The message is therefore not that women should not work but, rather, when giving priority to their careers, women should be aware that they could become a threat to men. A woman runs the risk of emasculating men, driving them 'into the arms of other women in order to rescue his manhood' (Brenner, 1999: 28). In this respect, the polygamy hype and re-assertion of masculinity, could suggest that middle class Indonesian men felt intimidated

---

15 'Puspo Wardoyo: Pria Mampu Wajib Berpoligami', *Male Emporium*, 5 May 2003.

or emasculated when women entered their professional realm. Rather than an affirmation, the discourse of hyper-masculinity then signals a crisis of masculinity. Here, 'acting out' polygamous behavior or 'acting out' masculinity, suggests the need among disempowered Muslim men to assert personal masculine potency against the hegemonic masculinity of the authoritarian New Order.

Although highly mediatized, this masculinist advocacy on behalf of polygamy was a marginalized discourse. Mainstream public opinion more often approached the phenomenon as a display of social status and cultural capital, dismissing Puspo Wardoyo's plea for a polygamous society as an act of hypocrisy (*munafik*). The media attention he provoked and the numerous debates that resulted from his campaign, however, do show us that polygamy as such is not generically dismissed or resisted in contemporary Indonesian public discourse. Quite the contrary, important politicians (Hamzah Haz), popular Islamic clerics (Aa Gym) and well-known celebrities (Rhoma Irama) either practice polygamy or endorse it. With the exception of a marginalized feminist discourse, it has become clear that many different Islamic groups, although not necessarily endorsing polygamy, were not planning to eradicate polygamy altogether.

Andrée Feillard, A French Indonesianist based in Jakarta, has conducted research on perceptions of issues such as the veil and polygamy among leaders of Islamic women's organizations. According to her findings, both modernist and traditionalist women accepted polygamy only conditionally. Considering it men's nature to be sexually needier, the modernist faction saw polygamy as a solution to adultery. The traditionalists, on the other hand, rejected the above idea and argued that polygamy should only be allowed as a form of social assistance, for instance when the woman is a widow, or when she's ill. Both groups would not publicly advocate polygamy. They see the recent arguments in favor of polygamy in Indonesia as an issue of a younger generation. The real debate, Feillard argues, occurs within these spheres of modernists, traditionalists, and the younger generation (Islamists). The other half of Indonesia's population that is non-Muslim or secular Muslim (*abangan*) does not meddle in the affair (1999: 19-23). The way in which this latter group of *abangan* Muslims are not welcome to join in the debate on Islamic issues became evident in the polygamy debate where self-identified Muslim were attacked when they appeared insufficiently knowledgeable about the Qur'an or traditions of the prophet (*hadis*). Some *abangan* Muslims were labeled 'orientalists' for meddling in the affair and were accused of wanting to slander or weaken Islam. This also became apparent in the tension between different women's organizations and feminist groups in their respective contributions to the debate. 'Secular' groups opposed polygamy from a legalist and internationalist framework, whereas Islamic women's groups opposed polygamy from a theological perspective by bringing in textual evidence that the Qur'an does not proclaim polygamy to be an Islamic duty. While 'Islamic feminism' seemed to be at the forefront of advocating religious re-interpretation of Islamic text and seemed less prone to attacks from Islamic authorities, the more 'secular' groups were often labeled as western feminists that aimed to spread secularism.

Hence, as in the case with the public discussions about the veil, the background of the actual debate, which goes beyond the masculinist discourse of Puspo Wardoyo's 'Polygamy Award' event, contributes to bringing into focus the role of religion in public life and politics. It emphasizes and makes visible the different positions of various Islamic groups in society. It also signals the ambiguous and contradictory positions of progressive movements or individuals that previously did not adhere to religious principles.

The Urban 'Middle Class' and New Muslim Bodies

The representations and discourses on the veil and polygamy as analysed above apply mostly to urban bodies. The global and trans-national flow of information, images and knowledge that reside in metropolitan centres distinguishes the production of urban bodies from rural bodies. Moreover, the rhetoric and polemic surrounding the debates on veiling and practising polygamy are consumed and 'monopolized' by urban Muslims (intellectuals, students, and feminists) who are mostly based in Jakarta, Yogyakarta, Bandung, and other major cities primarily on Java. As a result, Indonesian media representations make visible the Islamic discourse that is concerned with urban consumerism and urban Islamism while making invisible the production of rural or regional Muslim bodies.

The consumerist discourse of the veiled female body and the masculinist discourse of the polygamous male body seem to be a continuation of populist politicking where the stereotype of modernity (consumption) is packaged in the stereotype of anti-modernity wrap (veil and polygamy). These representations normalize the act of veiling and polygamy by linking their respective practice to modern consumer culture. Especially in the mediatized landscape and in public spaces of urban centres this process of normalization plays an important role in imagining the Indonesian nation-state through the image of the modern Muslim woman and the modern Muslim man. Here, the message that these discourses convey is that the personal choice to veil for the woman, or the choice to practice polygamy for the man, does not have to collide with modernity or with the legacy of New Order Indonesia that is depoliticized, consumerist and developmentalist.

Normalizing veiling and polygamy in a consumerist discourse suggests that political transition to democracy can occur without conflict or crisis. It presents an unproblematic transition from an authoritarian regime to an open and civil society. Nevertheless, the effects of commodifying Islamic practices and symbols, namely normalizing that which used to carry a stigma, depoliticizes it and makes political agency or identity difficult to emerge or develop. Rather than suggesting a transition to democracy, the normalization of the veil and polygamy in a consumerist discourse actually re-affirms New Order power structures through a perpetuation of its modernist and consumerist ideology. By incorporating unproblematic 'Muslimness' into the political realm, it adheres to the principle of 'sameness' as a unifying principle for the imagination of the nation.

At the same time religionization of the public and political sphere takes place where the process of 'Islamization' and the increasing influence of political Islam and Islamist groups have contributed to redefining citizenship from religious views and principles. It becomes visible how another Muslim middle class – represented by Islamists – is emerging and demanding representational space. This less wealthy, and previously disenfranchised middle class has different ideas about the ways in which Muslim identity should be embodied or expressed. Unlike the de-politicized consumerist strategies that normalize 'Muslimness' in public discourse, the discourse of these Islamist groups opts for the politicized strategy of constituting 'difference' in the symbolic realm of re-imaging the nation. Here Islamism as identity politics leads to the category 'Muslim' and considers this as the most important identity in defining the citizen-subject. As the discourse on the veiled political bodies reveals, these groups are becoming stronger and more visible. While in the past political Islam in Indonesia has had the status of a minority, it now tries to manoeuvre itself into a majority.

Moreover, in relation to the state, the Islamic presence in the public sphere challenges the strict separations between private religion and public secularism. It seems that with their attempts to blur and redesign the borders between the private and the public spheres through the political use of Islamic symbols, the new Islamist groups are reacting against the hegemonic position of the New Order that adhered to both 'western' secularization, neo-liberalist capitalism, and Javanese-centred culture.

Conclusion

The public contestation relating to the veil and polygamy in contemporary Indonesia refers back to both the legacy of Suharto's authoritarian New Order and to the process of 'Islamization'. In media representations, the consumerist discourse of the veiled female body, or the masculinist discourse of the polygamous male body, normalizes Islamic symbols in such a way that they adhere to the principle of 'sameness' which conveys political stability and unity. This affirms earlier authoritarian influence through a perpetuation of its populist politicking. However, at the same time, actual religionization of the public and political sphere also takes place. The increasing visibilities of political Islam and Islamist groups, and their respective contributions to the debate on veiling or the practice of polygamy have assisted a reconfiguration of the Indonesian citizen-subject. Insisting on the notion of 'difference' by representing their 'Muslimness' as politically powerful stigmas, these new groups have claimed their own space in public discourse. Nonetheless, going beyond these contemporary debates, it remains to be seen which groups will take up the hegemonic position in future Indonesian politics.

References

Abu Lughod, L. (1998) Feminist Longings and Postcolonial Conditions in L. Abu-Lughod (ed.), *Remaking Women: Feminism and Modernity in the Middle East,* Princeton: Princeton University Press.

Abu-Lughod, L. (1995) Movie stars and Islamic moralism in Egypt, *Social Text,* 42 (Spring 1995), 53-67.

Ahmed, L. (1992) *Women and Gender in Islam: Historical Roots of a Modern*

Debate, New Haven: Yale University Press.

Barton, G. and Feillard, A. (1999) Nahdlatul Ulama, Abdurrahman Wahid and Reformation: What does NU's November 1997 National Gathering tell us?, *Studia Islamika,* 6 (1), 1-40.

Brenner, S. (1996) Reconstructing self and society: Javanese Muslim women and 'the veil', *American Ethnologist,* 23 (4), 673-997.

Brenner, S. (1999) On the public intimacy of the New Order, *Indonesia,* 76 (April), 13-37.

van Bruinessen, M. (2002) Genealogies of Islamic radicalism in post-Suharto Indonesia, *South East Asia Research,* 10 (2), 117-154.

Fakih, M. (2002) Pengantar, in E. Prasetyo (ed.), *Islam Kiri Melawan Kapitalisme Modal: Dari Wacana Menuju Gerakan*, Yogyakarta: Institute for Social Transformation (Insist) Press.

Federspiel, H. M. (1995) *A Dictionary of Indonesian Islam*, Athens: Ohio University.

Feillard, A. (1999) The veil and polygamy: current debates on women and Islam in Indonesia, *Moussons,* 99: 5-28.

Fox, J. J. (2004) Currents in contemporary Islam in Indonesia, paper read at *HARVARD ASIA VISION 21*, 29 April - 1 May 2004: Cambridge, Massachusetts.

Geertz , Clifford (1976) *The Religion of Java*, Chicago and London: University of Chicago Press.

Göle, N. (2003) The voluntary adoption of Islamic stigma symbols, *Social Research,* 70 (3), 809-828.

Hasbullah, M. (2000) Cultural presentation of the Muslim middle class in contemporary Indonesia, *Studia Islamika,* 7 (2), 1-58.

Hatley, B. (1999) Cultural expression and social tranformation in Indonesia, in A. Budiman, B. Hatley and D. Kingsbury (eds), *Reformasi: Crisis and Change in Indonesia*, Clayton: Monash Asia Institute.

Hefner, R. W. (2000) *Civil Islam: Muslims and Democratization in Indonesia*, Princeton: Princeton University Press.

Heryanto, A. (1999) The years of living luxuriously: identity politics of Indonesia's new rich, in M. Pinches (ed.), *Culture and Privilige in Capitalist Asia*, London and New York: Routledge.

Hobsbawn, E. (1983) Introduction: Inventing Traditions in E. Hobsbawn and T. Ranger (eds.), *The Invention of Tradition*, Cambridge: Cambridge University Press.

Lev, D. S. (1996) On the other hand?, in L. J. Sears (ed.), *Fantasizing the Feminine in Indonesia*, Durham and London: Duke University Press.

Locher-Scholten, E. (2003) Morals, harmony, and national identity: 'compassionate feminism' in colonial Indonesia in the 1930s, *Journal of Women's History,* 14 (4), 38-58.

MacLeod, A. E. (1992) Hegemonic relations and gender resistence: the new veiling as accommodating protest in Cairo, *Signs,* 17 (3), 533-557.

Miichi, K. (2003) Islamic Youth Movements in Indonesia, *IIAS Newsletter* 32 (November 2003): 22.

Nagel, J. (1998) Masculinity and nationalism: gender and sexuality in the making of nations, *Ethnic and Racial Studies,* 21 (2), 242-269.

Ong, A. (1990) State versus Islam: Malay families, women's bodies, and the body politic in Malaysia, *American Ethnologist,* 17 (2), 258-276.

Porter, D. (2002) Citizen participation through mobilization and the rise of political Islam in Indonesia, *The Pacific Review,* 15 (2), 201-224.

Santosa, J. C. (1996) *Modernization, Utopia and the rise of Islamic radicalism in Indonesia,* Unpublished doctoral thesis, Boston University, Ann Arbor, Michigan.

Sen, K. (1998) Indonesian women at work: reframing the subject, in K. Sen and M. Stivens (eds.), *Gender and Power in Affluent Asia,* London and New York: Routledge.

Turner, B. S. (2003) Class, generation and Islamism: towards a global sociology of political Islam, *British Journal of Sociology,* 54 (1), 139-147.

Wieringa, S. E. (2002) *Sexual Politics in Indonesia,* Houndmills, Basingstoke, Hampshire: Palgrave Macmillan.

Wong, L. (2003) Market cultures, the middle classes and Islam: consuming the market?, paper read at 3rd Critical Management Studies Conference *Critique and Inclusivity: Opening the Agenda,* 7-9 July 2003, at Lancaster, UK.

Yuval-Davis, N. (1997) *Gender and Nation,* London: Sage.

Chapter 7

'Safe and Risky Spaces':
Gender, Ethnicity and Culture in the
Leisure Lives of Young South Asian
Women

Eileen Green and Carrie Singleton

Introduction

Although there is a wealth of knowledge within the social sciences about 'risk
society' (Beck, 1992; Giddens, 1991), there is comparatively less material that
engages with the experiences of young people and the ways in which they manage
aspects of risk as part of their everyday leisure lives (Mitchell *et al.*, 2004). This
chapter seeks to ground abstract theories of 'risk' using empirical data on young
South Asian women's perceptions of risk and risk management strategies in leisure
settings.[1] It explores the ways in which women create, negotiate and maintain 'safe'
spaces for leisure and argues that such spaces offer secure and appropriate arenas in
which young women develop networks of belonging and friendship. Leisure is a key
space in which women both encounter risk and danger to themselves and engage in
risk-taking behaviour, and it is also gendered, both in terms of the spaces and places
that young women occupy, and their behaviour within such spaces. Such behaviours
are also influenced by differences of class, sexuality, 'race', ethnicity and culture.[2]
There is a sizeable body of work on women and risk, safety and danger (Pain, 2001)
and the literature on young people in relation to spatialised aspects of safety and
danger is expanding (Valentine *et al.*, 1998), but less research has addressed the
issue of how young individuals perceive and manage risk in their everyday lives
and the ways in which aspects of young people's identities such as age, social class,
gender, 'race' and culture intersect to shape risk encounters and risk management

---

1   An earlier version of this chapter was presented at the Leisure Studies Association
annual conference 2004, Leeds Metropolitan University.

2   The authors adopt the widely recognised view that 'race' is socially constructed and
has no legitimate base in science (Brah, 1996) but can be represented at an everyday level as a
fixed and objective category of identity (Maynard, 1994). As discussed in relation to the young
South Asian women's narratives about 'race' and ethnicity, it is important to recognise that
individuals and groups continue to confront racial discrimination based upon such markers,
whilst whiteness as an identity and category of power remains largely unproblematised
(Brown *et al.*, 1999; Watson and Scraton, 2001).

strategies (Brah and Phoenix, 2004; Lupton, 1999). Some recent studies of risk have suggested that young people often reject conventional definitions of 'risky' behaviour in favour of constructing their own subjectivised 'risk hierarchies' (Mitchell *et al.*, 2004), many of which contextualise risk as closely bound up with spaces and places, particularly those frequented during leisure time. As Lupton (1999) has noted, risk is subjective and relates to a given socio-cultural and historical moment. Risk can also be linked to any number of phenomena and reflects different types of human anxiety dependent upon an individual's position in the social world. Our knowledge and awareness of risk is informative of how we conduct our everyday lives, our relationships with others, our relationships to our own bodies, and where we choose to live, work and engage in leisure.

A major concern of this chapter is with how young South Asian women 'construct' risk within their own socially embedded and culturally meaningful discourses and how they develop risk management strategies which enable them to enjoy their leisure in safe space. Drawing upon data from a broader qualitative study focusing upon Black and Minority Ethnic (BME) women's health, well being and leisure we draw attention to young South Asian women's accounts of risk taking and their management of risk in the North East of England, arguing that concepts of risk, safety and danger are located within contextually specific spaces and places and are related to ideas about the gendered body and discourses of respectability, responsibility and reputation. Their safe spaces are embedded in their local communities and offer women greatly sought after leisure settings in which they can develop meaningful social relationships with others and realise a sense of belonging and collective identity amongst peers in the local urban environment (Scraton and Watson, 2003).

'Risk' in Women's Leisure Spaces

As part of the well recognised thesis which sites risk as an organising principle of late modern industrial society, Beck and Giddens suggest that risk has extensive effects on the construction of contemporary identities (Beck, 1992; Giddens, 1991). Contemporary risk theorists also claim that a number of traditional features of industrial society, such as class, community and family are decreasing in influence, and relationships with strangers, encountered through increased national and global flows of people and cultures, are taking on greater significance. Characteristics of this change are postulated as increased reflexivity and 'individualization' in the processes of identity formation (Beck and Beck-Gernsheim, 1996), resulting in individuals experiencing greater choice and determination in the construction of the 'project of self'. Contemporary individuals are construed as being more able to build and fashion identities through self-monitoring and choice. However, some theorists, such as Furlong and Cartmel (1997) remain unconvinced by the 'disappearance' of social structures such as class and gender. Working in the area of youth studies, they critique the Giddens / Beck thesis suggesting that whilst processes of individualisation and risk have come to characterise late modernity, life chances and experiences continue to be impacted upon by an individual's location within social structures.

Additionally, research continues to show that women of all backgrounds experience risk and danger in local spaces in their everyday lives (Pain, 2001).

Adjacent to sociological theories of risk, a discourse has emerged in which young people are represented as 'risky' individuals and as posing a risk to others (Bunton *et al.*, 2004: 1). 'Risky youth' is also an aspect of a general prevalent adult anxiety about young people and their personal development and well being. As a consequence, adult 'regulatory regimes' such as surveillance and curfews serve to delimit young people's movement through time and space (Valentine *et al.*, 1998: 7). Such regimes alter across the course of youth and differ in relation to an individual's gender and cultural positioning. Studies have shown that young people, and women in particular, learn from an early age from parents where and where not to go in order to minimise risk and danger to themselves (Deem, 1986; Pain 2001). Parmar (1995), exploring young South Asian women's leisure, found that although parents did not want their daughters to socialise with young boys this was not the only reason for their reluctance to send their daughters to youth clubs. More crucially, it was parents' fears that their daughters might be victims of attacks on the streets, both sexual and racial, that influenced their decision-making around their daughters' leisure.

In addition, a related set of more recent debates within leisure studies has begun to draw upon the cultural and spatial 'turns' in geography (Soja, 2000) to explore and interpret the meanings of space and place (Aitchison *et al.*, 2000). We engage with the work of the 'new' cultural geographers who suggest that 'space' is in a constant state of transition as a result of 'continuous, dialectical struggles of power and resistance among and between the diversity of landscape providers, users and mediators' (Aitchison *et al.*, 2000: 19) and is invested with historical, social and symbolic meaning for its occupants. Contributions to leisure studies from feminist geographers and feminist leisure theorists have theorised the spatial nature of gendered relationships, critiquing theories that view space as neutral, and arguing instead for a critical appreciation of the social production of space (Rendell, 2000). Massey (1994:186) writes that spaces and places, and our perceptions of them, are gendered in ways that vary across time and between cultures. The gendered nature of spaces and places both 'reflects and has effects back on' the ways in which gender is constructed and understood. Within leisure studies, Deem's (1986) groundbreaking study of women's leisure in Milton Keynes highlights the spatial inequity of leisure opportunities for women and men, linking this both to women's fear of violence, men's control over women's leisure movements and men's ideas about where women should and should not go. Deem's findings are consolidated by other early feminist work on women's leisure that drew attention to the link between, sexuality, dress and leisure behaviours (Green *et al.*, 1990) and the importance of avoiding 'unrespectable' and 'unwomanly' behaviour or dress in public places. Skeggs (1997) also observes that women's access and entry to leisure space can alter according to their social position, for example, women can exclude other women on the grounds of class, 'race', ethnicity, age and culture.

More recent analysis has focused on the ways in which space and gender are defined through power and how power relations are etched in spaces and places (Rendell, 2000). Space, it is argued, is gendered, sexualised, classed and racialised; and ease of access and movement through space for different groups is subject to constant negotiation and contestation and is embedded in relations of power (Aitchison, 2003; Scraton and Watson, 1998; Skeggs, 1999). Public leisure space in Western society has long been claimed by white, heterosexual men who have dominated, controlled and excluded other groups through the exertion of an aggressive 'gaze' or the use of violence (Green *et al.*, 1990; Lupton, 1999). Other groups of people, including women, have had to 'struggle' to establish their own spatial positioning, with some groups having greater resources of power than others to 'enter into negotiation' (Skeggs, 1999). For example, Scraton and Watson (1998: 131) observe how certain spaces can become 'no-go' areas on the grounds of 'race' whilst, equally, spaces can be perceived as safer or more welcoming when the occupants share common identities (Watt and Stenson, 1998). Accordingly, women's use of public space for leisure and everyday practices can be fraught with danger and 'risk', both real and imagined, yet the way in which risk is perceived and experienced varies for diverse groups according to factors such as location, social position, community, culture, time and life course stage. Spatial exclusion, as our data shows, continues to be an important feature of women's leisure lives and what might be considered as 'safe space' for one person or group of people may not be for another (Aitchison *et al.*, 2000).

Leisure, Identity and Belonging

This chapter is also concerned with the ways in which young women designate places as non-risky or 'safe spaces', for example, the young women in our study refer, in particular, to community venues as safe leisure spaces. We explore the interplay of meanings attributed to safe and welcoming space, including the need for parental acceptance, and women-only space in which they can express their faith and cultural identities without the risk of prejudice and discrimination. Community spaces are places where these young women can convene with others and experience a sense belonging and collective identity around age, gender, culture, faith, class and ethnicity. Similar concepts of leisure as social and personal space are explored by Scraton and Watson (2003) in relation to older South Asian women. Here such spaces centre upon the family, community and faith and are both material and emotional, offering, amongst other things, belonging, companionship, intimacy and security. These spaces are also closely intertwined with other social and personal spaces such as the home and workplace. This research importantly brings a critical awareness to the historically narrow focus upon leisure as *activity* and seeks to challenge ethnocentric leisure theorising. The authors draw upon Wearing's notion of leisure as 'personal space' where space is 'physical or metaphorical' and exists for women to 'fill with whatever persons, objects, activities or thoughts that one chooses' (1998: 149). This is a space of resistance, a space for being and becoming, although Wearing acknowledges that this space may not necessarily be used in overtly positive ways. In addition, and significantly, Scraton and Watson (2003) argue for the inclusion of collective social meanings as well as individual meanings of leisure spaces.

Conceptualising leisure as social space highlights the importance of viewing women as agents in their own lives, resisting 'dominant' stereotypes related to gender, 'race' ethnicity, culture, class and age; and creatively constructing and reconstructing spaces of collective belonging and friendship (Green, 1998). However, this needs to be balanced with a recognition that women continue to encounter barriers to leisure spaces and, as Parmar notes, the institutional racism of British society continues to prevent 'Asian girls having an equal share of the provisions that exist' (1995: 155). Whilst community spaces for leisure are an important part of our women's leisure, feelings of exclusion and isolation from existing public leisure facilities permeate the women's narratives. The sense of belonging found in community spaces needs to be critically analysed against the notion that community spaces can be 'enforced' spaces for minority groups, rather than space constructed out of choice (Bauman, 2001: 89). Invoking 'community' can also conjure false notions of belongingness, sameness and reciprocity, where community is seen as a bounded, static entity. It is therefore necessary to pay critical attention to women's differences and individual identities (Ahmed and Fortier, 2003), to unequal distributions of power and to permeable spatial 'community' borders (Morley, 2001).

Methodology

This chapter draws upon qualitative data from the Nisaa Project,[3] an ongoing action research project financed consecutively by UK government and then European urban regeneration funds and based in 'Middletown', a large industrial town in the North of England. The research began in 2001 in the central district of an area with a tradition of employment in the steel and chemical industries and currently experiencing high levels of unemployment. This area has a history of social and economic deprivation and ranks high on most of the official deprivation indicators. The majority population in the central district is white British but the area has a large BME community (an estimated 19 per cent at the time of the 2001 Census (ONS, 2001)). Phase one of the project aimed to enhance opportunities for health and wellbeing for BME women residing in the local communities. Merging research with community development work, Nisaa was designed to actively address barriers to health and leisure services and develop community-identified initiatives. The project has provided support to local women's community groups and developed capacity building initiatives, many of which were centred upon enhancing women's well being through gender-appropriate and culturally-sensitive leisure and training opportunities.

The research on women's leisure was carried out between 2001 and 2003 with additional leisure focus groups with young women carried out in the summer of 2004. This chapter draws upon the personal narratives of 12 South Asian women aged between 15 and 25 years. Most interviewees were recruited through participation in the community development project and were involved in local women's groups or attended Nisaa training sessions. All of the participants featured in this chapter were born in the UK and their families originate from Pakistan, in particular, the Mirpur region. The women are multi-lingual and chose to conduct the interviews in English. They all self-identify as Muslim women discussing their faith as an integral

---

3   'Nisaa' is derived from the Arabic word meaning women.

aspect of their culture, family and personal identity. They demonstrate different and heterogeneous articulations of religious identity, for example around dress, some choosing to wear the hijab and others not, and participation in prayer. Although the class positioning of women is difficult to determine (Skeggs, 1997) all of the young women reside in the central area of Middletown, a locale perceived by our participants as a 'bad' area, experiencing high levels of socio-economic deprivation and characterised as being inhabited by 'druggies' and prostitutes.[4] The women tend to concur that the town as a whole was a nice place to live but that certain 'notorious' local areas were more 'risky' than others, especially after dark.

Seeking 'Safe' Leisure Indoors

All of the young women in our study perceived themselves to be at risk from male physical and sexual violence in public spaces and deployed diverse strategies for managing this type of risk. Risk is spatially distributed, with certain areas of their neighbourhoods and the town, and specific streets, being considered 'out of bounds' by the young women. Most of the young women living in Middletown thought that their locality was mainly a dangerous place to live, punctuated with pockets of 'nice' areas, usually closer to their homes. They generally consider most 'outside' public space to be dangerous, and portray 'inside' private spaces as safe, demonstrating complex mapping systems of where they felt could walk on their own, with others or not at all and diverse spatial 'techniques' for minimising risk, such as, travelling in cars and carrying mobile phones:

> ...places like [place name] or [place name]... Yeah I think it's just a bit rough for me (giggle) you know, you hear about people getting their handbags snatched off them... I will go through the park but only if someone else is with me, I won't just go on my own but a back alley, no way (laugh) ... If I do go out, I usually end up taking somebody with me, coz I wouldn't go out on my own, but if I do go out with people in my car, I'm a little bit secure anyway...

> (Uzma)

They expressed fear and anxiety about what might happen to them in outside spaces and linked this with perceptions of dangerous strangers and figures who are 'out of control' because of alcohol consumption and drugs. Outside space associated with the physical characteristics of darkness and enclosure also featured predominately in their narratives of risky places (Seabrook and Green, 2004). Regardless of whether such men actually existed or whether they had had personal experience of danger, fear of assault by men was a very real experience (Pain, 2001).

More often than not, the streets were not used as spaces for leisure by the young women, many preferring home or indoor community-based venues as 'safe' spaces

---

4   Women were asked for demographic data on occupation but there was a low response rate suggesting a reluctance to disclose this type of information because of its 'sensitive' nature in this community.

for leisure. Risk narratives featured in their conversations about travelling to and from venues rather than their actual occupation of outside space. These women walked in groups, went with male chaperones or took lifts from family and friends because of the perceived danger of walking alone. This was, in part, because parents and family members encouraged them to stay indoors for reasons of safety and also because these women's culture required that they protect their honour and modesty by participation in women only leisure activities and staying inside after dark, as the women in this focus group articulate:

Furzana: 'I'm trying to think which people would be allowed out, cos like young people ...'

Salma: 'We're not allowed out really late, like after seven or something or eight isn't it.'

Yasmin: 'Well as soon as it gets dark we stay just indoors.'

The women described parents having different rules for their brothers who play football in the park, go on their own to the gym and are free to walk around the town and use public transport at any time of the day. Interestingly, all of the young women share a common perception of the town centre in the daytime as a safe place to walk around either by oneself or with others, perhaps because the bustling central area with its shoppers, workers and safe spaces within the shops creates an aura of safety, reflecting Deem's (1986) assertion that women occupying town space feel safer when with children or carrying out domestic tasks because these are legitimates activities for women to pursue.

The threat of racialised violence is also a problem. The young South Asian women are keenly aware of the inter-racial tensions in their area and the risks and fears that this evokes as they move through space and negotiate other bodies within this space. As others have noted (Parmar, 1995), this impacts significantly on their ability to access leisure and other social spaces. The racialised and gendered risks posed to the young South Asian women in public spaces was also discussed in reference to being framed as 'outsiders' to the area. Women were made to feel that they did not belong in the town because they were from a 'different' ethnic background:

Salma: 'Yeah it's a really bad area coz, they just don't like you do they ...'

Yasmin: 'They just can't accept us being here ...'

Salma: 'It's like 'oh go back to your own country.'

Furzana: 'All they say is 'pakis get out'.'

Rashida: 'This is when we go 'this is our country'.'

Furzana: 'That's just like no, totally go away, go away, not interested.'

This group of women also describe being harassed by white individuals because they wear the *hijab* (headscarf), an example of cultural racism, where cultural difference is mobilised to vilify, marginalise and exclude different groups (Modood *et al.*, 1994). Women are experiencing a multi-layered form of racism based upon skin colour and national and cultural identities, where gender, 'race', ethnicity and culture intersect and serve to marginalise women from public space (Back, 1996). Yet, as the dialogue above demonstrates, the women do not readily accept outsider status, feeling that the local space is their home, that they belong in the area and continue to display pride in their cultural identity. They actively resist being 'othered' by responding to their abusers through a mixture of silent opposition and verbal countenance. However, as Jamila illustrates, she is aware that this mode of resistance has the potential to expose her to a position of heightened risk,

> Jamila: 'I don't care how big they are or men or women or whatever I'll start back. I've a really bad habit, it is bad really, but I can't help it.'

> Interviewer: 'What makes it bad?'

> Jamila: 'It is bad because you're starting on them aren't you? [You should] just leave and walk away.'

The use and meanings associated with leisure spaces and concomitant risks can vary both between and within genders, and ethnic and cultural groups. Different groups of young women living within the same locality experience and negotiate space and its occupants differently as part of their everyday leisure experience and they learn to find ways of active resistance to and management of, the recurrent risks that they face on a daily basis.

Risking Reputation

Narratives of embodied respectability are also central aspects of women's occupation of space and uptake of leisure pursuits (Green *et al.*, 1990). Women's embodied behaviour is regulated, monitored and judged by others, in particular by those seeking to explain male violence (Stanko, 1990), but also in relation to commonly-held assumptions made about what constitutes 'respectable feminine' behaviour (Mitchell *et al.*, 2004). In our study, the young women's experiences of risk and movement through public space and place were closely connected to the representation of them as bodies which need to be carefully managed. Women of all ages both monitor and control their own bodies and behaviour and those of other women in public spaces (Burgess, 1998). The young South Asian women regularly cited family and the extended family and female family members in particular as playing a pivotal role in regulating their leisure behaviour as young women with gossip and ostracism highlighted as mechanisms which facilitated an effective self-policing system. For some of the young women there appeared to be tension between wanting to 'go out' to socialise and exercise, alongside anxiety that being seen in public, in the wrong place at the wrong time and perhaps in inappropriate clothing, might damage their own and their family's reputations; a finding that replicates those of the Sheffield-based study of women's leisure conducted over fifteen years earlier (Green *et al.*, 1990). Central to this was the notion of honour, *Izzat*, which was explained to us by the women in terms of 'family honour' and reputation, the safeguarding of which was the responsibility of the young Muslim women themselves through respectable and chaste behaviour (Gillespie, 1995) and other female members of the family. In consequence, they articulated feeling that their behaviour and actions were under the scrutiny of other community members for potential transgression of this code (Alexander 2000; Dwyer, 1998). The issue of visibility, being 'seen' and then 'labelled' as 'good' or 'bad' is highlighted in Alexander's study of an Asian community in London and is clearly reflected in our study, as Jamila's comments illustrate:

> 'Cos ... people see you, like Asians right, whether it's a man or a woman or a young lad or a young girl they'll talk about them ... 'did you see her, did you see her walking over there, oh, what's she doing'. You get a bad reputation.

Women 'moderated' their behaviour in public to avoid being 'gossiped about' and labelled as 'unrespectable' and several women articulate views on this, making distinctions between 'good' gossip or 'chat' which operates as a harmless aspect of leisure and as a mechanism for sustaining networks of companionship (Gillespie, 1995), and 'bad' gossip, or the spreading of rumours, designed to jeopardise a woman's reputation within the community. The young women emphasise 'bad' gossip as something that is circulated amongst older women, mainly between grandmothers and women of their parent's generation. Women in all interview settings 'condemned' the type of gossip that they considered to be harmful although the extent to which they participate themselves is unclear. Uzma enjoys going to the sauna where she can sit and chat with friends and family, and 'catch up on the gossip' but she was strongly opposed to 'malicious' gossip because it could acutely damage a woman's reputation: 'A reputation is what somebody makes of themselves really and basically if somebody gossips about them their reputation is down the drain kinda thing...' (Uzma).

One focus group of young women described how they deployed diverse strategies to avoid being 'spotted' outside of the home by family, relatives and local community members. The use of public transport including taxis and buses for leisure was one such area where visibility and safety were important issues. Women narrated the different and complex approaches required in travelling to and from leisure venues. Some women described parents' anxieties about them using taxis and buses because they were unsafe, particularly for women travelling alone. Other participants also pointed out that they were not permitted by parents to travel in taxis: being 'visible' in a taxi driven by an unrelated Asian man could potentially form the substance of 'gossip' in their community, incurring the disappointment of their parents. For some of the women, white male and preferably female taxi drivers, although they were rare in the area, were necessary to avoid the risk of a negative association with an Asian male. Women described on some occasions making themselves less visible to the community gaze to avoid identification by, for example, 'hiding' in the back of taxis, demonstrating women's negotiation of their own identities in relation to family and community and within different social spaces (Dwyer, 1998; Qureshi and Moores, 1999). The relative compactness of this community space the women refer to also reduces their capacity to remain invisible in contrast to larger cities where a degree of anonymity is afforded.

Our interview data demonstrates the contradictory pull between women being aware of the need to maintain a 'respectable' reputation which is, of course, all about guarding the body against harm and dishonour and yet wanting to enjoy their leisure as young women. Our findings confirm Martin's (1988) claim that women tend to see their bodies as separated from themselves, as alienated or fragmented and in need of control. It can be argued, therefore, that women carry a multiple burden of risk, with leisure activities threatening to jeopardise their 'respectability', combined with the need to negotiate multi-layered aspects of risk and danger.

Accessing Public Leisure Spaces

Many of the young women's accounts of leisure do not feature the regular use of public leisure facilities and few women attend leisure centres or local gyms. During the Nisaa Project, the community development worker organised some weekly sessions at the local leisure centre. The women access the centre using dedicated community transport and, in conjunction with the local leisure service, a programme of keep fit and exercise was developed that incorporated the women's needs for women-only leisure space. Adopting the ideas presented by Skeggs (1999) we suggest that leisure buildings and their appropriation, often by dominant societal groups, can exclude 'minoritised' groups spatially, socially and culturally. Most of the young women stressed that they did not want to swim or exercise in the presence of men for faith reasons and that their use of public leisure space was dependent upon the provision of appropriate women-only facilities. For the women in our study this suggests that their marginalisation was heightened on the grounds of gender, ethnicity and 'race', culture and language needs and by a failure on behalf of service providers to provide appropriate services for them. Hargreaves (1994) shows that Asian women are still the least likely to participate in sports on account of experiences of racism, lack of culturally appropriate facilities and the low priority assigned to sport by communities. Women's opportunities for leisure appear to be limited because public leisure provision remains geared to the white majority population, a finding that echoes those of the Sheffield study conducted in the 1980s (Green *et al.*, 1990). Accessing information is also difficult because the young women explained that they cannot find anyone they can identify with and who has specialist knowledge to be able to signpost them towards appropriate leisure facilities and activities. Women are active agents in their own leisure lives but, as Yasmin highlights, a lack of appropriate provision and information increases the alienation experienced by these women (Scraton and Watson, 1998):

> I actually went down to the [community centre] to get some leaflets… the receptionist was English and he couldn't really help me, he goes 'oh the girl's gone out and', so I didn't really get the help that I wanted, but I actually went down there myself cos' I was interested so I went down myself to find out what sort of trips… but I didn't get any information…

(Yasmin)

Anecdotal evidence from the community development worker also shows that white women at the women-only sessions at the leisure centre adopt a racialised 'gaze' which serves to construct boundaries between themselves and the South Asian women in public leisure space. White women's embodied behaviours, such as departing from the sauna when the young South Asian women enter, re[produces] and maintains the women's perceptions of themselves as being 'outsiders' in public spaces and creates spatial and social boundaries which prevent the women from finding a sense of belonging in leisure settings.

'Getting Together' in Community Spaces

Youth provision in the UK also remains primarily geared to the white male population, for example in the provision of school trips, discos and early evening youth clubs (Parmar, 1995; Qureshi and Moores, 1999). Parmar emphasises that South Asian women have different needs to the majority population and that Asian girls-only groups provide an atmosphere free from threat and intimidation from white youth, making it possible to facilitate the development of positive cultural, racial and sexual identities. Our research shows that this continues to be an important issue for young South Asian women because their gender, ethnic, faith and cultural needs are often not accounted for by local schools, colleges and youth groups when organising group leisure activities, as Yasmin expresses:

> But I think when… the teachers like in college and stuff, they try to like unify the blacks and the whites kind of thing – it didn't work because they didn't understand, for example, 'ah let's all go and do paintballing' and then you know, we wouldn't be allowed that…

(Yasmin)

Women's groups provide the space and opportunity for the girls to meet in a comfortable, tension-free environment, giving girls and young women the opportunity of acquiring the skills necessary to cope with the consequences of the racism they face in their everyday lives: skills they are not taught or given a chance to develop by the institutions they pass through such as schools, colleges and employment schemes (Parmar, 1995). Our study found that many of the women's leisure activities were centred in and around 'community' spaces especially in local community centres.[5] The Mosque does not feature as a place for leisure, in part because it is site for the practice of faith but also because they feel that it is primarily a male space, where men can meet up and socialise but women cannot. Leisure in the 'community' is rarely referred to in mainstream leisure literature, partly because of the increasing attention to 'city' spaces and the night time economy (Scraton and Watson 1998,

---

5   We are attentive to the problems involved in using the term 'community' and use this phrase because it was referred to as such on numerous occasions by interviewees themselves to signify both a group identity and a geographical area of belonging.

2003). Local community centres, offer greatly sought after and, most importantly, 'safe' and welcoming spaces for women to engage in opportunities for leisure. The centres offer indoor sessions where women can convene and take up an activity such as keep fit, join a sewing class or food club, go to events such as Bhangra evenings, hold meetings or gather in groups to chat and exchange news. They are also a focal point for women to meet prior to going on a day trip, another very popular aspect of the young women's leisure time. Such spaces afford the interviewees' experiences of collective belonging amongst their peers and, as Uzma explains, they also offer space away from the family home and surveillance by parents:

> ...Well I am looking forward to a... women's night... it's a part of the mela... I can't wait for that!... I'll go there and just chill... Just dancing and prancing about, don't really care, don't give a toss about what my mam's saying... just enjoying it.

(Uzma)

Socialising in groups amongst peers is very important to the young South Asian women, whose interview narratives emphasise the value they place upon the social and communal aspects of leisure, rather than engagement in individual leisure activities. Phrases such as 'it's the getting together' and 'it's the social' were common in our discussions. Scraton and Watson (2003) also note the importance of such local spaces as key sites for the formation and reproduction of imagined community. In addition, they provide an insight into the complex forms of women's agency, evidencing women as active agents in their own leisure lives rather than passive recipients of gender and cultural constraints. Drawing upon Wearing (1998) we assert that such 'space' extends beyond the physical and material environment to encompass social and emotional space and offers the women an opportunity, through leisure, to find a sense of collective belonging, support and friendship. Wearing's re-evocation of leisure as space for 'enlargement of the self' (1998: 177) incorporates women's creativity, empowerment and agency into traditionally narrow definitions of leisure and moves away from a singular focus on what women 'can't do' to include what they 'can do'. Our participants frequently engage in creative and artistic activities, such as dress making, creating new clothing styles through contemporary interpretations and representations of their cultural and historical roots, thus reflecting shifting plural identities and subjectivities as young South Asian women (Qureshi and Moores, 1999).

Conclusion

This chapter has argued for the need to ground theoretical work on risk through an exploration of empirical data which might test and develop the concept of risk itself. We were particularly interested in the ways that risk emotions, risk calculations and management strategies are perceived and experienced as embodied and spatially-located experiences. Our data confirms that young women carefully manage their embodied and spatialised selves to avoid risk, but it also demonstrates that there are significant contextual differences within and between groups of women. Women's perceptions of 'risk' are complex articulations of historical, gendered, cultural, social, ethnic and age-related positioning. Such feelings and emotions are embedded in local discourses and knowledge, characterised by gender, 'race' and relations of power. Debates within both feminist and sociological theory more generally have moved towards recognition of diversity and 'difference', paying closer attention to the intersections of gender, race, ethnicity, sexuality, class and age (Scraton and Watson, 1998) but there remains insufficient empirical research in this area. Our interest in capturing commonality and difference amongst groups of young women engaged in leisure makes a contribution to both contemporary theoretical debates on leisure and more broadly to 'risk theorising'.

Interrogating how young women use and think about the meanings of space, enables us to construct an analysis of the ways in which individuals think or reflect 'through the body' as a process for understanding and coping with risk and change. Social expectations and cultural discourses have always mediated women's relationships with their bodies. As Skeggs (1997: 82) notes, the body is also a site upon which relations of class, gender, 'race', ethnicity, sexuality, culture and age interact and are embodied and practiced. Women must regulate and be responsible for their bodies and strive to maintain embodied respectability. Analysis of our data demonstrates young women alternately striving for and resisting respectability and social acceptance both of which are also linked to women's spatial and temporal positioning. Being seen in 'the wrong place at the wrong time', can compromise women's status and reputation. Additionally, our data demonstrate that constructions of the 'respectable woman' are linked to women's positioning within the cultures that they occupy. Drawing upon perspectives which stress the importance of gender, 'race', ethnicity, class and age, both as processes and as relational identities, assists us in highlighting how identity is linked to the continual and, at times, contradictory re-working of individual subjectivities via a complex interaction between personal agency and social context. This contributes to an understanding of how young women can both actively construct their identities, for example, by taking risks and contesting established risk discourses, and yet continue to be constrained by dominant discourses which represent them as submissive bodies striving for respectability.

Exploring space in different contexts such as the local community enables an understanding of leisure as a series of arenas in which identities are [re]affirmed, celebrated, negotiated and contested. The women creatively transform communal spaces into those in which they feel they belong, giving us insights into how women form groups and communities of belonging and where they feel comfortable with the other bodies within that space. It also provides an insight into young women's modes of resistance to dominant cultural norms and forms of structural oppression. Such spaces are thus important in managing risk in terms of personal safety and reputation and in creating safe spaces of belonging through shared histories, identities, faith backgrounds and interests.

References

Ahmed, S. and Fortier, A. (2003) Re-imagining communities, *International Journal of Cultural Studies,* 6 (3), 251-259.

Aitchison, C. (2003) *Gender and Leisure: Social and Cultural Perspectives*, London: Routledge.

Aitchison, C., Macleod, N. E. and Shaw, S. J. (2000) *Leisure and Tourism Landscapes: Social and Cultural Geographies*, London: Routledge.

Back, L. (1996) *New Ethnicities and Urban Culture: Racisms and Multiculture in Young Lives*, London: Routledge.

Bauman, Z. (2001) *Community: Seeking Safety in an Insecure World*, Cambridge: Polity Press.

Beck, U. (1992) *Risk Society: Towards a New Modernity*, London: Sage Publications.

Beck, U. and Beck-Gernsheim, E. (1996) Individualisation and 'precarious freedoms': perspectives and controversies of a subject oriented sociology in P. Heelas, S. Lash, and P. Morris (eds), *Detraditionalization: Critical Reflections on Authority and Identity,* Oxford: Blackwell.

Brah, A. (1996) *Cartographies of Diaspora: Contesting Identities.* London: Routledge.

Brah, A. and Phoenix, A. (2004) 'Ain't I a woman?': revisiting intersectionality, *Journal of International Women's Studies,* 5 (3), 75-86.

Brown, H., Gilkes, M. and Kaloski-Naylor, A. (eds) (1999), *White? Women: Critical Perspectives on Race and Gender*, York: Raw Nerve Books.

Bunton, R., Green, E. and Mitchell, W. (2004) Introduction: Young People, Risk and Leisure: an overview', in W. Mitchell, R. Bunton and E. Green (eds), *Young People, Risk and Leisure: Constructing Identities in Everyday Life*, London: Palgrave.

Burgess, J. (1998) 'But is it worth taking the risk?' How women negotiate access to urban woodland: a case study' in R. Ainley (ed.), *New Frontiers of Space, Bodies and Gender,* London: Routledge.

Critcher, C., Bramham P. and Tomlinson, A. (eds), (1995) *Sociology of Leisure: A Reader*, London, E and F Spon.

Deem, R. (1986) *All Work and no Play? The Sociology of Women and Leisure*, Milton Keynes: Open University Press.

Dwyer, C. (1998) Contested identities: challenging dominant representations of young British Muslim women' in T. Skelton and G. Valentine (eds), *Cool Places: Geographies of Youth Cultures*, London: Routledge.

Furlong, A. and Cartmel, F. (1997) *Young People and Social Change: Individualisation and Risk in Late Modernity*, Buckingham: Open University Press.

Giddens, A. (1991) *Modernity and Self-Identity: Self and Society in the Late Modern Age,* Polity Press: Cambridge.

Gillespie, M. (1995) *Television, Ethnicity and Cultural Change*, London: Routledge.

Green, E., Hebron, S. and Woodward, D. (1990) *Women's Leisure, What Leisure?,*

Hampshire: Macmillan.

Green, E. (1998) 'Women doing friendship': an analysis of women's leisure as a site of identity construction, empowerment and resistance', *Leisure Studies* 17 (?), 171-185.

Hargreaves, J. (1994) *Sporting Females: Critical Issues in the History and Sociology of Women's Sports*, London: Routledge.

Lupton, D. (1999) *Risk*, London: Routledge.

Martin, E. (1989) *The Woman in the Body: A Cultural Analysis of Reproduction*, Milton Keynes: Open University Press.

Massey, D. (1994) *Space, Place and Gender*, Cambridge: Polity Press.

Maynard, M. (1994) 'Race', Gender and the Concept of 'Difference in Feminist

Thought, in H. Afshar and M. Maynard (eds.) *The Dynamics of 'Race' and Gender: Some Feminist Interventions*, London: Taylor and Francis.

Mitchell, W., Bunton, R. and Green, E. (eds) (2004) *Young People, Risk andLeisure: Constructing Identities in Everyday Life*, London: Palgrave.

Modood, T., Beishon, S. and Virdee, S. (1994) *Changing Ethnic Identities,* Policy Studies Institute.

Morley, D. (2001) Belongings: place, space and identity in a mediated world', *European Journal of Cultural Studies,* 4 (4), 425-448.

Office for National Statistics (2001) Neighbourhood Statistics: 2001 Census, URL (consulted April 2005): http://neighbourhood.statistics.gov.uk/

Pain, R. (2001) Gender, race, age and fear in the city, *Urban Studies,* 38 (5-6), 899-913.

Parmar, P. (1995) Gender, race and power: the challenge to youth work practice, in C. Crichter, P. Bramham and A. Tomlinson (eds), *Sociology of Leisure: A Reader,* London: E and F N Spon.

Qureshi, K. and Moores, S. (1999) Identity remix: tradition and translation in the lives of young Pakistani Scots, *European Journal of Cultural Studies,* 2 (3), 311-330.

Rendell, J. (2000) Introduction: Gender, Space, in J. Rendell, B. Penner, and I.

Borden (eds) *Gender, Space, Architecture: An Interdisciplinary Introduction*, London: Routledge.

Seabrook, T. and Green, E. (2004) Streetwise or safe? girls negotiating time and

Space, in W. Mitchell, R. Bunton and E. Green (eds), *Young People, Risk and Leisure: Constructing Identities in Everyday Life,* Basingstoke: Palgrave Macmillan.

Scraton, S. and Watson, B. (1998) Gendered cities: women and public leisure space in the 'Postmodern City', *Leisure Studies,* 17 (2), 123-137.

Scraton. S and Watson, B. (2003) 'Leisure as a space for achieving a sense of belonging for South Asian women' paper presented to the British Sociological Association's Annual Conference, 2003.

Skeggs, B. (1997) *Formations of Class and Gender: Becoming Respectable*, London: Sage.

Skeggs, B. (1999) Matter out of place: visibility and sexualities in leisure spaces', *Leisure Studies,* 18 (3), 213-32.

Soja, E. W. (2000) *Postmetropolis: Critical Studies of Cities and Regions,* Oxford: Blackwell.

Stanko, E. (1990) *Everyday Violence: How Women and Men experience Sexual and*

Physical Danger, London, Pandora.

Valentine, G., Skelton, T. and Chambers, D. (1998) Cool places: an introduction to youth and youth cultures, in T. Skelton and G. Valentine (eds.), *Cool Places: Geographies of Youth Cultures*, London: Routledge.

Watson, B. and Scraton, S. (2001) 'Confronting Whiteness? Researching the leisure lives of South Asian mothers', *Journal of Gender Studies,* 10 (3), 265-277.

Watt, P. and Stenson, K. (1998) 'The Street: 'It's a bit dodgy around there': Safety, danger, ethnicity and young people's use of public space, in T. Skelton and G. Valentine (eds.), *Cool Places: Geographies of Youth Cultures*, London: Routledge.

Wearing, B. (1998) *Leisure and Feminist Theory*, London: Sage Publications.

Chapter 8

Daughters of Islam, Sisters in Sport

Tess Kay

Introduction

One of the divisive structures in multicultural Britain is the very varied access that young people from different backgrounds have to post-compulsory education. Non-participation among ethnic minorities often reflects their experience of pre-16 education, including lack of understanding and support from teachers, and 'ignorant comments based on stereotyping about career goals, family and community cultures' (Social Exclusion Unit, 1999: 40). Low educational qualifications have long-term consequences, acting as a barrier to the labour market and contributing to high unemployment and low income among many minority communities. One of the cornerstones of Britain's social exclusion policy is therefore to improve educational qualifications among groups at risk from exclusion.

Between 2003-2004, Loughborough University was involved in a 'widening participation' programme targeted at young people from local black and minority ethnic communities. The 'Widening Access Through Sport' (WATS) project was funded by the European Social Fund and was part of the UK government's policy to increase access to further and higher education among groups who were currently under-represented. As a university with particular strengths in sport, the Loughborough project offered a combined package of sport and education activities intended to attract young people to the university campus, give them experience of a Higher Education environment, and encourage them to consider continuing their studies beyond the age of 16.

The use of sport within the programme reflected a broader recent trend in the UK to incorporate sport in social policy. Since Tony Blair's New Labour governments first came to power in 1997, claims about the capacity of sport to contribute to social change have fuelled a wide range of sports-based initiatives directed at diverse groups from varied social and cultural circumstances. Most of these initiatives have focussed on young people, who are seen as a primary target for policies to promote social inclusion through increased educational attainment, improved health and reduced youth crime. In comparison to policy makers, academics have generally been more sceptical, acknowledging the theoretical benefits of sport but emphasising the lack of evidence that such benefits are actually achieved (e.g. Coalter, Allison and Taylor, 2000; Collins, Henry, Houlihan and Buller, 1999; Long, Welch, Bramham, Butterfield, Hylton and Lloyd, 2002). Notwithstanding this, there has been a marked increase in sports-based provision addressing social exclusion issues.

The Loughborough project generally found sport to be a successful vehicle for engaging young people. During its two-year lifetime, the project worked with young people from a range of backgrounds, but most continuously and intensively with young Muslim men and women. Three 'Education and Sport' Development Workers were appointed, one of whom was employed to run an activity programme for female Muslim youth. This activity programme proved to be particularly successful, attracting regular and continuous attendance. Informal feedback from participants and the activity leader indicated a high level of enjoyment and satisfaction among the young women taking part.

Despite the successes, there were some difficulties in the arrangements. The Muslim young women's elements of the project were often the most difficult to organize in practical terms because of their requirement for female-only activity areas from which males could be excluded. The project directors also learned that a number of girls who would like to participate in the project were forbidden to do so by their parents. As the project progressed, there were occasions when the young women were only allowed to participate after the activity leader had visited their home and explained the activities in full detail to their parents, and assured them that the arrangements met the requirements of Islam. At the same time, the girls themselves were confounding our expectations: they were far more responsive to the sports elements of the programme than we anticipated, to the extent of moving quickly from personal participation to taking entry-level coaching qualifications. To a westernized outsider, the assertiveness and energy they displayed appeared at odds with the 'constraints' surrounding them. As members of the project management team, we became interested in these apparent contradictions and in the role of the girls' families in influencing them. We also recognized that programmes such as our own that attempted 'social change' must take account of these factors. In 2004, we therefore undertook a number of participatory research activities to improve our knowledge and understanding of this context.

This chapter draws on this research to contribute to understanding of 'being a Muslim young woman in England'. It draws attention to the value of addressing family diversity and the dynamics of intra-family relationships as a core component of ethnic identity. It also explores how a focus on sport can facilitate understanding of the experiences of young Muslim women as they conduct their day-to-day lives in the context of the varied and sometimes contradictory influences of their religion, the culture of their family's country of origin and their exposure to western values and expectations.

Family and Identity

Increasing cultural diversity in Britain has fuelled a growing literature on the situation of minority populations, underpinned by a complex notion of 'ethnicity' that is socially constructed and embodies ancestry, history and culture. This conceptual approach emphasises diversity among minority ethnic groups and recognises that socio-economic positions and identities of their members are not structurally determined but are at least partially formed by their actions (Pilkington, 2003: 2). In Britain the Runnymede Trust's Parekh Report reflected current debates surrounding multi-culturalism in its exploration of the future of the country as a 'multi-ethnic' society (Parekh, 2000) in which individuals and communities actively engage in the process of identity negotiation, and ethnic identities are dynamic and fluid (Pilkington, 2003: 7). Early expectations of 'assimilation' have thus become outmoded: rather than experiencing a move to cultural homogeneity, we are witnessing growing cultural diversity both between the white majority population and non-white groups, and between different minority ethnic communities.

Elliott (1996) has argued that the most significant manifestation of this diversity is in family life. She places family very centrally at the heart of cultural identity and depicts different family arrangements and values as crucial distinguishing characteristics of different ethnic groups. Bhopal's (1999) research into women in east London found that a majority valued South Asian family traditions, including the practice of arranged marriages, precisely because they represented something distinctive about South Asian personal and collective cultural identity, while Harvey (2001), in her examination of minority families in four different countries, found the dominant theme to be the importance attached to 'maintaining our differences'. Similarly, Berthoud (2000: 2) claims that 'it is diversity between minority groups which is their most striking characteristic' and that 'nowhere is this diversity more apparent than in family structures'.

In Britain the most distinctive minority family arrangements are those of Muslim families of South Asian origin who follow a traditional interpretation of Islam (Elliot, 1996; Berthoud, 2000). 'Family' is a particularly strong defining feature of these communities, which draw on a complex legacy of values in which culture and religion are closely intertwined. The traditions of South Asia are particularly influential in defining dominant ideologies of family in many communities. Ballard (1982), to whom contemporary writers continue to refer, highlighted two central features: the gendered structure of family and its 'collective' or 'corporate' nature. He gave a particularly clear account of the privileged position of males, explaining how membership of a family unit consisted of a man, his sons and grandsons, together with their wives and unmarried daughters. Female children of a family were not, therefore, permanent members of their parents' household: at marriage, daughters left their natal home and became members of their husbands' family (Ballard, 1982: 3).

Ballard also addressed the corporate nature of South Asian family life. This provides a striking contrast with western notions of marriage as intimate partnerships between two people, based on romantic love. In contrast, South Asian families have been traditionally ideologically focussed on the family group with little regard for individual freedom or self-interest (Ballard, 1982). Verma and Darby (1994), writing about the British Bangladeshi community in the 1990s, describe it as 'essentially collectivist': 'that is to say that its members perceive themselves not as individuals but also as members of a group – the family' (1994: 45). Bhopal captures this well in her description of marriage as 'an arrangement between two families, not two individuals' (Bhopal, 1999: 120). The collective efforts of the individual members of the family are directed at maintaining and increasing family honour - 'izzat', which depends on the family's wealth and on its members' conformity with ideal norms of behaviour. As the most effective way for families to increase izzat is through arranging prestigious marriage matches for the families' daughters, it is women who are ultimately responsible for izzat: 'if a daughter steps out of line, she not only jeopardises her own respect in the community but her parents' social standing' (Bhopal, 1999: 121).

These influences are strongly evident in South Asian families in Britain. Although minority ethnic groups do modify their traditional family arrangements as a result of interplay with the majority culture, they do so in ways that are consistent with their own traditions (Elliott, 1996: 41), drawing on their own extensive cultural capital (Pilkington, 2003) to establish their identity in western contexts. Beishon, Modood and Virdee's (1998) comparison of the values and attitudes underpinning family life among different ethnic groups showed that Pakistanis and Bangladeshis were the most traditional: the majority believing in multi-generational households with parents and their adult sons' families, and any unmarried children, living together. The current parent generation in particular saw multi-generational households as an ideal living arrangement that fostered meaningful relationships within the family. Younger Pakistani and Bangladeshi adults were generally as much in favour of living in an extended family, although a few felt it was better to have parents living locally rather than with the household, for reasons of privacy and autonomy. Parents of Pakistani or Bangladeshi origin were the most concerned that their children should be involved in some form of cultural or religious activity and have access to Islamic teaching. They were also generally against marrying outside their ethnic group, although this might be acceptable if the prospective partner was Muslim or prepared to become a Muslim. Overall, interviewees of South Asian origin saw their families as very different from white families, and were critical of white parents' perceived lack of commitment to parenting, which they saw as fostering indiscipline and lack of respect among the young for their parents and elders (Beishon *et al.*,1998).

However, while the overall picture conformed to the idea of Asian households in Britain reflecting 'traditional' family structures, there have been other indications of a more complex picture. Although Berthoud (2000) found that Pakistani and Bangladeshi were clearly the most conservative of ethnic groups in the population, even here there were indicators of change. Firstly, many British Asians appeared to be moving away from the tradition of arranged marriages, although this development is much less common among Muslims than among Hindus and Sikhs (Berthoud 2000: 16). Secondly, although a clear majority of Pakistani and Bangladeshi women looked after their home and family full-time, this was becoming less common among the growing number of women who are obtaining good educational qualifications. Thirdly, and possibly associated with this shift in female career expectations, although Pakistani and Bangladeshi women have very high fertility rates from their teenage years to their early forties, there were clear signs of a reduction in the number of children being born to women from these communities.

The changes Berthoud describes centre mainly on shifts in the life patterns of women. Dale, Shaheen, Kaira and Fieldhouse (2002) throw more light on this, particularly in relation to changing patterns of education among Muslim females. They note that when the first generation of Pakistani and Bangladeshi women arrived in Britain, their lack of qualifications and limited fluency in English were major barriers to employment. Subsequently, young Pakistani and Bangladeshi women educated in the UK have had the opportunity to acquire language and qualifications that was not available to their mothers, and most have also been exposed to Western cultural values as well as the traditional Muslim values of their parents and family (Dale *et al.*, 2002: 943). Berthoud reinforces this, pointing out that while the fourth PSI survey found that a clear majority of Pakistani (70%) and Bangladeshi (81%) wives were full-time homemakers, Labour Force Survey data demonstrates a strong correlation between levels of qualification and employment status. Thus, while unqualified Muslim wives of the current parent generation were unlikely to take up low-status employment, there is a 'strong implication' that 'more Muslim women will find their way into the labour market as more of them obtain educational qualifications' (Berthoud, 2000: 18).

It is against this backdrop of tradition and change that young Muslim women in Britain are constructing their identities. The legacy of their family's country of origin is a critical component of their experiences as they do so. Changes in family life and educational experiences place Muslim young women in the vanguard of changing South Asian ethnic identities in Britain. Changes in family patterns combined with changing expectations of education and employment represent points of divergence and possible conflict between young girls and their parents.

The Research

It is in this context of complex and almost contradictory influences that our research was located. As researchers and project managers, we were able to establish a small-scale in-depth research project in partnership with seven of the young women participants. As well as identifying the influence of the girls' families on their daughters' involvement in the WATS project itself, the research was an opportunity to explore parental expectations of young Muslim females in relation to education, employment and domesticity, and to compare the girls' own views to those of their parents.

The study was conducted as an education and personal development element within the educational syllabus of the girls' activity programme during the Easter school holiday. The data collection took the form of a preliminary interview with the development worker to help define the parameters of the study; a detailed 'family profile' questionnaire completed by the girls, providing details of all household members concluding personal characteristics, employment status and English language competence; in-depth interviews, conducted by the girls themselves with their parents and other family members; and two focus-group discussions in which the girls responded to the views their parents had expressed in the interviews. The family interviews addressed three themes: views on the girls' involvement in sport; views on their involvement in education; and expectations of their adult lives, including employment and domestic roles. The girls were directly involved throughout the research process and had maximum influence in defining the parameters of the research through their input into the detailed design of the interview schedule. The format of the research had been designed to allow us to access a group with whom we had had no direct contact and with whom we might have limited credibility, but who were likely to be more responsive to their own children. The girls were also fully involved in the interpretation and analysis of the outcomes of the interviews and had the opportunity to respond to the findings.

Under the guidance of the researchers and the sport and education development worker, the girls met as a group on four occasions over a two-week period and, between meetings, undertook some additional independent work. An initial workshop was held to introduce the girls to social science research and to explain the researchers' interest in the role the girls' families played in their lives. The girls then worked in small sub-groups to discuss the issues to be addressed and drew up lists of questions to be asked of parents and/or older siblings. The researchers collated the information from the girls and compiled an interview schedule using their questions. No question topics were rejected although wording on some was edited and like questions were combined. At a second workshop, the researchers presented the completed interview schedule to the girls and trained them in the use of mini-disc recorders. The girls practiced using the interview schedule to conduct pilot interviews on each other, recording the conversation as they did so. Over the weekend following the workshop, each girl then conducted an interview with one family member and began to transcribe it. This work continued over the next week until all transcripts were complete.

Two further workshops were held when the interviewing had been completed. At the first of these, the girls reported back on the findings of their interviews. The activity leader, a Muslim female, led the discussion which was recorded on minidisk. In the final workshop the activity leader led a second discussion on the interviews, this time focusing on the girls' response to their parents' views and their own attitudes to the issues covered. The workshop discussion was again recorded on mini-disc. The reiterative structure of the data collection allowed comparisons to be made between the views of the parents and the views of the girls, and also allowed the girls' explanations for differences between the two to be considered.

Being a Daughter of Islam

Research Participants and Their Families

The research study was conducted with seven Muslim girls, aged 13 – 18. At the time of the research all were in full-time education at local schools/colleges. They varied in ethnicity, describing themselves as white and black Africans, Bangladeshi and Arab. Most (six) of the girls wore the headscarf, indicating conformance with a traditional interpretation of Islam.

Two of the girls were sisters so the number of families involved in the research was six. The girls' parents were first generation immigrants to Britain and their households were two-generational: some were 'large' households, but not all. Most of their parents (eight out of 12) were not in employment – three fathers and five mothers; of the remainder, two were employed part-time and two full-time. Parents varied in their ease of use of English, which was not always the first language used at home, and a number of parents were considered by their daughters to experience some difficulty in using either written or spoken English, or both. The combination of low employment and (some) English language difficulties indicated that this group might experience a degree of separation from the local majority population. Such separation may encourage strong internal community ties and also represents an important difference between the experiences of the parent generation and those of their children. In contrast to their parents, the girls involved in the study were fully competent in English and, through their schooling, had regular contact with young white people and those from other ethnic groups.

Family Life

The picture that emerged of how the girls lived their lives as members of their parents' household illustrated the prominence of 'family' in their day-to-day lives. It also highlighted elements of the girls' experiences that represented 'difference' in comparison to the westernised lifestyles of the majority of the local population. Two examples of this were particularly in evidence. Firstly, the research revealed something about the *extent* of family. A number of the girls came from large families, as did the WATS development worker who was one of nine siblings. In addition to this, however, families who had been living in Town for more than a generation were usually related to other families living locally. In these cases, the number of people to whom any individual was related could be very high. The development worker estimated that she was related to around 65 people living in Town and in the questionnaire completed at the outset of the research, three of the girls estimated that they had between 40 and 60 relatives living there. As members of the Muslim community tended to live in properties located near to each other, this could be very close proximity indeed. For the girls this meant that there was an extensive number of people with an interest in their behaviour. This echoes a point made by Singleton and Green (2004) about the sense of surveillance that young women can have in these close-knit communities in which cultural norms make the behaviour of young females a particular focus.

Secondly, the research revealed some interesting examples of the relatively constrained spatial scope of the girls' activities. In comparison to non-Muslim teenagers, they spent a high proportion of time in the home and travelled a limited distance beyond it. Even the development worker – an assertive and highly skilled 25 year-old graduate in full-time employment – described her life outside the home as taking place only in work hours: when she returned home at the end of each afternoon she was expected to remain in the house until re-emerging for work next morning. For the girls, this applied when they returned home from school. This pattern partly reflected the expectation that girls would contribute domestically to the household, and partly concerns about the activities they might engage in outside it. Beyond the home, the girls did not travel independently: when, in the course of the project, the development worker took the girls to nearby City 12 miles away, it was the first time that even the oldest members of the group had spent some time in the city centre unaccompanied by their parents. Their lives were therefore more localised than those of young people from other groups, much more home-based, and involved much less contact with friends and much more time in the company of immediate family.

Family Voices on Muslim Girls Participating in Sport

Islam does not forbid its female followers to participate in sport: on the contrary, taking care of the body through exercise is seen as a duty and participating in sport is condoned for this reason (Walseth and Fasting, 2003). Constraints do, however, arise from the circumstances in which girls and women can participate, for unless they are wholly concealed from the male gaze, girls participating in sport will infringe the religious requirement and cultural expectation of modesty in females. As we have seen, this has social consequences in that a daughter behaving in an unseemly way will damage family izzat.

The family 'voice' on participating in sport reflected these contrasting issues, expressing both approval and constraint. There was outright support for girls participating: in one sibling interview, a brother went so far as to say that 'Muslim girls just don't do enough sport' and criticised them for not doing more. The parent generation was also supportive, including mothers who had not been able to participate themselves under the more traditional restrictions of their generation and now wished to see their daughters enjoy a wider range of experiences. Family members also referred to the fact that taking part in sport conformed to Islam, and supported participation for this reason.

The family voice of constraint was also in evidence. Throughout the interviews, those who expressed support for sport stressed that this was only acceptable if the conditions conformed to Islam. If parents were uncertain about the suitability of the occasion and facilities, they could prevent their daughter attending. One of the female participants referred to a friend who was not allowed to take part in the project, while another recognised that the decision about her own and her friends' attendance rested wholly with parents:

> She did tell me at school that she likes taking part in sport but her parents don't have that understanding so… they object to her coming along. You have to realise that if the parents are going to say no…that is it, and you will just have to leave them with that choice.

The girls themselves were wholly positive about sport. By providing a guaranteed female-only environment, the WATS project was making opportunities available to them which they could not obtain elsewhere. They commented on the unease they could feel taking part in sport in less favourable situations that reinforced their sense of difference: 'It's like the leisure centre, if you go everybody is dressed in a different way to you and they are staring at you instead of doing what they are meant to be doing'.

The girls were particularly responsive to the elements of the project which had embedded education within sporting activities, e.g. through the coaching courses undertaken. Sport appeared to have been very effectively integrated into these elements of the activity programme:

1. You know that coaching thing that we did, I was thinking, God it has got so much to it.
2. When you think of sports like hockey, you think of playing the game but there is more to it, links with sociology and everything else.
3. Yes I thought how much do you need to study to be a coach?

Islam places a strong value on education as a matter of self-development and much of the WATS project 'syllabus' developed for this group focused on these matters. Here, too, sport appeared to contribute:

4. I have gained more knowledge on sports, [it is] not just something that you practically take part in, it is communicating with each other, learning to respect one another, helping one another, building your self-confidence and esteem.

The girls were also aware of the fact that by participating, they were confounding expectations of what Muslim girls could do:

1. I go on about it all the time, they're like 'ok shut up!'
2. They don't think we would be able to do something like that [karate].

1. Especially cos of the way we dress, they wouldn't think we could.
2. They are careful what they say to us now!

The girls also commented on the sense of solidarity that they obtained from meeting together through the WATS project. Most of the girls did not normally socialise outside school hours: there was a parental expectation that they would spend their time at home. It became apparent that they valued the opportunity to meet other young women who shared and understood their situation: 'I get the impression when I say something that you [the group] understand what I am saying. I feel that when I say something you get it and say, yeah right'. One of the consequences of this was that the girls felt more confident about their ability to express their faith:

1. I think I feel more comfortable now talking about my faith…like sometimes I get…I feel a bit awkward having to explain some things, like I can't do this because of this, this, this, and this. I don't mind the questions it doesn't bother me I just [used to] feel like a bit weird, I felt like an alien, because you know…
2. You feel like you are the only one.

1. Well not just the only one, it's because like you know this is multi-cultural Britain, not everyone has a faith, so if you do everything according to your faith some people might find it a bit odd, a bit strange. But now I feel that I can talk about my faith and feelings especially at school. Because before I wouldn't talk to anyone but now I feel I can, I have more confidence.

The overall situation in relation to sport was mixed. Family members were supportive, but the proviso was that sport must conform to acceptable behaviour for young women. This conformance was partly a matter of religious observance, but also one of social respectability. The family was a conduit for both these sets of values.

Family Voices on Muslim Girls Taking Part in Educational Activities

Levels of progression to further and higher education by young Muslims in Britain are low. A number of researchers have explained this in terms of the relative poverty of much of the Muslim community in Britain (Modood *et al.*, 1997; Parekh, 2000) and the need for young people to leave education to work and supplement family income from a young age. Our own earlier research into the Higher Participation Education Through Sport (HEPTS) project, the precursor to WATS, indicated that many young people from the Bangladeshi community in Town were leaving school at the minimum legal age for precisely this reason –to earn an immediate and necessary income for their families (Kay and Lowrey, 2003). In many cases it therefore appeared to be practical circumstances rather than attitudinal factors that limit educational progression. In other words, the under-representation of young Muslims in post-school education belies the extreme importance attached to education within Islam. The value attached to education was central to the activities programme provided by the WATS project for the Muslim girls' participant group. The Muslim female development worker was key in developing the programme to deliver a substantial educational syllabus, reflecting her certainty that families would be supportive of girls participating in educational activities. The research amply justified this assumption. The value attached to education was so entrenched that one older sibling found it almost incomprehensible to be asked to explain this: 'Education is important, it can't be overstated. You are asking me to explain the obvious'.

Family approval of education for girls was expressed in terms of conforming to Islam, and also in relation to material circumstances. Parents believed from their own experiences that educational qualifications were needed for financial security. However, more mixed views came to the fore when family members were asked about the suitability of further and higher education for the girls. Again, the views expressed related to Islam: how could the girls pursue education in an environment where they would be particularly exposed to western culture, and separated from their families and thus isolated from their guiding influence? An additional factor arose in relation to the role which education and employment might play in the girls' adult lives. Having a 'career' was very definitely seen as a secondary consideration, and even an inappropriate one. Although education was valued for girls in their current situation there were reservations about where it might lead.

The girls themselves held similarly contradictory views. On the one hand, they valued education and also expressed some resentment of the constraints they faced in comparison to their male counterparts:

1. Education I think it is important for a girl.
2. I don't think it is fair that the guy can go off to 'uni' no problem whatsoever and the girl, on the other hand, has to stay at home and be the good one.

The girls' discussion of education was also revealing for what it displayed about their uncertainties and how they intended to resolve them. The following exchange was an illuminating cameo, illustrating the ambiguities that sometimes surrounded the requirements of Islam, and providing an example of how the girls would actively seek out guidance from experts in Islamic religion (a 'scholar') on how to conform to these:

3. Well it has something to do with modesty doesn't it…. It's safer for girls to stay within the home… Islam has set down these laws, you can't travel 46-48 miles without…

1. But it says no matter where education is, then there is nothing wrong with that.

Development worker: With universities I am not sure, you would have to put it to a scholar and see what they say.

As well as being concerned about conforming to Islam, the girls were concerned at a more personal level about with how the experience of being at an educational institution might affect them. They had a very strong awareness of the issues of being exposed to western culture:

1. I would be worried that I would commit more sin if I moved away.
2. I actually agree with everything my mum said. The main thing was she said you can get influenced – and you can get influenced very easily. I would probably be scared to go on and even do A levels and stuff.
3. You'd be scared to do A levels? You'd be at college and everything.

2. But you'd have free periods and stuff…
3 Are you easily influenced?
1 She is…

The findings concerning 'education' raise a number of issues. While there is no question about the support in principle for Muslim girls and young women engaging in educational activities, there are, however, potential conflicts with religious and cultural requirements. It is interesting to see how these conflicts are experienced and articulated by the girls themselves. While there is some expression of dissatisfaction with the different freedoms ascribed to males and females, there is also considerable acceptance of the constraints that underlie this. The girls explicitly expressed fears about their own potential behaviour and their possible deviation from Islam. Perhaps of most interest, however, are the expressions of how the girls engage with the identity work required to resolve these dilemmas. This small group have recourse to specific teachings/guidance from religious leaders. Within the discourse surrounding Muslim girls' identity in Britain, there is a discernible discourse of 'what am I allowed to be?'

The very specific sources of guidance available on this position were rather different for these girls than from many other British youth.

Family Voices on Adult Roles

Family attitudes to girls' involvement in education were closely linked to views about the adult pathways that Muslim girls would take. Parental comments reflected both the power of tradition, and the pressure for change. For the most part, the girls' reported that their parents, and mothers especially, emphasised the role of mother as the primary one: 'My mum said education is important but being a mother is more important than education'. Some mothers were, however, keen that their daughters should have wider experiences, and showed some acceptance of women's ambition beyond the home: '[S]he said whatever I want to become I have to achieve it through education. So she said, [I should] try to achieve my goal and aim high'. The girls themselves displayed both attitudes. They valued motherhood:

1. I think being a mother is more important than having a career. My mum thinks being a mum is more important.
2. It is kind of like a career...
3. ...being a full-time mum.

There were, nonetheless, aspects of the traditional South Asian Muslim woman's role from which some wanted to distance themselves. The discussion of adult roles brought up the fundamental issue of girls' relationship to their family and the tension between the closeness of this relationship and any individual desire for independence:

> But I don't like to be scared of doing something... I want to be independent and think for myself. If you are always under your parents' guidance you don't always think for yourself, do you, you can't really be your own person...It is also I don't like when you are asked to make a decision and you're like, what shall I do, I'll go and ask my dad...I'd be calling them up when I was 50 or something... I'd rather think for myself.

Difference and Identity

This chapter has used sport as a vehicle for investigating the experiences of second-generation young Muslim females in Britain. 'Sport' is a useful focus for this type of investigation because of its special position in relation to Muslim women: it is an activity condoned by Islam but severely restricted by cultural restrictions on women. Hargreaves (2000) has, in fact, suggested that in some Islamic states, access to sport is synonymous with women's broader struggle for gender equity. Questioning Muslim young women about their participation in sport therefore requires them to explicate a broader range of issues relating to their situation and allows evidence of identity work to emerge.

The study revealed substantial family influence on the response to the sports project by the girls, whose participation was wholly conditional on their parents' approval. However, although authority lay with the parents, there were examples of views being mediated by older siblings, especially older sons. These family members acted as a bridge to the local community from which parents were relatively excluded through their lack of employment and sometimes limited English language skills. In the examples in this study, older siblings' contributions served to increase girls' opportunities rather than constrain them. Some mothers also supported their daughters having something to do beyond the home. There were, therefore, some indications of family support for a slight widening of opportunities for girls, but still within quite strict limits.

Daughters in Transition

The girls' responses to their families' expectations of their current and adult roles revealed some of the complexities of negotiating identity when positioned between cultures, religions, ethnicities and generations. For the most part the girls were accepting of parental authority and shared their parents' views on appropriate behaviour. Again, however, it was evident that some questioned a number of the traditional expectations of them, with some expressions of individualism emerging. While this might indicate a step towards 'modern' values, there was, however, strong evidence of alternative influences that countered this. Discussions of what was permissible under Islam showed that the girls continually made reference to their faith for guidance on practical matters. Their identity work was concerned, therefore, not just with what they wanted to be, but with establishing what they were 'allowed' to be.

This combination of small indications of movement towards more liberal lifestyles, counterbalanced by explicit reference to Islamic teachings in relation to day-to-day activities, is in accordance with recent analyses that reveal the complexity of ethnicity in Britain. On the one hand, there was evidence of the fluidity described by the Parekh report (2000): parental and sibling attitudes towards the girls' involvement in the project suggested that rather than being 'permanently locked into unchanging traditions', the Muslim community in Town was 'constantly adapting and diversifying their inherited beliefs and values in the light of the migration experience' (Parekh, 2000: 27). The girls were not only experiencing, but also actively creating, a fusion of the traditions of their origins with elements of the majority culture (Modood, Berthoud *et al.*, 1997). This identity work was evident in the girls' dialogues, especially when they confronted uncertainties and differences amongst themselves about what was appropriate and/or required of them as young Muslim women. It was also, however, evident in the voice of the parents, who gave approval to their daughters' involvement in activities which signified change. Some of these changes were modest: for example, participating in sport within a very controlled environment that conforms to Islam is not in itself a major departure. The support for girls' education and higher level qualifications, however, contrasts strongly with their mothers' generation and has the potential to produce more fundamental long-term shifts.

Conclusions

The experiences of the young are an inevitable focus in analyses of processes of cultural adaptation. Minority ethnic youth have been described as 'skilled cross-cultural navigators' (Parekh, 2000: 29) who draw not only on their own and the majority culture, but also on the cultures of other minorities in the population. There can be a danger, however, that this navigational process is assumed to be unidirectional: Muslim youth are often presumed to be moving only towards the 'progressive' elements of other cultures. Our experience did not suggest this: rather than abandoning Islam, the girls quite specifically referred to Islam as a source of guidance for how they should conduct their present and adult lives. This very much accords with the work of other writers who have suggested that the 'navigation' process of the younger generation is complex. Modood (1997), for example, talks of young people seeking ways of adapting that accord with their own culture.

In the case of Muslims, these acts of adaptation mean that 'new ways of living and the process of gradually becoming a part of British society have to be ultimately justified in terms compatible with a Muslim faith' (Modood, 1997; in Parekh, 2000: 31). It is important, therefore, to recognise ethnicity as a source of very positive identity. This may be especially the case among groups which westerners might naively assume have most to 'gain' by casting off their more 'restrictive' traditions. Young women, whose positions in their host culture raise particularly obvious differences with the majority culture, can be especially significant in this. For example, many are active and vocal in criticising aspects of western gender arrangements as more progressive (Barot, Bradley and Fenton, 1999). However, illustrating the complexity of gender and ethnicity, the same Muslim women under scrutiny for maintaining traditions such as arranged marriages, whilst receptive to a degree of change, may also reject views of their cultures as inferior.

Acknowledgements

The researchers who worked alongside me on this project were Nadira Ahmed, Sayeda Camp, Amina Gani, Yasmin Gani, Sami Reza and Ghyda Senussi, participants in the WATS project, and James Lowrey and Ruth Jeanes, both Research Associates in the Institute of Youth Sport at Loughborough University. Rahmanara Chowdhury, the development worker for the WATS female activities programme, played a pivotal role in the study.

The research reported in this paper was first presented at the annual conference of the Leisure Studies Association at Leeds Metropolitan University in July 2004.

References

Ballard, R. (1982) South Asian Families in R.N. Rapoport, M.P. Fogarty and R. Rapoport, (eds), *Families in Britain*, London: Routledge and Kegan Paul, 86-97.

Barot, R., Bradley, H. and Fenton, S. (1999) *Ethnicity, Gender and Social Change*,

London: Macmillan Press Ltd.

Beishon, S., Modood, T. and Virdee, S. (1998) *Ethnic Minority Families*, London: Policy Studies Institute.

Berthoud, R. (2000) Family formation in multi-cultural Britian: three patterns of diversity, Working paper, Institute for Social and Economic Research, University of Essex.

Bhopal, K. (1999) South Asian women and arranged marriages in East London, in R. Barot, H. Bradley, and S. Fenton, *Ethnicity, Gender and Social Change*, London: Macmillan Press Ltd, 117-134.

Coalter, F., Allison, M., and Taylor, J. (2000) *The Role of Sport in Regenerating Deprived Urban Areas*, Edinburgh: Scottish Executive Central Research Unit.

Collins, F., Henry, I., Houlihan, B. and Buller, J. (1999) *Research Report: Sport and Social Exclusion*, A Report to the Department of Culture, Media and Sport, London: HMSO.

Dale, A., Shaheen, N., Kalra, V. and Fieldhouse, E. (2002) Routes into education and employment for young Pakistani and Bangladeshi women in the UV, *Ethnic and Racial Studies*, 25 (6), 942-968.

Elliott, F. and Robertson, (1996) *Gender Family and Society*, Basingstoke: Macmillan.

Hargreaves, J. (2000) *Heroines of Sport: The Politics of Difference and Identity*, London: Routledge.

Harvey, C. (ed.) (2001) *Maintaining Our Differences*, Aldershot: Ashgate.

Husain, F. and O'Brien, M. (2001), South Asian Muslims in Britain: Faith, Family and Community; in Harvey, C. (ed.), *Maintaining Our Differences*, Aldershot: Ashgate, 15-28.

Kay, T.A. and Lowrey, J., (2003) *Interesting Times Ahead: the potential of sport for encouraging access to higher education by young people from ethnic minorities*, unpublished report to the Higher Education Funding Council for England, Loughborough: Loughborough University.

Lowrey, J. and Kay, T.A (2005), Doing sport, doing inclusion: an analysis of provider and participant perceptions of targeted sport provision for young Muslims, in Flintoff, A., Long, J. and Hylton, K. (eds) Youth, Sport and Active Leisure: Theory, Policy and Participation, Eastbourne: Leisure Studies Association.

Kay, T.A. (2004) The voice of the family: influences on Muslim girls' participation in sport; in Flintoff, A., Long, J. and Hylton, K. (eds) Youth, Sport and Active Leisure: Theory, Policy and Participation, Eastbourne: Leisure Studies Association.

Kay, T.A (2005) Research by proxy: reaching across the divide, Leisure Studies Association Newsletter No. 70, Eastbourne: Leisure Studies Association.

Long, J., Welch, M., Bramham, P., Butterfield, J., Hylton, K., Lloyd, E. (2002) *Count Me In: The Dimensions of Social Inclusion Through Culture and Sport*, Leeds: Centre for Leisure and Sport Research.

Menski, W. (1999) South Asian women in Britain, family integrity and the primary purpose, in R. Barot, H. Bradley and S. Fenton, *Ethnicity, Gender and Social Change*, London: Macmillan Press Ltd, 81-98.

Modood, T., Berthoud, R., Lakey, J., Nazroo, J., Smith, P., Virdee, S., and Beishon,

S. (1997) *Ethnic Minorities in Britain*, London: Policy Studies Institute.

National Statistics (2004) *Social Focus on Ethnicity and Identity*, London: HMSO.

Parekh, B. (2000) *The Future of Multiethnic Britain: The Parekh Report*, London: Profile Books.

Pilkington, A. (2003) *Racial Disadvantage and Ethnic Diversity in Britain*, Basingstoke: Palgrave.

Singleton, C. and Green, E. (2004) 'Safe' Spaces: an analysis of the interrelationships of gender, ethnicity and culture in South Asian women's leisure lives, paper presented at the annual conference of the Leisure Studies Association, Leeds Metropolitan University, July.

Social Exclusion Unit (1999) Bridging the Gap: New Opportunities for 16 -18 Year Olds Not in Education, Employment or Training, CM 4405.

Verma, G.K. and Darby, D.S. (1994) *Winners and Losers: Ethnic Minorities in Sport and Recreation*, London: Falmer Press.

Walseth, K. and Fasting, K. (2003) Islam's View on Physical Activity and Sport: Egyptian Women Interpreting Islam *International Review for the Sociology of Sport,* 38 (1), 45-60.

Chapter 9

Cultural Muslims:
The Evolution of Muslim Identity in
Soviet and Post-Soviet Central Asia

William Rowe

Throughout most of its history, Central Asia[1] was the crossroads of the Eurasian landmass. The famed Silk Road crossed Central Asia from China to the Middle East and on to Europe. Culture, arts, technology and peoples came from north, south, east, and west, sometimes staying and leaving a solid imprint, sometimes merely passing through and leaving only the merest trace of their passage. Among the most important of these groups to move among the people of Persian origin in the region were: the Arabs, who brought Islam to the region; the Turkic peoples, who settled among the Persians who had lived in Central Asia from the earliest known periods; and the Russians who colonized the area and later imposed communism. To understand the role of Islam in relation to the various groups of people in Central Asia and how it has evolved over the past century, at least a cursory knowledge of the region's history is needed to explain the importance and place of each of these groups and the place of religion in their lives and to their identity today.

Background

The history of Islam in Central Asia goes back to the early eighth century and the invasions of the Muslim armies under Qutayba bin Muslim. He succeeded in conquering the main oases and cities culminating in a series of defeats of the Soghdian prince, Ghurak, for Samarqand in 711. Although prior to the invasion of the Islamic armies Central Asians were mainly adherents to Buddhism, Manichaeism, and, more widely, Zoroastrianism (elements of which remain as a cultural part of the lives of Central Asians), Islam was more readily accepted in Central Asia than in Zoroastrianism's motherland of Iran. This does not mean that these religions were either exterminated or immediately converted, as evidence of individual communities continued until well into the ninth century. However, because of various economic and social pressures, Islam was firmly established as the dominant religion by the tenth century in the agricultural areas along the Amu Darya, the Syr Darya, and the

---

1 Although the term 'Central Asia' can refer to many geographic configurations, here it is used to mean Kazakhstan, Kyrgyzstan, Tajikistan, Turkmenistan, and Uzbekistan.

Zerafshan River Valleys. Islam eventually extended beyond the cities and oases to the villages and, ultimately, to the deserts and steppes surrounding them, with the extension into the Steppes being more difficult due to the nomadic and sometimes transitory nature of the people that inhabited these areas who, in many cases, did not fully accept Islam until as late as the 18th century. Many scholars consider this later acceptance of Islam more superficial in its application than that of their urban and agricultural neighbours as it was over a longer period of time and often became mixed in with local shamanistic practices that are in evidence today in rural areas particularly (Abdullayev, 1998; Bartol'd, 1963; Chavannes, 1942; Gibb, 1970; Polonskaya and Malashenko, 1994; Sagdeev 2000).

At the end of the ninth century, the Samanid Dynasty began their rule of Central Asia from their capital in Bukhara. The Samanids were eastern Persians who had previously administered the region for the Arab, Abbasid Empire. Under the Samanids, and later under the Turkic dynasties (including the Turkmen) that swept through Central Asia and politically dominated it from the beginning of the eleventh century, Sunni Islam flowered before the Mongol interlude wrought its destruction on the region. Although the immediate outcome of this interlude was the devastation of many of the urban centers (including Samarqand and Bukhara in modern Uzbekistan, and Balkh, in Afghanistan) and agricultural areas, the area quickly rebounded under the *pax mongolica*, and the Silk Road, now freely traversing the length of the Mongol Empire, flourished. This economic and cultural boon continued under the following Timurid Dynasty, began by the Turco-Mongol leader Tamerlane, and which brought wealth, glory and renewed culture in the form of education, religion, architecture and literature to his capital of Samarqand.

The sixteenth century saw the introduction of three of the Turkic groups that are associated with Central Asia today: the Uzbeks, Kyrgyz, and Kazakhs. The Uzbeks finally conquered the region at the beginning of the sixteenth century and, although the riches previously amassed due to the Silk Road would decrease considerably over the next four centuries with the founding of the sea route to the east by Portuguese traders, Islam remained a potent force in the region and the famed *medrassas* and libraries of Bukhara and Samarqand continued to lure young scholars to the area. With the takeover by the Uzbeks of the main agricultural regions, three entities,[2] the Emirate of Bukhara, the Khanate of Qoqand, and the Khanate of Khiva – ruled by Uzbek dynasties, controlled the settled regions of Central Asia. Outside the river valleys, the Kazakhs ruled much of the steppes, the Kyrgyz the more northerly mountainous regions, and the Turkmen the desert areas of the southwest. The other major group in the region, the Karakalpaks, related linguistically and ethnically to the Kazakhs, became localized around the western coast of the Aral Sea. This continued until the nineteenth century when the creeping acquisition of Central Asia by the Russian Empire began. This period of colonial acquisition coincided with increased unease by the British government in relation to Russian goals and has been variously described as 'The Tournament of Shadows' (by the Russians) or 'The Great Game' (by England

---

2   Although here separated, the Kyrgyz and Kazakhs were generally known as Kazakh-Kyrgyz prior to the Soviet era. Any real differences between the two was geographic rather than ethnic.

and other European countries). Eventually, the two powers agreed on a border (mostly along the Panj/Amu Darya Rivers), that separated the Tajiks, Turkmen, and Uzbeks of Central Asia from their brethren in Afghanistan, which was seen to be at least nominally under the British sphere of influence. Although Russia had previously held close ties with Islamic people due to centuries of interaction with the Tatars, with the annexation of much of Central Asia, it became the only imperial, European government to incorporate entire Muslim lands within the borders of the country itself.

In the 19th century, it was common for Russia and other colonial powers to denigrate most Muslims as 'fanatics', and to view Islam as 'fanatical' which, as David Edwards points out in *Mad Mullahs and Englishmen*, denies the other moral authority and renders one's own cause as enlightened (Edwards, 1989). Adeeb Khalid takes this further in pointing out that this method underlines the feeling of superiority of civilization felt by Russians and implemented in their administration of Central Asia both during the Tsarist period and later during the Soviet Union. Although the general attitude of the Tsarist government was not to interfere directly with Muslim spiritual affairs (although administratively they did appropriate some of the best *waqf* land and tied up all requests for new mosques in the bureaucracy), they felt that the advantages of Russian civilization would soon become apparent to everyone in the region and they could therefore avoid direct religious conflict (Curzon, 1889; Khalid, 1998; Vambéry, 1906; see also Becker, 1988; d'Encausse, 1988; and Polonskaya and Malashenko, 1994). This was to change with the coming of the Soviet Union. Central Asian communists tried to find a way by which Islam could be 'secularized', and would allow the cultural heritage of Muslim civilization to remain integrated in the daily lives of Muslims (Polonskaya and Malashenko, 1994). The government at first accommodated this idea during the civil war and, later, the repression of local rebellions, but ultimately began to systematically 'de-Islamicize' the region in everything from language to activities in daily life.

According to several early speeches by Joseph Stalin, the criteria for nation status include language, culture, territory and economics, so any attempt to officially equate nationalism and Islam (i.e. religion) would lead to harsh retribution from the government (Stalin, 1940). This was later expanded upon and codified by Article 124 of the 1936 Constitution, which stated: 'In order to ensure to citizens freedom of conscience, the church in the USSR is separated from the state, and the school from the church. Freedom of religious worship and *freedom of anti-religious propaganda* is recognized for all citizens' (italics added). It is this last, italicized statement however that set the official rhetoric for the Soviet government. The problem was that the people of Central Asia had never specifically identified themselves according to either language or culture although geography and economics had played a part. In the agricultural regions especially, Tajiks and Uzbeks had lived side-by-side for centuries, spoke each others' languages and at times could be hard pressed to tell who was 'Tajik' and who 'Uzbek' because of intermarriage (Atkin, 1997; Critchlow, 1989; Lane, 1978; Ro'i 1984).

Stalin, however, had a high regard for the power of language and linguistics. In a letter to linguists in 1950, he stated:

Marxism holds that the transition of a language from an old quality to a new does not take place by way of an explosion, by the destruction of an existing language and the creation of a new one, but by the gradual accumulation of the elements of the new quality, and hence, by the gradual dying away of the elements of the old quality.

(Stalin, 1950)

With this in mind, the government commissioned linguists to begin the extraction of 'Arabic' influences from Central Asian languages and to begin their 'democratization' (Rakowska-Harmstone, 1970). This was accompanied by the promotion of Russian for all governmental and scientific activities and using only Russian words to denote any political ideas (i.e. *revolutsia* for revolution, *demokratia* for democracy, etc.) or new technology. Anyone familiar with Central Asian linguistics would know that it would be a nearly impossible task to take out every Arabic word from the local languages; however, specifically *Islamic* terminology was mostly deleted from everyday usage. The use of 'Arabic' however was not accidental as it appealed to linguistic chauvinism that Tajik, Uzbek or words of any of the other national languages (and where lacking, Russian words) should be used whenever possible.[3]

According to early Soviet thought, local languages had to be used because Central Asians could not be educated in communism unless literacy rates were drastically raised. Accompanying this, the government, in 1929, began changing the alphabets of the various languages from an Arabic-based alphabet to the Latin alphabet (which was originally viewed as a script to which Russian might switch). In 1940 however, Cyrillic became the script for all Soviet languages. The government stated that the initial reason for using Cyrillic was because it corresponded better to Turkic and Persian sounds; however, Cyrillic proved no better at this than the Latin alphabet. This reasoning was soon amended to state that the transliteration would better aid people in studying Russian, the intended, future *lingua franca* of the Soviet Union, and to facilitate the inculcation of Russian culture to the people of Central Asia. Through this 'Russification' process, the Soviets reasserted the colonial maxim of Russian cultural superiority in an effort to raise local people out of their perceived backwardness. These moves had a concomitant benefit of severing (to a degree) linguistic and religious correspondence between Central Asia and Middle Eastern countries including Iran, Afghanistan, and Turkey and in precluding young people from reading texts written prior to linguistic reform. The Muslim clergy noted this immediately and, although with no effect, complained to the Soviet authorities through the leader of the All-Union Committee for the New Turkic Alphabet, Agamaly Oglu, that abandoning the Arabic script would be tantamount to sinning (Anon. 1964, Kreindler, 1995; Niedermeier, 1952; Winner, 1952; Wurm, 1954).

Although outwardly deprived of its institutional underpinnings due to Soviet elimination of *shari'a* courts and religious schools and the complete nationalization of *waqf* lands, Islam and Islamic practices did not wither in the daily lives of the

---

3   A note must be made here that the Soviet government's preoccupation with language reform centred on the creation of local *literary* languages that schools would teach throughout each republic. Use of Islamic terminology continued in dialects for considerably longer (see also Baskakov 1952).

citizenry. Instead, it became more personalized or, as many people in Central Asia have stated, it became an expression of family life and personal guidance as authorized by the constitution. It was when one needed further spiritual guidance that people had to be careful. The official Islamic clergy continued to exist in Central Asia after 1928, but firmly under the observation of Soviet authorities. This interference spawned the rise of 'unregistered clergy'. These men, though undergoing no formal training as clergy, were frequently members of Sufi communities which, due to the highly decentralized nature of the local Naqshbandia Order, allowed them to function individually and not risk being persecuted as a group. They would dispense advice based on Islamic traditions, organize readings of the Qur'an, and officiate at life ceremonies. Meetings would often take place in teahouses, with the understanding or complicity of the proprietor, or in the guestrooms of their own homes. Teahouses were the preferred meeting places of Central Asian men although, because people sometimes perceived the teahouse as dangerous, they could use the area reserved for guests – an important part of every Central Asian Muslim home. These rooms are usually spacious and comfortably equipped so that men could meet unobtrusively to pray and hold discussions. One author has compared this period (and the subsequent post-Soviet period in Uzbekistan) to a standard practice amongst the *Shi'a* minorities, that of concealment of religious practices and adherence, or *taqiya*. This further led some authors to coin some interesting identity terminology for local populations such as 'atheist Muslims' and people who only practiced 'Everyday Islam' (Alimov, 1998; Bennigsen and Lemercier-Quelquejay, 1979; Bennigsen and Lemercier-Quelquejay, 1981; Bennigsen and Wimbush, 1985; Bräker, 1989; Byelyayev, 1935; Critchlow, 1989; Keller, 2001; Olyeshchuk, 1939; Poliakov, 1992; Soper, 1979; Trofimov 1995).

The Soviet authorities were aware of these practices and unregistered clergy and particularly Sufis came under attack in the Soviet press. Local governments tried to usurp the local tea culture by setting up 'red teahouses' where patrons could discuss atheism and councils were formed to divert attention towards more ideologically safe topics. An example in Tajikistan was the creation of the Commission for Establishing New Rites and Customs formed by the Tajik Academy of Sciences to replace the more obvious Islamic rituals with atheistic ones. The Soviet government also tried sanctioned spiritual councils set up during World War II, but these did not turn into the apparati for control of the Muslim population the Soviet government had intended and official publications like *Muslims of the Soviet East*[4] occasionally succeeded in showing the dynamic spirit of Islam (Bräker, 1969; Keller, 2001; Rakowska-Harmstone, 1983; Ro'i 1990; Rorlich, 1991; Sukharyeva, 1960; Varabov, 1966).

---

4   Published in Persian, Uzbek, Arabic, English, and French (it should be noted that it was *not* printed in Russian, the now official *lingua franca* of the Soviet Union), articles in this publication ranged from travel pieces to Muslim commonalties, regardless of nationality, as well as articles on establishing the Soviet line on such issues as Afghanistan after the 1979 Soviet invasion. For different examples, see Abdullah 1975, Anon. 1983b, and Rahimdjan 1982. The small pamphlet *Soviet Power and Islam* by Burkhanov and Gusarov, also addresses issues from Palestine to cooperation between the Soviet government and Muslim clergy, at least those 'particularly close to Muslim workers', in a very pro-Soviet way. For an opposite point of view, see Baymirza Hayit's *Islam and Turkestan under Russian Rule*.

Other factors the government hoped would aid their cause and better integrate the region into the Soviet Union such as its extensive expenditures in Central Asia, particularly in infrastructure and education, had quite the opposite effect. This outlay, however, effectively served to heighten the differences felt by people in the region towards their consciousness of their cultural heritage based on Islam and their lack of association with a European cultural heritage, especially that of Russia and the Russian culture propagated through education (Bräker, 1983; Bräker, 1989). The final hope of the Soviet government was that Islam could be eradicated with the demise of the older generations. However, towards the close of the Soviet Union, the Soviet observers of Islam began sounding the alarm. T. S. Saidbayev wrote that the age profile of observant Muslims was considerably lower than the age profile in Christian areas. His research demonstrated clearly that Islam was *not* dying out, but continuing to maintain its presence and power (Saidbayev, 1984). By the time of independence, Islam had proved too vigorous in the face of outright suppression and, through its ability to adapt, had continued as a mainstay in the lives of individual Muslims.

Cultural Islam

Given the resilience of religious observance in Central Asia, the fact remains that over seventy years of a communist political environment and state sponsored cultural interference did have a significant effect on Central Asian Muslims and their identity *vis-à-vis* Islam. For some people, official intolerance has the effect of stiffening one's resolve to maintain their religiosity and spirituality at whatever cost. Others will fall in with the official line, but most will find a middle ground. The costs of outright resistance could be enormous. This was especially true early in the Soviet period during the first five-year plan and the late 1930s when waves of arrests and show trials swept Central Asia in an effort to subvert the moral authority of the clergy and serve as examples to ordinary citizens of the price of counter-revolutionary activities. During these periods and particular subsequent periods, it was equally as dangerous to be over zealous on the other side of the spectrum as the violent party purges under Stalin exemplified. However, for most Muslims of Central Asia, the way to work within the system, and not become a victim of it, was to pay lip service to communist ideals and develop a sense of religion whereby the daily exercises of religion would become more familial or personal. In Islam, the declaration of faith, praying, observing holidays inclusive of Ramadan and even almsgiving can be done privately; it is not incumbent upon the individual to perform such practices publicly. Soviet authorities vigorously attacked all of these practices, but all of them continued to have varying levels of observance in society. The pilgrimage to Mecca was a virtual impossibility for the Muslims of Central Asia as the government only allowed thirty-six people per year to exit for such a purpose (Karklins, 1980); however, this pillar of Islam is not mandatory and is binding only to those who have the means to go.

Of course, the five pillars of faith do not represent all rituals important to Muslims; and ways were developed in which they could subsume other rituals under the more politically safe rubrics of nationalism or culture which, from the earliest times until the

1980s, were not generally topics attacked by the government. From this practice the concepts of 'cultural Muslim', 'ethnic Muslim' and, less frequently, 'national Muslim' evolved. These terms are sometimes used interchangeably in both the literature and in conversations in Central Asia although 'cultural Muslim' is the term I heard most often applied to (and by) both the Muslims of Central Asia and the way they approached religion. These ideas did not emerge uniquely in Central Asia as Muslim populations in other communist countries, notably the former Yugoslavia, also used similar terms (more often 'ethnic Muslim') to refer to the personalization of their religion, adherence to specific rites and the separateness they felt from the Catholic Croats and Orthodox Serbs (Höpken, 1989; Ramet, 1989a; Ramet, 1989b). The Yugoslavian census of 1961 even had a category 'Muslim in an ethnic sense' as a means of identity for those who wished to distinguish themselves from Croats and Serbs (Brunner, 1989).

This development allowed Muslims to then address the important life ceremonies that set the course of a Muslim's life and afterlife. Among these rituals were the circumcision of boys, marriage rites and burial rites. The Soviet government at various times attempted to co-opt these practices into more acceptable terminology that reflected the 'local' culture, the 'heritage' and the 'history' of each ethnic group. Although every one of these 'cultural' practices in each Central Asian country had at their roots the same Islamic doctrines (although sometimes mingled with pre-Islamic vestiges including Shamanism and remote practices from Zoroastrianism) this was not generally discussed. Any public discussion revolved around how these practices reflected 'Uzbek' culture, 'Turkmen' culture, or any of the other republics' culture. Communist officials allowed them as national anomalies and their relationship to Islam was either willfully ignored or overlooked through cultural ignorance or ideological shortsightedness. The people of Central Asia did not, however, differentiate between issues of religion and nationalism, so when told they could not have religious observances, but they could have national observances, in the end it was one and the same to them.[5] However, this allowed officials to downplay the context of Islam as well as any greater Turkic or Persian solidarity, two other potential movements the Soviet government was keen to avoid.

Of the three ceremonies listed above, the only one that the Soviet government tried actively to stop was circumcision. Alternately calling it cruel, barbarous, and backward (terms also used for veiling) as well as forcing the Muslim Spiritual Administration of Central Asia and Kazakhstan to issue a *fatwa* against it, the Soviet government tried, through all official means, to stop the practice. However, Muslims in Central Asia did not stop the practice and, as a dodge from the religious argument, would offer a medical argument much as American doctors have erroneously done over the past century. Social opinion was adamantly for the practice and each ethnic group did not consider a male to be a member of that ethnic group unless he was circumcised, no matter what the government said. Circumcisions were then carried out secretly by doctors, unregistered clergy, or family members (see also Anon. 1983a; Ashirov, 1975; Ashirov, 1978; Rakowska-Harmstone, 1983; Saidbayev, 1984).

---

5   The similarities between religion and nationalism was also noted by T. S. Saidbayev in his work *Islam: Istorii i Sovryemyennost'* especially in relation to ceremonies.

Circumcision ceremonies are always enormous and very expensive affairs. The parents are not only aware of their duty to their sons to have them circumcised, but also are aware that the neighbours are watching to compare how the ceremony ranks with others in the neighbourhood. Parents who have their son circumcised without a ceremony (either through lack of funds or desire) will garner social rebuke by family and neighbours alike, who will see the child as having been denied an important life event. A typical ceremony (or *tui*) is an all-day affair and the extended family, friends, colleagues and neighbors are invited. Guests will arrive early for lunch and will either stay the entire day or come and go several times if they live nearby. Two or three meals are served during the course of the afternoon and evening and dancing (led by women in traditional dress) will take place. Women generally congregate on one side of the home's enclosure, in a home built along traditional lines, while men will stand or sit on the other. To cut costs, an entire generation of a family will often be circumcised at the same time so it is not uncommon to see three or four boys ranging in age from six month old babies to ten year old boys (usually brothers, but sometimes also cousins) sharing a celebration. Ideally, the ceremony will take place when the boy is around eight as it is theoretically a choice, but no male I interviewed ever said that there was any real choice in the matter. The ones with whom I talked who had been older at the time of the event said that they had attended celebrations previously and looked forward to their own. At the ceremony, the boys will wear a special costume for the occasion, sometimes a Western-style suit and sometimes a more ceremonial outfit with an intricately detailed hat, coat, and trousers. The boys sit in the centre of the house, courtyard or enclosure in the evening and, during the dancing, the guests will place money in the laps of the boys. The actual surgery takes place the next morning unlike in areas of the Middle East. Ceremonies involving very prominent members of communist society frequently occurred under the guise of 'birthday parties' and could last as long as three days with guests staying the night either at the home or in the neighbourhood (see also Karklins, 1980). All Central Asian men view this ceremony (unless they had it done as an infant) as an important milestone in their lives and one that, in essence, makes them one with the nation and ethnic group.

Like circumcisions, marriages are big community celebrations on which the family will spend even more money. Today, a typical 'small', i.e. poor, marriage can cost upwards of the equivalent of US$6,000-10,000. The limit on a large wedding is only restricted by the imagination of the family, but weddings of US$30,000 are not unheard of since independence. This should be viewed within the context of a society where the gross national income in purchasing power parity (GNIPPP) ranges between US$930 (Tajikistan) to US$5,630 (Kazakhstan) (Haub, 2004). Clearly, families must find creative ways to pay for this. In some cases, a nuclear family will canvass the entire extended family for money for the ceremony. Another way is to appeal to the *mahalla*, or traditional Central Asian society of neighbours, in which the family resides. In many cases, within the *mahalla* there is a central store of money that is maintained for events such as weddings and circumcisions. A family can avail itself of the money with the implied knowledge that it will be replaced as the family can afford to do so. Given the sometimes impromptu nature of these ceremonies, it is a relief to many families to have this fund available. *Mahallas* are much institutionalized in Uzbekistan and Kyrgyzstan; however, although Tajiks in Tajikistan claim that this system does not exist *de jure* there, it does exist *de facto* in a much more informal way. Neighbours help out neighbours during these ceremonies, but they do not officially devote themselves to all the community issues undertaken by a *mahalla* in Uzbekistan.

Marriage as an act is an obligation for both Islam and the nation, but the ceremony itself would, in most circumstances, be made under Islamic (*shari'a*) guidelines. Generally, the bride and groom marry early relative to Western couples, the bride frequently while a teenager and the groom before his 25th year.[6] Ceremonies range from one to three days, depending on the prominence and wealth of the family. Pre-Islamic rituals are often part of the ceremony, particularly in rural areas. Examples, such as those in Tajikistan where the groom and his friends jump over a bonfire, an act of purification that comes from Zoroastrianism, and rituals involving Shamanistic overtones in Kyrgyzstan abound. The ceremony itself is entirely paid for by the groom and his family, inclusive of the materials for the bride's trousseau and the making of *korpachas* for the new home (made by the bride and her family). The ritual of bride price,[7] *kalym*, was prohibited early on by the Soviet government; however, quietly and sometimes in unique ways it was still widely carried out as a sign of a family's prestige (see also Krader, 1966; Rakowska-Harmstone, 1983).

In attending a ceremony, it was possible to see 'expressions of nationality and culture' in people's outward appearance. Many urbanites, both male and female, adopted clothing similar to that worn in Russia or Eastern Europe. But unlike China with their 'Mao jackets', government control did not extend down to this level despite a command economy. Most rural young men in Central Asia dressed similarly to their compatriots in Russia and the rest of the Soviet Union and Eastern Europe. Older men, however, tended to wear more traditional clothing and to grow beards. Women (particularly in rural areas) dressed far more traditionally than their male contemporaries and often wore pantaloons and long smocks with recognizable and often vivid patterns distinct to their region along with some form of hair covering. The hair covering is usually a scarf and did not include the Middle Eastern *hijab* or head scarf that entirely covers the hair and neck, or the *burka* or veil that covers the face, which is more often seen in Afghanistan.

It is still usual for a family to arrange a marriage, although amongst the urban elite marriages of love are not uncommon. The mother of the groom will begin to seek out an appropriate bride sometime prior to his 25th birthday, or much earlier in the countryside. When an appropriate woman has been found, the groom and potential bride will get the chance to meet each other and decide whether the other is acceptable. The date and any monetary transactions are then agreed upon and the groom's family

---

6   This number is very important in Central Asia as I observed on several occasions in Tajikistan. Four examples come to mind of young men who had stated their age as "24'when we met, were suddenly 26, 27, 27 and 32 on their next birthdays *after* they were married.

7   The term 'bride price' that has entered Western languages is not wholly indicative of the transaction involved in Central Asia. A woman is not treated like livestock and is not bought and sold; however, when a woman marries her dowry goes to the groom, the groom's family pays for the wedding and the bride's family will be compensated for this 'loss' of a daughter from the family home (see also Krader 1966).

will begin the process of securing the money necessary and planning the day of the wedding. It is very unusual for a Muslim man to marry a non-Muslim woman even in an urban environment and the societal prohibition about a Muslim woman marrying a non-Muslim man is very evident throughout Central Asia (see also Halbach, 1991). Long engagements are rare and frequently the date of the wedding is set long before a bride is picked. Several contacts of mine in Tajikistan who were getting married made me promise to be available on a certain date during the subsequent month so that I could be a guest at their weddings. In each case when I asked who the bride would be, the man would shrug and say that had yet to be finalized.

As this ceremony is guided by strict tradition, on a typical wedding day the guests will assemble at a very early time. The groom invites the guests of honour to his house for an early meal and time with his family, while the bride and her family will get together at her house to prepare her for the ceremony. The first meal is eaten and the preparations for the ceremony are begun. Around 12:00, everybody at the groom's house gets into vehicles that have been specially hired and decorated for the day and are taken to the bride's house where the party will separate into three groups: women, older men and younger men: the younger men will sit with the groom and the bride's younger male relatives. After the meal, the groom collects the bride from the women's area and takes her to the first car while both parties crowd into the cars to go back to the groom's house. In more secular households, the wedding party will stop at a prominent statue where the bride will leave a bouquet of flowers, a tradition adopted from the Russians. At the groom's house, the head table is reserved for the bride and groom, the bride's maid, and the best man. Rarely do the bride and groom leave the table during the course of the evening. The guests dance, eat and socialize until very late at night and sometimes until the next day. For weddings among urban families with more wealth and prestige, the ceremony itself will often happen at a hotel or banquet hall with a larger ceremony at the groom's home for the men the day before.

Perhaps the most surprising aspect of marriage within the former Soviet Union where bigamy was prohibited were the cases where men took more than one wife. This is just one instance where the Soviet government tried and failed to instill a more western, nuclear model of a family in place of the traditional, extended family in Central Asia. The first wife would be the 'official' wife registered in a civil ceremony with a very public wedding, while the second wife would receive a 'private' (*shari'a*) ceremony from an unregistered clergy. Many times, the families involved felt that there were extenuating circumstances whereby the groom could do this without offense to the first wife. A second marriage generally (but not always) occurred after it had become apparent that the first wife had proved unable to bear children. Such is the importance of family and bearing children (there were more 'Heroines of the Soviet Union', i.e. woman with ten or more children, in Central Asia than anywhere else in the country) that this practice was quietly overlooked by local officials. Divorce was a possibility although the bride's family could often not afford to send back the money they had received nor did they want the societal disgrace of having a daughter sent back home to them (see especially Krader, 1966; Massell, 1974; Rakowska-Harmstone, 1983; Tokhtakhodjayeva, 1995). In the 1980s and into the years since independence, it has become more of a mark of affluence and power to take more than one wife (especially in the countryside) even if the first wife has given birth to several children.

Depending on the family, brides and bridegrooms can wear a range of different wedding clothes. Couples will wear clothes as diverse as Western-inspired, white wedding dresses and Western-style business suits, to traditional, hand-made, hand-stitched clothing that completely covers the body and face of the bride, accompanied by an absence of ties and other western accoutrements on the suit of the bridegroom.[8] However, when you observe the clothing worn during the days following the ceremony itself when the couple have moved into their new quarters and are spending their first days together, few, if any, differences are apparent. Both the 'modern' and 'traditional' brides and grooms wear the same traditional clothing sewn for them for the day after the ceremony (i.e. the first full day as a married couple). For the women this will be a long smock over a pair of pantaloons and a loose scarf over her hair; for the men, a traditional long, quilted coat worn over pantaloons and a loose shirt. On this day the newlyweds will move into their new quarters. Extensions to a family compound, or a new compound will be built for older sons in the countryside. Urban families will secure apartments, preferably in the neighbourhood, but as some cities continued to have severe housing shortages, they often had to live wherever one could be procured. The people of Central Asia do not practice primogeniture and the youngest son inherits the family house and he and his wife are expected to care for the parents in their old age.

Burial rites were by far the most observed ceremony and according to some reports no one, not even highly placed communist leaders, would be buried without them. As one contact in Uzbekistan mentioned, "it is always best to be safe when dealing with death and the afterlife, so no one wants to be laid to rest without the requisite religious rites". Women as a group were more likely to go to mosques or surrogate religious sites, but as men retired or simply grew older and became a *musafed* or *aksakal* (literally 'white hair' or 'white beard' in Tajiki and Uzbeki respectively), they also would frequently became more outwardly spiritual. This is not uncommon among groups, whatever their religion but, as men in focus groups in Kyrgyzstan told me, once they had retired and become old, they worried less about official displeasure and worried more about their soul. The burial ceremony would consist of readings from the Qur'an and even when there is a civil burial, a religious one for the family would follow. Muslims were buried in specially-made shrouds separate from Russians and other non-Muslims in cemeteries that would frequently be further segregated by ethnicity (see also Ashirov, 1975; Karklins, 1980; Rorlich, 1991; Saidbayev, 1984).

With regard to Islamic buildings and architecture, the Soviet government either allowed mosques, and to a lesser extent *mazors* (tombs of famous Sufis or local religious men of great learning), to deteriorate or else, as was the case with the Registan in Samarqand and other historically important buildings, fossilized them into museums or 'buildings of cultural heritage'. Surreptitiously however many people

---

8   This is not to imply that covering the face is an Islamic practice, when in fact it is a regional habit. Historically, it was often a part of rural areas of the Persian-speaking world (particularly Afghanistan) and people have tried to use Islam to justify this culturally-based practice. The point herein merely illustrates the diversity encountered.

continued to visit them either at night, especially *mazors*, which are quite common throughout rural areas, or under the guise of taking their children and grandchildren to see a building reflective of local history and culture. This was made still easier when the *mazor* was located in or by a cemetery, which is the case with a great many of them. For this reason cemeteries became one of the most important (if not the most important) site for religious pilgrimages. Although they are not segregated like a mosque, the vast majority of pilgrims were (and continue to be) women and many *mazors* could be categorized as a safe religious space for women since many of those who maintained and sometimes oversaw the complexes were also female. According to these same sources the people who performed small pilgrimages to these or more distant holy sites (inclusive of sacred springs and wells in addition to *mazors*) saw them as a way of performing an act of penitence or purification before God. It was therefore very unusual for someone to make a pilgrimage without a specific need or request. The reasons for going included not only spiritual fulfillment, but also often a desire to seek help in curing an illness, in getting pregnant, or settling family problems. Because of the volume of writings done on this subject during communist times, Soviet officials obviously recognized that these pilgrimages posed an ideological threat to them. They tried repeatedly through official Islamic channels to stop them as counter-revolutionary *and* a threat to Islam by categorizing such practices as saint worship (see also Atkin, 1989; Bennigsen and Wimbush, 1985; Broxup, 1989; Poliakov, 1992; Rashid, 2002; Rorlich, 1991; Saroyan, 1997).

In viewing these practices, from superficial considerations such as clothing through to important spiritual considerations, it becomes clear that Central Asia displayed a spectrum of ideas, observances, and manifestations of its Islamic history throughout the Soviet period and into the independence of the various countries. Among the various social groups within Central Asian society, the two that adhered the most to communist party guidelines both culturally and linguistically were government, party and industry leaders and academics. The effects of Russianization and communist ideals had the greatest impact on their lack of an outward adherence to Islam because they were the representatives of Soviet and communist thought enforced from Moscow. Most members of these groups lived in large urban centres like Bishkek, Almaty, Tashkent and Dushanbe where Russian was the main language of communication. However, in the countryside traditional attitudes are stronger and it remains rare to hear Russian spoken except among collective or state farm presidents and local government authorities. But even the people in these two groups would have their sons circumcised and hold wedding and burial services in line with Islamic law (Ro'i, 1990; Ro'i, 1995; Vagabov and Vagabov, 1988). These groups were the elite of the Soviet republics and they continued their political dominance into the post-Soviet period. Therefore, it is these people who have attempted to set an official course for each new country and an identity for its citizens.

Post-Soviet Identity Issues

Although there were significant religious movements in Central Asia prior to the fall of the Soviet Union and a noticeable shift within the local communist parties to cooperate with the clergy, it is really after 1991, when the uncertainty of independence was thrust upon the Muslim populations, that ideas of religion became more prominent in national politics and in local affairs, especially in Tajikistan and Uzbekistan (Dudoignon, 1997; Polonskaya and Malashenko, 1994). As far as national politics went, much of this attention was negative as regional communist leaders who had towed the official party line while quietly participating in Islamic practices became national presidents and were reluctant to share power, particularly with groups who confessed political Islam. With the events that have unfolded over the past sixteen years, it is clear that Central Asians, although aware of the varying nature of political support (or lack thereof) for observant believers, continue to maintain their Soviet era views of cultural Islam. This has varying degrees of profession amongst the different groups. Among the Kazakhs and Kyrgyz, Islam does not have the long history in the lives and lore of the people for Islamists to cause the governments as much concern. Kazakhstan also had a unique demographic situation in that the population at independence was almost evenly split between Kazakhs and Russians. With a nervous Russia on their western and northern borders, the government of Nursultan Nazarbayev has had to be careful about defining nationalism and identity in the country and took steps early in the independence years to reassure Russians that they respected their Russian identity while promoting Kazakh identity. However, in the three southern tier countries, appeals to ethnicity played a greater role in Turkmen politics while adherence to clan-based or locale-based relationships have formed much of the political issues (especially in the civil war) of Tajikistan and, to a lesser extent, Uzbekistan (Atkin, 1997; Chatterjee, 2002; Kolsto, 1998; Olcott, 1997; Rakowska-Harmstone, 1983; Trofimov, 1995; Wheeler, 1960).

Although all five Central Asian countries continued with governments avowedly secular in nature, nationalism still plays a key component in the promotion of Islam with very different effects, particularly in Tajikistan, Turkmenistan, and Uzbekistan. The governments of Turkmenistan and Uzbekistan were quick to understand the importance of Islam to nationalism and culture within the newly independent states. They therefore moved to co-opt Muslim identity into a cultural identity reflective of their determination of what was going to become 'Turkmen-ness' and 'Uzbek-ness'. The remnant communist leadership used Islam (by claiming to be a champion of the faith), history and pre-Soviet national figures to claim legitimacy to lead the new republics. The government of Tajikistan, however, posed itself against Islam allowing an Islamic opposition group to position itself as the overseer of legitimate Tajik national identity. This was a major factor in the devolving of the country into civil war following independence. As Tajikistan was the most artificial of Soviet republic constructs, due to there being no 'Tajik' or Persian governmental entity since the 10th century in Central Asia and problems relating to the definition of the word Tajik itself, it proved nearly impossible for the government to find common ground on which to base itself and the new country. This was further hampered by the fact that the ruling elite had traditionally come from Khojand, in the north of Tajikistan (that area of the country in the Ferghana Valley), which represented only a small part of the country, had had the most prominent positions in the communist government and was the only section which did not encounter first hand the violence of the civil war (Akbarzadeh, 1994; Ashirov, 1975; Rashid, 2002; Thöni, 1994).

The war would be fought mostly in the southern half of Tajikistan, primarily in the Vakhsh Valley, Dushanbe, and the Qaroteghin Valley to the east of Dushanbe. The coalition of Kulobis (from the Vakhsh Valley) and the Khojandis, backed by Russia and Uzbekistan, finally forced a peace treaty in 1997, which did allow an Islamic party to form in the Republic and included Islamic rhetoric in official statements and in national identity. This identity began to form around pre-Russian, pre-Turkic Central Asia and focused primarily on the Samanid Empire of the 10th Century and implies backwards a 'Tajik' identity to that Persian empire and beyond to the ancient, pre-Islamic Soghdians and Bactrians (this last to distinguish themselves further from Iran). Under this form of current government propaganda, Tajik would come to mean anyone who is a Central Asian, eastern Persian-speaking Muslim, which geographic, linguistic, and religious definitions would constitute the major components of their culture.[9] It must be remembered, however, that the capital of Tajikistan, Dushanbe, is almost entirely a Soviet construct. In 1920, there were approximately 235 families in the village. The current city was built along Soviet lines, which does not include any sites or architecture to aid the government in defining their heritage nor does it include any high profile religious structures. The most important city to this new Tajik identity is Bukhara, now in Uzbekistan, where the tomb of Ismail Samani is located. The Uzbeks, perhaps understandably, have shown that they are extremely uncomfortable with Tajiks basing a good portion of their identity on a city not within their own national borders. The only significant structures in Dushanbe today that could impute current local identity are a mosque built by the Iranians after independence and a large statue complex of Ismail Samani in front of the Parliament. The mosque has had some degree of controversy attached to it because of its Iranian funding and attendants there are at pains to stress the fact that Iran only contributed the money for the mosque and that those who attend are Tajik and Sunni, with both adjectives applied.

The Tajik government and Tajik linguists have also attempted through the Soviet and post-Soviet periods to influence Tajik identity by promoting the idea that Tajiki was older and distinct from Farsi (spoken in Iran) and Dari (spoken in Afghanistan), and that it pre-dated the Arab invasions (Rakowska-Harmstone, 1970). The famous Russian historian, V. V. Bartol'd, disputes this, claiming that pre-Arab inhabitants spoke a form of Soghdian, now only found in the Yaghnob Valley, and that Persian settlers brought the current language in the later centuries under the Samanids. However, he credits the people of Central Asia at that time for reviving the Persian language in the face of Arab expansion and their emphasis, through Islam, of Arabic. Thus in this scenario, literary Persian passed from the Iranian Plateau to Central Asia and then back to Iran with the founding of the Samanid Empire (Atkin, 1994; Bartol'd, 1956).

By no means were issues of nationalism, linguistics or ethnicity, along with attendant difficulties, unique to Tajiks. Soviet ideology had defined each of the Turkic groups similarly and sought to defeat Islam through non-religious nationalism.

---

9   Implied in this statement is an expression of Sunni Islam because of the emphasis on 'eastern' Persians. It is not often expressly said though as the majority of the lightly-populated Badakhshan Autonomous Mountain Oblast, located in the Pamir Mountains in eastern Tajikistan, is Ismaili.

However, this ultimately failed because Muslims, instead of relinquishing Islam, suffused this new nationalism with its practices, albeit with the new nomenclature. This has however produced levels of differences in tolerance between the countries both of Islam and of their Soviet past. Currently, Tajikistan is the only country with a recognized Islamic opposition party that participates in elections. On the other hand, Tajikistan, along with Kyrgyzstan are the two countries that have not tried to 'erase' their Soviet history, like neighboring Uzbekistan and Turkmenistan. With the exception of major streets and squares in Dushanbe, statues of Lenin and other prominent communists are still in place. In Bishkek, there has been even less change. Kazakhstan has also shown restraint since Russians represent about 38% of the population and they have made a further linguistic accommodation by calling Kazakh the 'state language' and Russian the 'language of interethnic communication' (Banuazizi and Weiner, 1994; Kolsto, 1998). This contrasts heavily with Uzbekistan's position, which is to distance itself from Russia and their Soviet past as much as possible, and from Turkmenistan where Turkmen ethnicity has been made indistinguishable from the current leader, Saparmurad Niyazov, and statues of him have replaced Soviet iconography.[10]

In interviews with Kazakhs, Kyrgyz, and Tajiks, these actions of integrating their Soviet history with their pre-Soviet history are actively supported because many people view their recent history of communism, secularism and, in many cases, atheism as a very real part of their current heritage. Many of these people attempt to fuse a 'return to Islam' and a revitalization of the religion with their general secularity. This view tends to marginalize Islamists as threats to society (Olcott, 1995), that such places as Iran, the still unstable Afghanistan and, in the view of the Turkic republics, Tajikistan could potentially 'export'. Uzbekistan particularly has been waging what some writers have called a 'religious war' against its own people and using Islamists as terrorist bogeymen to justify a repressive, single-party dictatorship (Anon., 1998; Anon., 2001a; Makarenko, 2000; Peterson, 2000). Much of the activity against the government of Uzbekistan is centered geographically in the area known as the Ferghana Valley. This bowl-shaped depression is split between Uzbekistan, Tajikistan and Kyrgyzstan and is potentially the area that could cause much unrest in the region. As this is the prime agricultural area of Central Asia, the population in the depression is densely settled reaching 2,315 people per square kilometer in some districts. It is home to one quarter of Uzbekistan's population (26.9%), nearly one-third of Tajikistan's population (31.4%), and over half of Kyrgyzstan's population (50.3%). Uzbeks are the dominant group in the depression with 61.7% of the population. They also represent 84% of the population in Uzbekistan's portion of the depression and the largest minority in Kyrgyzstan and Tajikistan (Lubin 1999).

To many in Uzbekistan, the Ferghana Valley is considered the most conservative part of the country, particularly around the city of Qokand. Ethnic tensions run high

---

10 Niyazov has also taken on the moniker "Turkmenbashi'or Father of the Turkmen as an honorary title and has set up a cult of personality that connects patriotism with a love for him. See Akbarzadeh 1994, "Why the Sun Shines On Niyazov", and "A Trip Around the 'Stans", Foreign Reports, *Jane's Information Group*, January 20, 2000 and February 8, 2001.

here and the imposition of strict border crossings and the Uzbek policy of mining the borders in the valley have caused a great deal of tension between the three countries. Heightening these tensions was the 2000 attack by the Islamic Movement of Uzbekistan (IMU) against the Kyrgyz military inside the mountainous southern border of the depression in an attempt to destabilize the Kyrgyz government. That this group had avowed Islamist aims for the entirety of Central Asia and ties with *al-Qaeda* only made the situation more inflammatory to the government of Kyrgyzstan situated in Bishkek, located in the much more heterogeneous and secular northern area of the country. Against this backdrop the three governments view the attempt by the people of the Ferghana Valley to tie Muslim identity more to a renaissance of Islam and a higher amount of daily observance with suspicion, a fact brought home all too publicly with the brutal government crackdown against the citizens of Andijan in 2005 whom the government called 'Islamic extremists' but eyewitnesses called unarmed citizens expressing religious beliefs (Anon: 2005). Much of the local observance is also ethnically based as the Uzbeks represent the greatest percentage of mosque attendees in each district and country, although the numbers for the other ethnic groups are rising and new mosques self-segregate themselves by ethnicity (see also Rashid 2002; Tabyshaliyeva, 2000).

One of the central issues to occupy those either promoting Islamism or those concerned about it is the place of women in the society. The new governments have mostly continued to uphold the secular rights of women that they had during the Soviet period. However, towards the end of the Soviet era and into the independence years, the issue of women's dual roles in society has become an important identity issue. In over 300 interviews in Tajikistan, Kyrgyzstan, and Uzbekistan, I found that only the most conservative segments of society (i.e. the clergy and Islamists) wish to see women's secular rights changed to better reflect traditional Islamic norms. They stress that this is not a move to reduce their rights, but to reassert religious values over atheistic ones. This attitude has put women's non-governmental organizations (NGOs) and other urban groups on alert as many of them have as their stated goal not new rights, but the preservation and continuance of the rights that women garnered under the Soviet Union. When asked directly in informal interviews amongst make family members, most women referred to themselves as 'Soviet women' who may in many cases have been housewives, but these were positions that they chose and if they had wished to work in factories or taught in schools, then they would have done so. They therefore strongly support a woman's ability to choose what role in life she wishes to pursue. Women have a very public face in Central Asia and most have to work to support their family. However, when these women return to their family, they are almost never seen as equals in that sphere, but are expected to take care of the children, cook, clean and, in short, do all things that women have traditionally done. Attention was called to this issue in horrific fashion at the close of the Soviet era because of a number of women who chose self-immolation out of despair. When asked about this, a variety of answers have been given by the women who survived and by others, but the common denominator is that women feel exhausted trying to uphold both their traditional and modern roles of both mother/wife and worker in the face of the deterioration of health programmes, pensions, infrastructure and, especially, education (see also Fernea, 1998; Poliakov,

1992; Smith, 1990; Tokhtakhodjayeva, 1995). Education led to a woman's right to equality in the work place; however, it did nothing for her position at home. In the current post-Soviet era amidst a declining standard of living, women fear that their rights and privileges are at grave risk. Moreover, as education becomes less available and unemployment continues at such high levels, local NGOs believe that future generations of women will not have the advantages and choices enjoyed by their mothers and grandmothers.

Be that as it may, education is often cited as the greatest gift that the former Soviet Union bestowed on the region. With a literacy rate at 98% in 1990, even the most isolated herders and farmers had access to schools and the means to educate their children. In part because the Brezhnev years particularly were marked by an intensification of Russianization in schools and amongst workers, Russian was (and still remains) the *lingua franca* between Central Asian countries although each Central Asian country was allowed to continue to maintain part of local education in its own language. However, a growing gap exists in common knowledge of Russian. It is no longer a given that any citizen of a Central Asian country will be at least conversant in Russian, although this is less true in Kazakhstan. In urban settings, most, if not all, people will use Russian daily, but this is not the case in rural areas. A dearth of language teachers in villages, coupled with a reduction of funds for education and the concomitant necessity for individual families to now pay for books and other school supplies, has forced many parents to remove their children from school and has caused Russian to become a low priority (see especially Bauer, Boschmann, Green, and Kuehnast, 1998). In effect, anyone twenty and under, living in a rural setting, and not a member of the transition elite is unable to converse in Russian, although they will still understand much of the language from television and dubbed movies. This gap will undoubtedly continue to widen with each passing year. I witnessed this first hand many times, but my experience of travelling to a glacial valley in the Fan Mountains where herders brought their cattle for summer pasturage stands out. I had arrived with an aid worker who could converse proficiently in Russian, but knew no Tajiki. Amongst the herders, he could only talk with the elder and middle-aged men in the group whereas I could converse in Tajiki with all members of the group (a fact which made the older men clearly uncomfortable about their sons' inability to speak Russian).

With the absence in many cases of Russian instruction and a multilingual approach, the younger generation's education is already suffering. The only positive trend is that in many cases knowledge of their own language and literary heritage is increasing. The drawback is that there are currently very few books available in the local languages which severely limits the diversity of learning material. With these changes, one can already see shifts in local identity, especially with the youth. For those who remember little of the Soviet era, few of them look exclusively to Moscow or Russians for entertainment, education or political knowledge. They now also look to India, Pakistan, the Middle East, America or Europe. According to one source, a disproportionate number of the population turning to Islamism are young people, roughly those 16-24 (particularly unmarried men like those in similar situations in the Middle East) who reject Russia and their communist past and sometimes, by extension the West, (Polonskaya and Malashenko, 1994). Along with the renaissance of Central Asian languages and the rise in the number of observant Muslims, the youth have to deal with more than their share of the harsh realities of transitional economies. Issues of expanding unemployment, moves towards traditionalism and/or Islamism, and a significantly shrunken employment base in various stages between capitalist and communist are problems they will face for the foreseeable future.

Conclusion

According to Mark Saroyan, the Soviet government displayed an 'orientalist' approach to Islam by assuming that Central Asian Islam was defined by the Qur'an and *Hadith* and was therefore 'unchanging'. They did not understand that Islam '… is also constituted by the lived experiences and religious practices of those who identify themselves as Muslim' (Saroyan, 1997). Because of their unwillingness to understand the way Islam impacted the lives of Central Asian Muslims, the Russian-dominated, Soviet government succeeded in undermining the official Islamic clergy who could not maintain the hold on religious society they had had in pre-Soviet times. Unofficial clergy and, especially in the countryside, members of the Naqshbandi Sufi Order began to usurp this role and to fulfill the spiritual needs of the people of Central Asia. However, this in no way weakened the influence of Islam in the daily lives of the people of Central Asia. They adapted in ways that allowed them to maintain their Muslim identity in the face of official atheistic propaganda and Islam remained the standard by which they set their morals and structured their private space (see also Bennigsen and Lemercier-Quelquejay, 1979; Polonskaya and Malashenko, 1994).

It has been observed that most religious people call themselves observant because they participate in religious rituals. Many people call themselves Christian or Jewish even if they may never go to a church or temple except perhaps for the more important religious holidays ('Chreaster' Christians come to mind, those who only attend church for Christmas and Easter). Perhaps also they will be married and buried within the rites of their religion or if they are Jewish, perform circumcision on their sons. In this case, many Jewish people refer to themselves as 'culturally Jewish', although I have never heard anyone refer to themselves as 'culturally Christian'. Within Central Asia, it is common to hear people refer to themselves as 'cultural Muslims', signaling the adherence to specific rites and the observance of religious holidays. However, I only heard this terminology amongst urbanites within any of the countries and generally amongst those urbanites that had been a part of either the intellectual or political elite (or aspired to either). Amongst rural people and the urban proletariat, it was rare to hear this phrase. Rural people particularly were more likely to practice Islam in a much broader sense throughout the Soviet era especially in the later years when observance grew more open. Whenever I mentioned the term in rural Tajikistan, men would laugh and say that was a "Dushanbe expression", meaning that those in the capital, or those working within the party as a collective farm leader and answerable to the capital, would use that phrase to politely deflect talking about personal spirituality or because they did not want to be seen as either 'too secular', and therefore out of step with the population at large, or 'too Islamic', and out of step with the secular government.

If that is the case, it could be argued that most Muslims in Central Asia are observant Muslims and deserve the full respect of other Muslims. There has been aspersion cast on the religiosity of the people of Central Asia because they lived within the Soviet Union and in many ways changed culturally and religiously. However, it should be apparent that they did *not* forego Islam or what they perceived to be important Islamic rituals. To impute that the people of Central Asia are not 'really' Muslims, is to imply that Islam is monolithic and unvarying, an unfortunate trend in the West and a thought that should be negated by the very nature of this book. Islamic practices have always varied greatly since the early centuries of the Islamic era. These variants have included Sufism and the local compromises and intermingling of pre-Islamic practices within everyday observance as Islam spread from the Arabian Peninsula. According to Richard Bulliet there is great potential for individual action in Islam not found in Judaism and Christianity. This can be further extended to Islamism as the same author notes that in its individualist, private nature heightened attention to religious observation carries with it a heightened awareness of cultural identity (Bulliet, 1994).

Since the fall of the Soviet Union, the people of Central Asia display a wide range of religious identity. Many people in the countryside mostly maintained their Islamic identity throughout the Soviet era, but in a very private way that allowed them outwardly to conform to government dictates. After independence, they can be more open about their identity, but much of the private nature of observance has been maintained. Urbanites, and especially those people who have become the transition elite in the country, are openly Muslim, but many chose to retain the observance of life identity events within a framework of secularity. The term 'cultural Muslim' is used today primarily by those people who will circumcise their sons, marry with the blessing of the clergy and be buried with Islamic rites. These people do not deny their Muslim identity, but they do take pains to offer further markers of identity based on geography, linguistics, culture and nationalism nurtured by the Soviet government. Most recently, the governments have tried to augment this with an additional emphasis on pre-Soviet, historical figures who can be shown as indicative of the place the group has in Central Asia. Whether it is Tamerlane for the Uzbeks, Ismail Samani for the Tajiks, or the Turkmen raiders who so harassed the Russian army before Geok-Tepe, the governments wish to maintain Islam as *one* source of identity, not *the* source of identity, within a framework of secularity that they hope will allow them to preserve their political hegemony. In this way, the linguistic and nationalist borders and cultures that were meant to destroy Islam failed. Where they were successful was in destroying a *united* Muslim land in Central Asia.

The promotion of sovereignty based on linguistics and the Soviet perception of local geography could be the lasting legacy, however artificial, for the countries of Central Asia. For the people, each country's independence has allowed more public expression of their religiosity, but has not yet allowed full expression for many. Especially in the post 9/11 years, there is still an 'official Islam', one guided by the governments in a way that promotes what they perceive to be a moderate form of religious observance, i.e. one that mostly conforms to how Muslims lived in the later years of the USSR. At the same time, they keep close tabs on anyone suspected of promoting Islamism or wishing for a change to theocratic rule. The governments, much like Russia, use the current international situation and the war on terror to crack down harder on people perceived as Islamist in the name of fighting terrorism. With the example of the Tajik Civil War in most people's minds, it is unlikely in the short term that this policy will prove widely unpopular. So the people of Central Asia continue, much as they have throughout their lives, to keep their Muslim identity a private issue; a strategy with which they feel comfortable yet which allows them to stay in the Muslim *umma*.

References

Abdullayev, S, (1998) 'Religious Practices under the Samanids', in Bashiri, I., (ed.) *Samanids and the Revival of the Civilization of Iranian Peoples*, Dushanbe: Academy of Sciences of the Republic of Tajikistan.

Abdullah, SA., (1975) 'Samarkand as It Is,' *Muslims of the Soviet East* No. 1, 25th in the series: 18-20.

Akbarzadeh, S., (1994) *Islam in Perspective: the Truimph (sic) of Islamic Traditions in Central Asia*. Discussion Papers No. 1, 1994. Carlton: The University of Melbourne, Centre for Soviet and East European Studies.

Alimov, K. (1998) 'Theology and Mysticism during the Samanid Era', in Bashiri, I., (ed.) *Samanids and the Revival of the Civilization of Iranian Peoples*. Dushanbe: Academy of Sciences of the Republic of Tajikistan.

Anon (1964) 'Razvyertyvaniye Kul'turnoi Ryevolyutsii', in Antonyenko, BA., (ed.) *Istoriya Tadzhikskogo Naroda*, vol. III, no. 1, Moskva: Izdatyel'stvo "Nauka".

Anon (1983a) *Islam v SSSR*, Moskva: Izdatyel'stvo "Mycl'".

Anon (1983b) Muslims and Freedom of Religion in the Soviet Union. *Muslims of the Soviet East* No. 2, 58th in the series: 1-2.

Anon (1998) 'The Crusade against the Wahhabis', *The Economist* 348 (8075) 36-7.

Anon (2000) Why the Sun Shines on Niyazov. Foreign Report *Jane's Information Group Limited*.

Anon (2001a) 'Nervous Spring', *The Economist* 358 (8206) 40.

Anon (2001b) A Trip around the 'Stans, Foreign Report *Jane's Information Group Limited*.

Anon (2005) 'Uzbekistan: The Andijan Uprising' International Crisis Group Asia Briefing No 38, 25 May 2005. http://www.crisisgroup.org/home/index.cfm?id=3469.

Ashirov, N., (1975) *Islam i Natsii*, Moskva: Izdatyel'stvo Politicheskoi Lityeratury.

Ashirov, N., (1978) *Musul'manskaya Propovyed'*, Moskva: Izdatyel'stvo Politichyeskoi Lityeratury.

Atkin, M., (1989) *The Subtlest Battle: Islam in Soviet Tajikistan*, Philadelphia: Foreign Policy Research Institute.

Atkin, M., (1994) 'Tajikistan's Relations with Iran and Afghanistan', in Banuazizi, A and Weiner, M., (eds) *The New Geopolitics of Central Asia and Its Borderlands*, Bloomington: Indiana University Press.

Atkin, M., (1997) 'Thwarted Democratization in Tajikistan', in Dawisha, K., and Parrott, B., (eds) *Conflict, Cleavage, and Change in Central Asia and the*

Caucasus, Cambridge: Cambridge University Press.

Banuazizi, A., and Weiner, M., (1994) 'Introduction', in Banuazizi, A., and Weiner, M., (eds) *The New Geopolitics of Central Asia and Its Borderlands*, Bloomington: Indiana University Press.

Bartol'd, VV., (1956) *A Short History of Turkestan: History of the Semirechy'e. Four Studies on the History of Central Asia*, vol 1., Minorsky, V. and T., transl. Leiden: E. J. Brill.

Bartol'd, VV. (1963) Khlopkovodstvo v Sryednyei Azii s istorichyeskikh vryemyen do prikhoda russkikh, *Akadyemik V. V. Bartol'd Sochinyeniya* v. II, part I. Moskva: Izdatyel'stvo Vostochnoi Lityeratury.

Baskakov, N. A. (1952) 'Razvitiye Yazykov i Pis'myennosti Narodov SSSR (na Matyerialye Tyurkskikh Yazykov),' *Voprosy Yazykoznaniya* **1**(3) 19-44.

Bauer, A., Boschmann, N., Green, D., and Kuehnast, K., (1998) *A Generation at Risk: Children in the Central Asian Republics of Kazakstan (sic) and Kyrgyzstan*, Manila: Asian Development Bank.

Becker, S., (1988) 'Russia's Central Asian Empire, 1885-1917', in Rywkin, Michael, (ed.) *Russian Colonial Expansion to 1917*, London: Mansell Publishing Limited.

Bennigsen, A., and Lemercier-Quelquejay, C., (1979) "Official'Islam in the Soviet Union, *Religion in Communist Lands* **7**(3) 148-159.

Bennigsen, A., and Lemercier-Quelquejay, C., (1981) *Les musulmans oubliés: L'Islam en U.R.S.S. aujourd'hui*, Paris: François Maspero.

Bennigsen, A., and Wimbush, SE., (1985) *Mystics and Commissars: Sufism in the Soviet Union*, Berkeley: University of California Press.

Bräker, H., (1969) *Kommunismus und Weltreligionen Asiens* 1(1) Tübingen: J.C.B. Mohr.

Bräker, H., (1983) *The Implications of the Islamic Question for Soviet Domestic and Foreign Policy*, Köln: Bundesinstitut für ostwissenschaftliche und internationale Studien.

Bräker, H., (1989) 'Die Sowjetische Politik gegenüber dem Islam', in Kappeler, Andreas; Simon, Gerhard; and Brunner, Georg, eds. *Die Muslime in der Sowjetunion und in Jugoslawien: Identität, Politik, Widerstand*. Köln: Markus Verlag.

Broxup, M., (1989) 'Politische Tendenzen des Islam in der Sowjetunion seit dem Afghanistan-Krieg', in Kappeler, A., Simon, G., and Brunner, G., (eds) *Die Muslime in der Sowjetunion und in Jugoslawien: Identität, Politik, Widerstand*, Köln: Markus Verlag.

Brunner, G., (1989) 'Die Stellung der Muslime in den föderativen Systemen der Sowjetunion und Jugoslawiens', in Kappeler, A., Simon, G., and Brunner, G., (eds) *Die Muslime in der Sowjetunion und in Jugoslawien: Identität, Politik, Widerstand*, Köln: Markus Verlag.

Bulliet, RW., (1994) *Islam: The View from the Edge*, New York: Columbia University Press.

Burkhanov, S., and Gusarov, V., (1984) *Soviet Power and Islam: The Soviet Government's Experience in Cooperating with the Muslim Clergy*, Moscow: Novosti Press Agency Publishing House.

Byelyayev, E. (1935) 'Islam', in Meshchyeryakov, N. L. (ed.) *Malaya*

Sovyetskaya Entsiklopyediya, Moskva: Gosudarstvyennii Institut "Sovyetskaya Entsiklopyediya".

Chatterjee, S., (2002) *Society and Politics in Tajikistan in the Aftermath of the Civil War*, Gurgaon: Hope India Publications.

Chavannes, E (1942) *Documents sur les Tou-Kiue Occidentaux*. Paris: Librairie d'Amérique et d'Orient, Présenté à l'Académie Impériale des Sciences de St-Pétersbourg le 23 Août 1900.

Critchlow, J., (1989) 'Islam and Nationalism in Soviet Central Asia', in Ramet, P (ed.) *Religion and Nationalism in Soviet and East European Politics*, Durham: Duke University Press.

Curzon, GN., (1889) *Russia in Central Asia in 1889 and the Anglo-Russian Question*, New York: Barnes & Noble, Inc.

d'Encausse, HC., (1988) *Islam and the Russian Empire: Reform and Revolution in Central Asia*, Berkeley: University of California Press.

Dudoignon, SA. (1997) 'Political Parties and Forces in Tajikistan, 1989-1993', in Djalili, M-R., Grare, F., and Akiner, S., (eds) *Tajikistan: The Trials of Independence*, New York: St. Martin's Press.

Edwards, D., (1989) 'Mad Mullahs and Englishmen: Discourse in the Colonial Encounter', *Comparative Studies in Society and History* **31**(4) 649-670.

Fernea, EW., (1998) *In Search of Islamic Feminism*, New York: Doubleday.

Gibb, HAR., (1970) *The Arab Conquests in Central Asia*, New York: AMS Press.

Halbach, U.,(1991)*Islam, Nation und politische Öffentlichkeit in den zentralasiatischen (Unions-) Republiken*, Köln: Bundesinstitut für ostwissenschaftliche und internationale Studien.

Haub, C., (2004) *2004 World Population Data Sheet*, Washington, D.C.: Population Reference Bureau.

Hayit, B., (1987) *Islam and Turkestan under Russian Rule*, Istanbul: Can Matbaa.

Höpken, W., (1989) 'Die jugoslawischen Kommunisten und die bosnischen Muslime', in Kappeler, A Simon, G and Brunner, G, (eds) *Die Muslime in der Sowjetunion und in Jugoslawien: Identität, Politik, Widerstand*, Köln: Markus Verlag.

Karklins, R., (1980) 'Islam: How Strong Is It in the Soviet Union?', *Cahiers du Monde Russe et Soviétique* XXI(1) 65-81.

Keller, S., (2001) *To Moscow, Not Mecca: The Soviet Campaign Against Islam in Central Asia, 1917-1941*, Westport: Praeger.

Khalid, A., (1998) *The Politics of Muslim Cultural Reform: Jadidism in Central Asia*, Berkeley: University of California Press.

Kolsto, P., (1998) Anticipating Demographic Superiority: Kazakh Thinking on Integration and Nation Building, Europe-*Asia Studies,* 50 (1) 51-69.

Krader, L. (1966) *Peoples of Central Asia*, Bloomington: Indiana University Publications, Uralic and Altaic Series, volume 26.

Kreindler, IT. (1995) 'Soviet Muslims: Gains and Losses as a Result of Soviet Language Planning', in Ro'i Yaacov (ed.) *Muslim Eurasia: Conflicting Legacies*, London: Frank Cass.

Lane, D., (1978) *Politics and Society in the USSR*, London: Martin Robertson.

Lubin, N. (1999) *Calming the Ferghana Valley: Development and Dialogue in the*

Heart of Central Asia, New York: The Century Foundation Press.

Makarenko, T., (2000) Crime and Terrorism in Central Asia, *Jane's Intelligence Review* July 1, 2000.

Massell, GJ. (1974) *The Surrogate Proletariat: Moslem Women and Revolutionary Strategies in Soviet Central Asia, 1919-1929*, Princeton: Princeton University Press.

Niedermeier, H., (1952) Schriftreform und Nationalitäten in der UdSSR. *Osteuropa* 3(6) 413-16.

Olcott, MB., (1995) 'Islam and Fundamentalism in Independent Central Asia', in Ro'i Yaacov (ed.) *Muslim Eurasia: Conflicting Legacies*, London: Frank Cass.

Olcott, MB., (1997) 'Democratization and the Growth of Political Participation in Kazakstan (*sic*),' in Dawisha, K and Parrott, B (eds) *Conflict, Cleavage, and Change in Central Asia and the Caucasus*, Cambridge: Cambridge University Press.

Olyeshchuk, F. (1939) *Bor'ba Tserkvi Protiv Naroda*, Moskva: Gosudarsvyennoye Izdatyel'stvo Politichyeskoi Lityeratury.

Peterson, S., (2000) 'Central Asia's Islamist Crucible', *The Christian Science Monitor* November 28, 2000.

Poliakov, SP. (1992) *Everyday Islam: Religion and Tradition in Rural Central Asia*, Armonk: M. E. Sharpe.

Polonskaya, L., and Malashenko, A., (1994) *Islam in Central Asia*, Reading: Ithaca Press.

Rahimdjan, U. (1982) 'Solidarity with People of Afghanistan', *Muslims of the Soviet East* 3, (55th in the series) 12-13.

Rakowska-Harmstone,T. (1970) *Russia and Nationalism in Central Asia*, Baltimore: The Johns Hopkins Press.

Rakowska-Harmstone, T. (1983) 'Islam and Nationalism: Central Asia and Kazakhstan under Soviet Rule', *Central Asian Survey* 2 (2) 7-88.

Ramet, P. (1989a) 'Die Muslime Bosniens als Nation', in Kappeler, A., Simon, G., and Brunner, G, (eds) *Die Muslime in der Sowjetunion und in Jugoslawien: Identität, Politik, Widerstand*, Köln: Markus Verlag.

Ramet, P., (1989b) 'Religion and Nationalism in Yugoslavia', in Ramet, P (ed.) *Religion and Nationalism in Soviet and East European Politics*, Durham: Duke University Press.

Rashid, A., (2002) *Jihad: The Rise of Militant Islam in Central Asia*, New York: Penguin Books.

Ro'i Y., (1984) The Task of Creating the New Soviet Man: 'Atheistic Propaganda' in the Soviet Muslim Areas,' *Soviet Studies* XXXVI (1) 26-44.

Ro'i Y., (1990) 'Islam and Nationalism in Soviet Central Asia', *Problems of Communism* XXXIX (4) 49-64.

Ro'i Y., (1995) 'The Secularization of Islam and the USSR's Muslim Areas,' in Ro'i, Yaacov, ed. *Muslim Eurasia: Conflicting Legacies*, London: Frank Cass.

Rorlich, Azade-Ayse (1991), Islam and Atheism: Dynamic Tension in Soviet Central Asia', In Fierman, W (ed.) *Soviet Central Asia: The Failed Transformation*, Boulder: Westview Press.

Sagdeev, R., (2000) 'Central Asia and Islam: An Overview', in Sagdeev, R. and Eisenhower, S., (eds) *Islam and Central Asia: An Enduring Legacy or an Evolving*

Threat? Washington, D.C.: Center for Political and Strategic Studies.

Saidbayev, TS. (1984) *Islam i Obshchestvo: Opyt Istoriko-Sotsiologichyeskogo Isslyedovaniya*, Moskva: Izdatyel'stvo "Nauka'Glavnaya Ryedaktsiya Vostochnoi Lityeratury.

Saidbayev, TS., (1985) *Islam: Istorii i Sovryemyennost'*, Moskva: Znaniye.

Saroyan, M., (1997) *Minorities, Mullahs, and Modernity: Reshaping Community in the Former Soviet Union*, Berkeley: International and Area Studies, University of California at Berkeley.

Smith, H., (1990) *The New Russians*, New York: Random House.

Soper, J., (1979) 'Unofficial Islam: A Muslim Minority in the USSR', *Religion in Communist Lands* 7(4) 226-31.

Stalin, J., (1940) *Marxism and the National and Colonial Question*, Moscow: Foreign Languages Publishing House.

Stalin, J., (1950) *Marxism and Linguistics*. New York: International Publishers.

Sukharyeva, OA (1960), *Islam v Uzbyekistanye*, Tashkent: Izdatyel'stvo Akademii Nauk Uzbyekskoi SSR.

Tabyshaliyeva, A (2000) The Kyrgyz and the Spiritual Dimensions of Daily Life. In Sagdeev, Roald and Eisenhower, Susan, eds. *Islam and Central Asia: An Enduring Legacy or an Evolving Threat?*, Washington, D.C.: Center for Political and Strategic Studies.

Thöni, J. (1994) *The Tajik Conflict: The Dialectic between Internal Fragmentation and External Vulnerability, 1991-1994*, Geneva: Programme for Strategic and International Security Studies, Occasional Paper No. 3.

Tokhtakhodjayeva, M., (1995) *Between the Slogans of Communism and the Laws of Islam*, Lahore: Shirkat Gah Women's Resource Centre.

Trofimov, DA. (1995) *Islam in the Political Culture of the Former Soviet Union: Central Asia and Azerbaijan*, Heft 93, Hamburg: Institut für Friedensforschung und Sicherheitspolitik.

Vagabov, M. and Vagabov, NM., (1988) *Islam i Voprosy Ateisticheskogo Vospitaniya*, Moskva: Izdatyel'stvo "Vysshaya Shkola".

Varabov, MV (1966) Bol'shye Vnimaniya Sovyetskomu Islamovyedyeniyu. *Voprosy Filosofii* xx (12) 172-5.

Vambéry, A. (1906) *Western Culture in Eastern Lands: A Comparison of the Methods Adopted by England and Russia in the Middle East*, London: John Murray.

Wheeler, G (1960) *Racial Problems in Soviet Muslim Asia*, London: Oxford University Press.

Winner, TG. (1952), 'Problems of Alphabetic Reform among the Turkic Peoples of Soviet Central Asia, 1920-41', *The Slavonic and Eastern European Review* vol. XXXI, no. 76: 133-47.

Wurm, S, (1954), *Turkic Peoples of the USSR: Their Historical Background, Their Languages and the Development of Soviet Linguistic Policy*, London: Central Asian Research Centre.

Chapter 10

Islam and National Development: A Cross-Cultural Comparison of the Role of Religion in the Process of Economic Development and Cultural Change

Samuel Zalanga

Introduction

Since the classical work of German sociologist Max Weber in *The Protestant Ethic and the Spirit of Capitalism,* research in the social sciences has broadened discussions of economic development to include the role of cultural values and ideas in general in the process of economic development and cultural change. Much of this work focused initially on the experience of Western societies and, particularly, the role of Christianity in the process of socio-economic transformation. The implicit assumption in such analysis is the lack of internal capacity in other faith traditions to facilitate socio-economic transformation such as the type that took place in Europe and North America following the industrial revolution. However, with the phenomenal success of East and Southeast Asian societies in economic development and cultural change during late modernity, researchers started to focus on the ideas, beliefs and values that perform roles that are functionally equivalent to the 'protestant ethic and the spirit of capitalism' within other religions. Yet even with this concession, scholars like Samuel Huntington (1984) have argued that the religion of Islam is not conducive to the promotion of economic development and democracy, both of which are integral elements of modernity.

This chapter contributes to this debate by discussing the role of Islam in the process of economic development and cultural change by engaging in a cross-cultural comparison of the role of Islam in national development in Malaysia and Nigeria. The chapter adopts an interdisciplinary perspective to demonstrate how, through the intersection of geography, history, politics, organizational leadership and nationalism, Islam has played different roles in shaping national development in the two countries. It is argued here that the dominant strand of Islam in Nigeria is not only conservative but emphasizes past time-orientation, while the dominant strand of Islam in Malaysia emphasizes the need for rapid economic development and cultural change, and therefore underscores future time-orientation. Based on the comparative data, I argue that the issue is not simply whether a religion is conservative or progressive, as some scholars naively assume. Rather, the appropriate question to ask is under what conditions a religion does becomes a force for promoting desirable social change and under what conditions does it become a fetter. The chapter concludes by arguing that comparative analysis suggests the need for scholars to be cautious in characterizing any religion with a single orientation across time and space.

The Central Theoretical Argument

The main thesis of this chapter is that geography, locality and culture interact with and serve to complicate the process of class, state, ethnic group formation and articulation and the ways in which religion is empirically conceptualized and practiced (Murphy, 1991). This articulation, in turn, has consequences for development policy formulation and implementation. If, as I argue here, the specific or particular form of the practice of a universalistic religious faith is contingent on geography, locality, history and socioeconomic realities then we cannot argue that because a variety of people believe and practice the same universal religion, the practice of that religion will be the same across space and time. For instance, in both the case of Malaysia and Nigeria, coastal people for the most part were integrated into the modern capitalist economy dominated by the West prior to the people of the interior or the people in the Northern part of each country. When geographical differences intersect with cultural, religious, economic, regional, and ethnic differences the each resultant mix can metamorphose into powerful social forces that operate on their own accord. This broad difference between coastal and interior population results in the uneven integration of different social groups into the colonial economy. This uneven integration, in turn, results in distrust among pre-colonial social groups and the creation of different social movements to protect their varied social interests. Using insight from the central thesis of this paper, one might even argue that we can account for the variation in how Christianity was practiced and articulated publicly in the United States between the New England states and the Southern slave plantation economy before the civil war and reconstruction in the South (Emerson and Smith, 2000). Given how the Northern region of the United States was then more developed than the South, slave labor was less relevant to the industrial production structure of the region's economy vis-à-vis the Southern region, which was predominantly agricultural. Consequently, there is some systematic variation in how Christianity was publicly articulated or used to justify or not justify slavery in the United States. In this chapter I argue along the same lines; that the intersection of geography, history, culture, economics and ethnicity has shaped the way Islam has been practiced and articulated in the public sphere in Malaysia and Nigeria.

Islam and Social Change in Malaysia under British Colonial Rule

Islam, like any other religion, is critical in shaping development because, by and large, it shapes people's worldview. In any religious society, religious tenets are critical in shaping morality – what is to be desired, what is to be avoided, etc.

Given this influence of religion, Islam has significantly shaped social change and development in the two countries.

In Malaysia, Islam contributed positively to development because, through their teachings, many influential Islamic 'Ulamas' (experts) emphasized the need to modernize, to reform the status quo within Islam, to embrace science and to develop critiques of the nobility (Milner, 1995). The impact Islam had in Malaysia during the colonial period can indeed be deduced from an examination of the editorial comments of Malay Islamic journals. The journals addressed many issues connected to development and social change in Malaya (i.e., Malaysia) as they particularly affect the Malay people who are Muslims. I intend here to focus on two of the numerous issues that they addressed. The two issues are the critique of the Kerajaan (i.e., Malay traditional political elite) and the stress on the importance of knowledge acquisition. For instance, in January of 1908 a popular Malay Islamic newspaper journal wrote the following as a critique of the Malay traditional political elite. The criticism reads:

> If the Raja (i.e., traditional political ruler) happens to be ignorant, of bad character, low ambition, greedy, narrow-minded and so forth, then his action will lead to the downfall of the community (umat)... It will fall under the government of another race because of the evil policy of the Raja and because the ministers feared opposing him. In such a situation the people too are foolish... if there existed some spirit in the umat, and if they had the slightest reason ('akal') in their heads – even the size of an ant – they would root out the poisonous tree'.

(Al Imam January 5, 1907 cited in Milner, 1995: 140).

This is not only a criticism of the Malay ruling elite but virtually a call to the Malay people to revolt against an unjust regime, much like the call by social philosophers of the Enlightenment tradition in Europe in the early modern period.

In another issue, *Al Imam* (i.e., the Islamic journal) identified and criticized people in society who ought not to be honoured or respected. Of course, the particular group the journal identified was the Malay traditional political elite. The journal asserted that:

> Some of our rajas in this region who gained their medals and ranks in states inherited from their ancestors, states which they later surrendered to other races. [These rajas] surrendered the law of their community ('umat') and group ('kaum') to foreign religions and allowed the cream of the revenue of their states to flow to foreigners. In such countries all the Muslims must endure the difficulties and burdens loaded upon them, one after another, by foreign races.

(Al Imam cited in Milner, 1995:143)

Although operating within the realm of Islam, the Malay Muslim intelligentsia expressed their broad nationalist feelings in ways that could be accommodated within secular movements. In the preceding quotation, they were asserting their deep concern about the way the Malay people had been subordinated to other races and civilizations in their own land. They blamed this situation on their traditional political elite. The quotation brings to light the fact that the Malay Muslim intelligentsia causally associates progressive development in a society with the kind of political leadership existing within the same society. In addition, there is also evidence that *Al Imam* consciously elevated history to the level of epistemology for understanding the world and using that understanding to plan for the future. This position is asserted in the quotation below:

> There is one matter which will not escape the notice of all those who observe the movement of this universe by examining the history ('tarikh') of people in the past, and who use these observations as their guide ('murshid'), as a flare which throws light on all events. It is known by these people that the community ('umat') is divided into two parts. First, there are those who are active, performing good works for the advantage of their groups in the future. People of this part of the community do not limit their perspectives to their own affairs. People of the second part of the community possess concerns, which are limited to themselves and their own homes. There is no doubt that it is the first part of the 'umat' which follows the injunction of God and thus obtains whatever is promised by Him.

> (*Al Imam*, cited in Milner, 1995:169).

Undoubtedly the Malay Muslim intelligentsia indirectly called not only for broad-mindedness, but also for the need to put the interest of the community before one's own or the interest of one's relatives suggesting strong opposition to nepotism. Yet we should observe that, even with this kind of call, the scholars were not agitating for the restoration of Durkheim's type of mechanical solidarity consciousness where the individual's consciousness was submerged by collective consciousness. They expected leaders to put the interest of the community first, out of an individual rational understanding that was based on what God expected of individuals.

Regarding knowledge ('ilmu'), the Islamic journal asserted that it is 'the foundation on which every pillar of victory stands'. It is 'the sun which obliterates the utter darkness of night'. All the good things that characterize human existence, according to the paper, have, at their heart, the application of knowledge. Examples of some of the good things cited are 'tranquility, fertility, profit and high rank'. *Al Imam* also maintained that knowledge is the 'channel of perfection and the light of reason'. Knowledge, according to the journal, is not restricted to knowing what is legitimate and illegitimate in Islamic religion. While that is important, the newspaper asserted that knowledge entails understanding all 'matters which are brought into being by God in ourselves, on the earth and in the sky' (Milner, 1995: 177).

Al Imam was blunt in asserting that the advantage Europeans and Japanese had over Malay people, and which made their (European and Japanese) countries successful, was their superior knowledge (see Milner, 1995, p.177). In another issue, the journal attempted to establish a relationship between failure to acquire education and the continued persistence of human degradation and failure to realize self-actualization in human society. The quotation reads:

> History has already shown us that every community ('umat') which has been unable to rise from degradation, unable to escape a position of humiliation, unable to achieve its

desired level of honor and its portion of greatness, has failed in these respects because it has failed to obtain education.

(*Al Imam* cited in Milner, 1995: 169)

The foregoing analysis of the role of Islam in development in Malaysia raises several issues about the Malaysian development experience. First, by criticizing the traditional elite, the Malay Muslim intelligentsia constituted an indigenous reform movement in Malaya. Their critique of the Kerajaan (i.e., the traditional political elite) clearly demonstrated their desire to hold leaders accountable for their leadership responsibilities in society. As Wilbert Moore (1963) asserted, a modernization project is more likely to succeed if there is an indigenous group that has committed itself to seeing it accomplished, in contrast to a situation where the push is from outside the country.

Secondly, the quotations above strongly articulate the intellectual orientation of Malaysian Muslims as believers who saw the possibility of social, political, economic and cultural reforms based on Islamic inspirations. As far as they were concerned, it was not Islam that was the problem. Rather, the problem was the way people were practicing it, along with their incomplete understanding of what Islam really was. They did not see themselves as committing heresy by using Islam to legitimize the desire to reform Malay society, given that they believed refusing to reform could result in the wiping out of the Malay race (i.e., by implication Muslims) by people with superior civilization.

Third, the Malaysian Muslim intelligentsia, in contrast to the Nigerian case or traditional Malay society, adopted the use of history as an epistemology for positive reasoning and elevated it to the centre of human discourse. They stressed the need for people to observe the past and compare it with the present in order to see the necessity for planning to change for a better future. This position contrasts with the way Hausa-Fulani people used history in Nigeria. For them, they validated the future by using the sanctity of their past heritage as yardstick.

Fourth, the Malay Muslim intelligentsia was quick to admit the relative superiority of other cultures as compared to theirs. This was done in a positive and empowering manner, given that it was aimed at making people understand the need to work hard and change the old ways of doing things in order to be a part of human progress represented by the achievements of Europe and Japan. The readiness to concede their national deficiencies as a people was an important step in legitimizing and rationalizing a programme for change. Of course, in doing this, the Malay Muslim intelligentsia believed that their society too could excel. They just insisted that the preconditions for them to excel were social, cultural, political and economic reforms. Malay Muslim intellectuals also emphasized the need for their people to use reason ('akal') in whatever they do about their society. The emphasis on reason was an important innovation in Malay society because it was a call for individuation, whereas in traditional Malay society the emphasis was on the collectivity, which often submerged the individual's ability and capacity to reason, to have initiative and to engage in reflective consciousness (see Munshi Abdullah, cited in Milner, 1995, chapter one).

Islam and Social Change in Northern Nigeria Under British Colonial Rule

Although Islam had the upper hand in terms of getting converts in West Africa *vis-a-vis* Christianity in the 19th century, it lost its momentum as a reformist and liberating religion under colonial rule. The main explanation for this is the policy of indirect rule in Northern Nigeria, which sought to shield native authorities constituted on the Islamic caliphate system from agents and forces of social change during the colonial period. Michael Crowder's critical reflections on the relative decline of Islamic liberating influence in the 20th century in West Africa as a whole, including Nigeria, are contained in the following quotation:

> Islam under colonial rule became a force of conservatism rather than change, as it had been in the 19th century... Administrators supported established Islam in the form of emirs and marabouts of whose loyalty, they were sure, and saw in them a dam harnessing Western ideas to African society whilst holding back what they considered its disruptive influences. Christianity, which gained only a tenth of the converts Islam did, nevertheless made a much greater impact on African society, far from trying to control the flow of ideas from the West, the missionaries positively pumped them into West Africa.

(Crowder 1968: 362-363)

Only the Ahmadiyya group that originally started in Pakistan adopted a policy that tried to convert people to Islam, while also providing the converts with modern Western type education. Yet by the 1940s, the Ahmaddiyya group in Nigeria, and indeed British West Africa in general, had but a small following.

The Muslim emirs were the custodians of Islamic religion after the Islamic holy war in Northern Nigeria in the first decade of the 19th century. Subsequently, the emirs were entrenched in their position by the British colonial rulers under the indirect rule system, which fully took off in the early 20th century. Under joint agreement between the emirs of the Islamic caliphate in Northern Nigeria and the British, which protected the religious institution and beliefs of the caliphate, the emirs had to give their approval before missionaries were allowed to live in areas under their jurisdiction. Even when they allowed missionaries to stay in their areas, their continued stay was at the pleasure of the emirs and if the missionaries upset the emirs in any way, the emirs would request the colonial officers to direct the missionaries to leave. This policy was strongly supported by the colonial office in London. Indeed, Lugard, who was the colonial governor general of Nigeria was angered by the position of the colonial office in restricting the missionaries from the emirates when he asserted that no government can 'permanently deny access to missionary effort in a British dependency' (Lugard in response to Harcourt, see White 1981: 106). Lugard's view was that inasmuch as it was wrong to leave Western education totally in the hands of Christian missionaries, it was also an error to believe that missionaries could not provide any desirable contribution in the area of education in the colony. Indeed, the colonial government's budget for education was very limited. The colonial government relied on missionaries to establish schools and provide Western education to the local people all over Nigeria. One might argue that Muslims have a legitimate concern about Christian missionaries using their schools to proselyte students but, by the same token, it is fair to say that the response could have been more constructive.

For instance, the emir of Zaria in Northern Nigeria requested Governor Clifford to expel the Church Missionary Society (CMS) mission. The bone of contention was that a CMS missionary by the name of Miller, who was living in Zaria, was under so many restrictions, and what he considered discrimination by British colonial officers, that he wrote a petition to the governor in which he made a scathing attack on the abuses of the Fulani emirs of Kano, Zaria, and Katsina, which were all major Islamic cities and centres of learning in Northern Nigeria. He described the British residents as blind, and the native administration as a 'hideous travesty of rule' and 'a historical nightmare' (see White 1981: 109). It was reported that Miller lived with peasants and commoners in Northern Nigeria who felt free to tell him about the corruption, oppression and exploitation occurring under the British indirect rule system of government by the emirs. Similarly, the emir of Biu in North-eastern Nigeria once requested the Governor to expel two missionaries of the Brethren Mission living among the Burra people of Garkida, in spite of the fact that the 'pagan' community they lived in enjoyed their presence.

The Muslim society of Northern Nigeria had and still has a social structure that is very hierarchical, such that if change was not initiated from above, the typical conservatism of peasants predominates (Ikefa and Stride, 1969). Although the general situation in the emirates of Northern Nigeria was one of conservatism and resistance to change, there were a few emirs such as those of Kano, and Muhammadu Dikko of Katsina who were open to Western education. If the colonial residents had exploited such opportunities they could have used the influence and authority of the emirs to introduce Western education and, in that way, prepare Northern Nigeria for the future. The following is an extract from a letter written in 1930 by the emir of Kano to the Colonial Lieutenant Governor of the Northern provinces of Nigeria. The main theme of the letter was to explain why the Hausa people had a carefree attitude to Western education. Yet the letter also expressed the emir's openness towards the idea of Western education. Part of the letter reads:

> The reason that pupils do not of their own accord enter the schools under discussion and the reason that parents will not send their children to these schools to the same extent as their own, which they are accustomed, is simply that they are not used to them. Their fathers and grandfathers did not know them nor did they inherit them from their fathers and grandfathers. In this respect man is a creature of habit...

> ...There is yet another reason. The Hausas do not care for any type of literature other than religious or educational works – or what is closely connected with religion: such as the Unity of God, Sufism, jurisprudence and the law as Almighty God Himself said in His Book.

> ...Also the Hausa do not look ahead. They do not think of the future, of what will benefit their children and grandchildren. And this is especially true of those in the Sudan: for it is commonly said of him of the Sudan: he cares for naught but his belly and his wife.

...Furthermore let it be said that the best policy of all is for a man to learn as much as God wills of our knowledge and also to learn in the English schools what cannot be learnt save therein: her writing, her script, her methods of calculation and the like...

(see White, 1981: 302).

From this letter we can draw some conclusions about the situation of Northern Nigerian Muslims at this historical moment regarding social change. It is evident that tradition and Islamic religion (as perceived by the Hausa Muslims of Northern Nigeria) stood as obstacles to the process of desirable social change. In the case of Malaysia, the Muslims there established Muslim schools that taught English and Science and made it a strong part of their curriculum to teach the students that Islam was not opposed to science and one could be a Muslim and at the same time be modern. Here we find one of the greatest variations in the relationship between Islam and development in the two countries (Andaya and Andaya, 1982). It is very clear that Malaysian Muslims were more future-oriented in their conception of time and human history. They recognized their past, but insisted that the future requires new strategies and new ways of doing things. On the other hand, the Hausa Muslims of Northern Nigeria had a significant past subjective time orientation in their conception of time and history as they judged the future by the sanctity of past traditions. As the emir indicated, his subjects resisted Western education because it was not part of the heritage of their forefathers, and it was not part of Islamic literature. Yet the emir's own personal position on education seems to be similar to that of Malaysian Muslims, even though one wonders why he was unable to see his vision transformed into public policy in his native authority. The philosophical resistance of British colonial officers in Northern Nigeria to Western education in the emirates might have been one reason. Yet we must note that the position taken by the emir of Kano in Northern Nigeria, whose letter is quoted above, was the exception rather than the norm.

Because of the influence of the emirs and the commitment of the British colonial officers to please them, the government schools established by the colonial government in Northern Nigeria were basically concentrated in the Muslim emirates and districts, establishing very few in the pagan areas. The pagan areas were, however, helped more by missionary schools, given that the missionaries were generally allowed to operate in the pagan areas, even though at certain times the emirs were unhappy with this, as indicated above (White, 1981: 118-119).

In addition to the foregoing problems that bedeviled Western education in Northern Nigeria, the British colonial government aggravated the problem by insisting on only providing education in an elitist fashion in the North. Recruitment into the colonial government-established schools was essentially restricted to persons connected to the royal families, either as princes, nobles, slaves of the palace or clients to people in the ruling class. Only on rare occasions were the sons and daughters of commoners allowed to be enrolled.

Islam, Social Change, and Development Under British Colonial Rule: Contrasts Between Malaysia and Nigeria

Compared to Malaysia, Islam in Northern Nigeria could be seen to have retarded development in the 20th century by emphasizing the status quo, attempting to uncritically conserve traditional institutions, opposing Western education and by attempting to exonerate traditional elites from serious scrutiny and accountability to the general public. The emirs of Northern Nigeria by and large collaborated with conservative colonial officers in Northern Nigeria to resist Western education, primarily because they believed it would produce many people with critical minds who would question the legitimacy of the traditional social structure. I want to provide some evidence here to demonstrate how the practice of Islam in Northern Nigeria under colonial rule promoted conservatism – a conservatism that cannot be justified strictly on a thorough understanding of Islamic theology. For instance, when cultural changes started taking place among the Hausa-Fulani people because of contact with people from Southern Nigeria and British officials, a poem composed by a member of the Northern Muslim intelligentsia close to the ruling class demonstrated the in-built desire of the elite to resist change. The poem reads:

Today unbelief is established, and so also innovation,

Well, as for us, we have no use for this in our time.

This that I am about to say, there is no jesting in it,

Now I am going to warn you, O people,

Whoever heeds it, he will be happy.

Whatever article of their clothing, if you wear it,

I tell you that you may understand.

If you pray a thousand times you will not be vindicated,

And the same applies to the maker of hurricane lamp globes.

Your short trousers together with your tight-fitting trousers,

Whoever puts them on, his unbelief is wide.

Whoever wears suits with buttons, he has apostatized,

He has no religion at all, only pride.

His state is the state of the makers of silver dollars,

They are beyond our power to imitate.

One who wears shirts with collars,

Whoever wears them, his unbelief is wide.

Khaki and pyjamas, whoever it is,

Who wears them and prays in them, he has committed a crime.

Here they are, three things, do not use them,

All of them, avoid them, without arguing.

For to use them is not right, you have seen them,

Towel and washing-blue, and powder, whoever uses them,

Certainly on the Last Day the Fire is his dwelling.

(cited in Hiskett, 1973: 164-165)

Another poem composed by Mallam Sa'adu Zungur, a highly respected Northern Islamic scholar, not only demonstrates xenophobia, but the desire to keep away members of other pagan ethnic groups that had then become more educated than the Hausa-Fulani. The composer was also concerned about the danger of the spread of ideas of republicanism. Abdullahi, who features in the poem, was a brother to the leader of the Islamic holy war in Northern Nigeria which started in 1804, and he later became the leader of the caliphate. The poem reads:

O chief Abdullahi, help us,

You have the Chiroma Sanusi to spread knowledge.

Protect your whole community,

In order that our country shall remain for ever a monarchy.

Kano City and Fage and Tudun Wada

Villages, wattle and daub huts,

Do not let the pagan enter into them

To spread the poison of republicanism.

(Sa'adu Zungur 1960, 1964, cited in Hiskett, 1973: 167)

As for why Northern Nigerian Islam in the 20th century did not scrutinize the people in authority with the aim of making them accountable, one can identify two reasons. First, the leaders of the Fulani jihad of Northern Nigeria traced indirect genealogical connections to the Prophet Muhammad and therefore justified whatever they did on that basis. Thus the sacred and emotional attachment Muslim believers have towards the Prophet spilled over to the leaders of the Fulani jihad in Northern Nigeria and those who succeeded them. The poem below affirms this assertion:

The Shehu, the Renewer of the Faith, to the country of the Sudan,

God gave him, that he should perform good works.

By his blessedness we obtain dominion,

The Shehu, the Renewer, here is his line,

He came, he obtained his genealogy,

Both he and Abdal-Gadir al-Jilani,

Both are Sharifs, hold to this clear explanation.

Descendants of the Prophet Muhammad.

He who would argue, let him look at the book of genealogy,

Only see it there, you will set aside doubt

> (Abubakar Atiku, Sokoto poet and scion of the ruling
> house, cited in Hiskett 1973: 163).

The Shehu referred to in the poem was Shehu Othman Dan Fodio, the leader of the Sokoto Jihad that started in 1804 in Northern Nigeria. Sokoto was the capital of the Sokoto caliphate in Northern Nigeria.

As I observed above, criticizing or going against some public policies of the Northern Nigerian Fulani jihadists and political authorities amounted to going against the legacy of the Prophet and Islamic religion as a whole. The Shehu's family believed they had divine right to rule and expected people to recognize them as such. The idea of democratic mandate to govern is totally out of the question. This situation left little room for reform within the system unless it came from above. Otherwise any reform from below was interpreted by the leaders as being ideas of the infidel, and those who wanted to revolt against Islamic tenets and tradition. Few Muslims in Northern Nigeria would risk being described in this way and so religion was used for social control in a way that did not promote desirable social change. Any progressive reform would definitely undermine the power, influence and prestige of the ruling class, who were also the religious leaders.

Secondly, Northern Nigerian leaders who succeeded the leaders of the Fulani jihad later formed a political party to represent their interests in the federal republic (i.e. the Northern People's Congress), as Nigeria approached independence from Britain in 1960. But they carried their religious values and expectations into the presumably secular political landscape of the new nation state. Prior to the formation of the nation state, the Fulani jihadists and rulers of Northern Nigeria believed not only that they descended from the Prophet Muhammad, which qualified them to rule as indicated in the quotation above, but also to continue ruling until the time when another reformer by the name MAHDI appears to rejuvenate their theocracy. This belief ruled out the question of receiving consent from the population or renewing their mandate to rule regularly. The two points made above are supported by the following quotation:

Sardauna, Ahmadu Bello, praise to Allah,

Descendant of the saint, Usman, who does not sleep,

The high-ranking one, Sir Ahmadu Bello, is the light,

The Alhaji [pilgrim returned from Mecca] who removes the darkness of hypocrisy.

We pray the Glorious God, the King in truth,

NPC [Northern People's Congress] may it have mastery over Nigeria.

For the sake of Sidi 'Abd al-Qadir al-Jilani,[1]

Your rule will last until the appearance of Mahdi.

(cited in Hiskett, 1973: 163)

Sardauna was the leader of the NPC (the Northern People's Congress, the political party that represented the interest of the Hausa-Fulani Muslim oligarchy of Northern Nigeria during the 1950s as Nigeria approached independence from Britain. It can be seen that the situation in Northern Nigeria was one in which the combination of political and religious power and authority made hero and personality worship an integral part of the political landscape. The leaders were conceptualized as never making any mistake, and were never to be publicly criticized. To question the validity or legitimacy of the actions of the leaders or to dispute their position on anything was the same as revolting against one's religion or the will of God.

---

1   Sidi 'Abd al - Qadir al - Jilani traces his descent to Prophet Muhammad. Usman Dan Fodio, the leader of the Islamic jihad that took place in Northern Nigeria from 1804 to 1810 traces his descent to Sidi 'Abd al - Qadir al - Jilani and therefore ultimately to the Prophet Muhammad. Consequently all influential politicians from Northern Nigeria who trace their descent to Usman Dan Fodio, e.g., Sardauna of Sokoto, Sir Ahmadu Bello who later became the Premier of Northern Nigerian government in the 1950s and the first republic i.e., from 1963, also indirectly claim blood relations to the Prophet Muhammad. In this respect, politics in Northern Nigeria becomes inextricably connected to religion, in so far as the core of the Hausa-Fulani oligarchy claims special relationship to the origin of Islam.

Though there have been some changes, this situation by and large remains the same for most ordinary people in Northern Nigeria even today. In this respect, the Islamic religion becomes central to any program aimed at promoting social change and development in Northern Nigeria because it has a strong influence over the methods used to legitimize the existing social structure and resist any desirable program of social change. However, Islam is not unique in being viewed here as a force that has served to hold back social change; in medieval Europe Christianity was used in the same way (Bloch, 1961).

The difference in the nature of Islam in Northern Nigeria and Malaysia demonstrates how, even though the spread of Islam from the Hejaz region of Saudi Arabia became a world historical process, the manifestation of this one historical process has varied from one region of the world to another (Hitti, 1940). This variation can be explained by many factors, most of which are beyond the scope of this study, but one point is clear. The pre-existing situation intersects with new ideas, institutions and individual actions to give birth to something unique. Islam did not spread in the same way all over the world and did not encounter the same conditions everywhere in the world. Furthermore, Islamic religion, like many other religions, in its long historical trajectory of evolution has had many phases of variation even within the same country. Thus, in addition to its variation across different regions of the world within the same time frame, Islam has also varied across time within the same spatial location or country. Thus, the spread of Islam can be seen as a global historical process punctuated by many other intervening variables.

Closely related to the local variation in the global spread and manifestation of Islam is an important methodological issue about the meaning of time. The issue clearly brings into focus the analytical distinction between the objective meaning of time and its subjective meaning. If we broaden our analytical scope here to view the issue from a global perspective, we find that while the beginning of the 20th century was the era of consolidation and plunder of colonial empires in colonial territories, that same time period meant different things subjectively. For Muslims in Malaysia it was a time for Islam to evaluate itself with a future-oriented perspective and the hope of modernizing society and culture in such a way as to strengthen Islam *vis-à-vis* Christianity and Western civilization, which colonialism represented. However, in Nigeria, the same time was one of trying to appeal to the past, to the heritage of the leaders of the jihad who traced their origin to Prophet Muhammad, in order to perpetuate themselves in power and to protect and guarantee the survival of Islam. Thus Nigerian Muslims felt it was time for Islam to shield itself from external influences, while Malaysian Muslims were willing to methodically and strategically integrate Western science into their worldview.

This varied conception of time and the construction of social reality was shaped by other happenings in their geographical and social environment. European capital had invested heavily in Malaya, transforming the society beyond anything that the Malay people and their leaders imagined or anticipated. Furthermore, other ethnic groups such as Chinese and Indians had migrated to Malaya *en masse*, creating a niche for themselves, superior to that of the Malays, in the Malayan economy. Such factors helped to convince the Malay people that the way forward was to change in a purposeful and meaningful direction in order to develop rather than preserve or conserve society. The new social order convinced them that much in their traditional society could not compete with foreign ideas, innovations and institutions. The colonial government introduced better administrative organization which undermined the power of Malay rulers.

On the other hand, developments in broader Nigerian society during the colonial period tended to give security to the emirs of Northern Nigeria. Not only were they protected by the British, but the British also convinced them that they were a superior race with a more advanced civilization than that of Southern Nigeria (Lugard, 1929). Some of the emirs became as powerful as the British residents, such that the British resident could not accomplish anything without their cooperation. The native authority system was considered most successful in Northern Nigeria with its success due to the pre-existing structure of government established after the Islamic Jihad of 1804. Furthermore, even the colonial office in London was protective of Northern Nigerian emirates. Thus the emirs of Northern Nigeria felt very secure and saw no need to change. Indeed, they expected other Nigerian people to continuously accommodate to their ways. Consequently, they did not see any reason or need to critically re-examine their social structure and religious theology in terms of its relevance to contemporary and future challenges. By shielding themselves from the agents and forces of social change, they appeared to believe that things would remain the same indefinitely.

Northern Nigerian Muslims did not begin to seriously realize their 'relative lag' in modern development until the 1950s when, because of social and political developments after the Second World War, the liquidation of colonial empires became inevitable. But, while Southern Nigeria was relatively prepared for this due to the social changes they had accepted (or that were forced on them) much earlier under colonial rule, Northern Nigeria had to start almost afresh in the 1950s in order to prepare herself institutionally for a modern democratic government and to grasp the processes of the emerging new social order.

Religion and Economic Development

My main concern in this section is to document how religious values, beliefs, ethics, and behaviour contribute in facilitating economic entrepreneurship, economic development, social change and political stability. On the other hand, religion may promote political instability, maintain the status quo, and even slow down the process of economic development. Religion fits into this discussion in two broad ways: first, in how state elites use it to promote social change, particularly economic development, thereby legitimizing their regimes and, secondly, in how social groups in civil society can use religion to shape voting behavior, outcomes of political party contests, and the kind of public policies that elected state officials are able to formulate and implement. In the remainder of this chapter I focus only on the first part of this discussion.

I first begin by demonstrating some of the classic evidence in the sociological literature on the role of religion in shaping both the social structure of a society and the perpetuation or changing of the socio-economic order. Secondly, I provide evidence of empirical research from Indonesia, which illustrates the intricate nature of the relationship between religion and economic development. Using Nigeria as a backdrop, I show how one important way the regime of Prime Minister Mahathir Mohamad of Malaysia transformed his country economically and socially was by consistently evangelizing against traditional Islam and attempting to reform it.

Weber was fascinated by the process of rationalization taking place in Western Europe. It was evident to Weber that there was a clear break between feudal Europe, which emphasized traditionalism, and capitalist Europe, which emphasized instrumental rationality as an integral element of both social structure and social processes (Kalberg, 1994; Weber, 1958). Traditionalism made people have fixed and standardized preferences, with established ways of attaining them. Rationality, on the other hand, entailed constant weighing of cost and benefits and assessing of the best means of achieving the end using the most efficient technical means possible. As Birnbaum asserted:

> The application of the canon of rationality unloosed an intrinsically dynamic force in economic behavior. A given producer was no longer obliged to confine his activities to a limited sphere, if he could maximize gain in another one. The effects of this continuous calculation of mean-ends relationships were experienced in all other aspects of capitalist society as well: rationality, so destructive of precedent, could hardly be confined to economic life. It gave a decisive cast to the entire modern cultural ethos.

> (Birnbaum, 1953: 4)

Weber's fascination with the study of the process of increasing rationalization in western society was empirically illustrated by his study of the evolution of capitalism in Western European society (1958). In pursuing this theoretical agenda, Weber traced the origin of this new economic rationality to the religion and ethics practiced by certain ascetic Protestant sects. It is in this respect that religious worldviews and ethics become an integral part of the process of economic development. The central question about the relationship between capitalist economic development and religious beliefs, values, and ethics, which is my main interest here, is articulated by Nevaskar as follows:

> Capitalism rests on the inclination of men to adopt certain types of practical rational conduct. Since the magical and religious notions, as well as the ethical ideas of duty based upon them, have influenced the conduct of all men in the past, Weber reasoned that religious ideas may also have influenced the development of the present Western economic system ... because rationalization played a central role in Western capitalism, Weber proposed to investigate the influence of religion on its development.

> (Nevaskar, 1971: 5-6)

Once we accept the theoretical premise outlined by Nevaskar above then we can extend the insight by generally studying whether or not there exist similar sorts of facilitating value and ethical factors for capitalist development embedded in the religious beliefs of non-Western people. Indeed, following Weber's seminal work, several studies have been conducted in developing countries in order to examine the relationship between religious beliefs, values, and ethics on the one hand and behavioral conduct in general on the other. The evidence strongly supports the existence of the functional equivalent of the Protestant ethic.[2]

Although strong evidence also exists concerning the relationship between religious asceticism and instrumental rationality in non-Christian religion which, as in the West, had promoted capitalist development (albeit at rudimentary level), Martindale, commenting on Nevaskar's study of the Jains of India and the Quakers of America, sounds a word of warning:

> In the case of neither is it necessary to assume that their religiosity was exclusively caused by their economic practices or their economic practices exclusively caused by their religiosity. However, that these two components of their life styles were linked stands beyond any question. This linkage appears to have developed in a spiral of mutual reinforcement over time, increasing the solidarity and effectiveness of the respective sub groups within the context of their wider societies.

(Martindale, 1971: xx)

Martindale raises a methodological question which, in effect, warns of equating correlation with causation.

Of particular interest to this comparative study is research by Geertz (1963) undertaken in Indonesia and exploring the relationship between religious values, or values in general, and economic transformation in late developing societies. He discovered a close association between religious values and economic entrepreneurship in two rural towns of Indonesia, but with contrasting trajectories that can be summarized in two concepts: *Home economicus* and *Homo politicus*. Geertz (1963) was interested in unraveling the process of change from a *'bazaar economy'* to a *'firm economy'*. The bazaar economy was characterized by fragmented and disconnected person-to-person transactions while the firm economy was characterized by trade and industrial activities taking place within corporate institutions that were impersonal in how they organized production and distribution. A major finding of the first study carried out in Modjokuto, Java, Indonesia, was his discovery of how reformist Muslims played a decisive role in the economic transformation of the town based on their ascetic religious ethic, which was similar to the Christian Protestant ethic that Weber discovered in Europe. Geertz found that for the reformist Muslims, it was a source of pride to work hard, to dress and eat simply, and to avoid large ceremonial expenditures. They placed strong value on individual effort or 'raising oneself by one's own bootstraps'. Geertz asserted that the ethic of the reformist Muslim group had 'in abundance the classic free enterprise virtue of the rational pursuit of self-interest' (Geertz, 1963: 126). He further maintained that in Modjokuto, the process of economic development was 'at least in part religiously motivated [and a] generally disesteemed group of small shopkeepers and petty

---

2   See Kennedy (1962) for a study on the Parsis, Pieris (1969) for documentation on Sikhism, Nevaskar (1971) on the Jains of India, Nafziger (1971) on the Quakers of America and Bellah (1971) for the case of Japan.

manufactures [was] rising out of a traditionalized trading class' (Geertz, 1963: 50). Geertz provided ample evidence showing the involvement of this religious reformist group in the burgeoning commercial and manufacturing business of Modjokuto.

While the experience of this Muslim reformist group clearly reflects an equivalent Protestant work ethic, the second example demonstrates how ruling elites can use their position of influence in combination with religious beliefs to initiate the process of structural change in an economy. In Tabanan, another Indonesian rural town studied by Geertz, the social composition and value orientation of the entrepreneurial social group was quite different from that of Modjokuto. In this case the entrepreneurial group was made up of local people of aristocratic status, but their goal was not transforming a bazaar economy to a firm economy. Rather, their aim was to readjust an agrarian society. The aristocratic reformers of Tabanan were Hindu and, unlike the Muslim reformist sect, they belonged to the mainstream Hindu religious traditions and, in cultural terms, were therefore a model of conformity. The town of Tabanan was a palace town with an aristocratic descent line that existed for more than five centuries. The nobility was transformed into a class of civil administrators by the Dutch during the colonial period, but it still maintained its economic ascendancy and privileges as a noble social group. When new economic opportunities arose later in the area of trade and industry, the religiously conservative economic and political elite enlisted the help of the bulk of the peasant population to mobilize capital and labour in order to secure the wherewithal to float large-scale corporate enterprises.

From Geertz's two case studies in Indonesia, we can raise critical questions about the relationship between religious or ideological beliefs and values on the one hand and economic development on the other. First, Geertz's study suggests how difficult it is to isolate one factor and assume it is the only one that can be responsible for economic development. It is always a combination of factors and processes. Secondly, we cannot also say that there is a direct immutable relationship between a particular form of religious ideology (reformist or conservative) and the propensity to engage in entrepreneurial economic activities. Thus while it is definitely true that ideological factors shape the process of economic development, it is difficult to totally isolate economic relations from the workings of other social processes in society. Thirdly, the study suggests that the same role (e.g., mobilization of capital) can be performed by different institutions, private individuals or political elites (Gerschenkron, 1962). Fourthly, economic transformation can come through a group-focused approach (i.e., homo-politicus) engineered by political elites on behalf of a national population, or through an individual-focused approach (i.e., homo-economicus), as was the case with Puritan groups during the rise of capitalism in Western Europe. The example from Tabanan represents a group-focused approach while the example from Modjokuto represents the classical free-enterprise approach which is more individual-focused.

All the above suggest strongly that religion cannot be assigned one role across historical time and space. The preceding statement is also buttressed by more contemporary research on religion in society. For instance, Wuthnow (1980) identified six broad ways in which contemporary religious movements could be conceptualized *vis-à-vis* social change. The six types are: revitalization, reformation, military, counter-reform, accommodation and sectarianism. Similarly, after surveying a large number of comparative historical studies on how religion is used for political legitimation, Lincoln (1985) identified four ideal-type categories of religious legitimation. These are: religion of status quo, religion of resistance, religion of revolution and religion of counter-revolution. The existence of each of these will have a different implication for economic development and cultural change.

Similarly, in a review article by Billings and Shaunna (1994), one can deduce five ways in which religion shapes public policy in the contemporary world. First, it influences the legitimacy of certain public policies by sanctioning them; secondly, it influences the shaping of political constituencies, coalitions and the levels of political participation of people in elections; thirdly, religious groups and organizations may help people to see the connection between conservative religious beliefs and public policy; fourthly, religious political mobilization can produce mass cognitive restructuring and the reorientation of people's mindsets, predisposing them to support or oppose certain public policies, and, finally, in developing societies in particular, religion assumes a very strong capacity when it becomes the cultural medium of political protest by marginalized cultural groups against internal colonialism or against external colonialism by subordinated national groups.

These are by no means the only ways religion shapes public policy, but they serve my purpose here in drawing attention to the strong connection between religion and the process of economic development. Since space does not permit me to raise some comparative issues concerning how religion in society impacts the state in Malaysia and Nigeria, I will therefore end this section of the chapter by showing how Malaysia's ruling elite differed from Nigeria's in the way it used religion to legitimize itself and the goals it set for the nation.

Prime Minister Mahathir's critique of traditional Islam started in the early 1970s with his publication of *The Malay Dilemma* (1970). This continued in his second book *The Challenge* (1986). In addition to this, Mahathir has consistently sought to clarify his view of what Islamic religion should be through his public speeches during his tenure as Prime Minister. Some of the key elements in Mahathir's critique of traditional Islam are: first, to change the categories of thinking of his people; knowing fully how Islam is the most important identity of the traditional Malay person, he needed to undermine traditional Islam and replace it with modern Islam. Secondly, he has recognised that religion could be used to either promote desirable change or for reactionary purposes. He detested Malay Muslim groups that used Islam for reactionary reasons thus preventing people from participating in the modern sector of society. Thirdly, in his critique of traditional Islam, Mahathir emphasizes practical theology in order to convince Malays to change.

He asserted that unless Muslim nations modernize, they will continue to turn to the West for development assistance. Moreover, the survival of Islam as a religion and civilization will be at the mercy of the West. He argued that Islamic civilization lost ground in relation to its initial spectacular accomplishments because conservative Ulamas took control of the interpretation of the scriptures at a certain point in Islamic history and then made the study of areas of knowledge other than Islam sinful (Mahathir bin Mohamad, 1986). Mohamad continued to evangelize his fellow Malays: if for religious reasons they refused to engage in business, and they refused to participate in the modern capitalist economy, they would permanently remain poor employees of Chinese capitalists. Polemically, he asserted that if an atheist was materially more blessed than a Muslim, practical theology would suggest that Islam does not matter for one's life. But he insisted that Islam was not a religion of poor people although its practitioners could decide to practice it in a way that they remain permanently poor (Mahathir bin Mohamad, 1986). In an attempt to generate a modern economy the Malays, all of whom are defined in the Malaysian constitution as Muslims, are offered computer education classes organized and held in rural mosques (Interview, June 1997). Mahathir's type of Islam was one that encouraged Muslims to study modern science and technology and to think scientifically in order to maintain a competitive edge in the modern global market economy.

On the other hand, in the case of Nigeria, the northern-dominated ruling elite primarily structure public policies in ways that protect, and even extend, the interests of their Muslim supporters in the north of the country (Lubeck and Watts, 1994). To some extent, this is the case in Malaysia too. The difference, however, is in how the ruling elites in Nigeria failed to embark on a campaign to change the categories of thinking of the people especially in northern Nigeria where the practice of Islam is even more traditional than in rural Malay society (Hisket, 1973). Since the Northern Nigerian economy lags behind that of Southern Nigeria (Lubeck and Watts, 1994), structuring public policies essentially based on the political concerns and interest of the North means slowing economic development in the South and thus the country overall. Indeed, the crisis of legitimacy of the governments of Generals Buhari, Babangida and Abacha primarily revolved around the fact that within their cabinets all strategic positions were assigned to Northern Nigerians. Babangida narrowly escaped death from a *coup d'etat* carried out as a protest against his cabinet reshuffle of 1989 in which he removed all or most Christians from strategic cabinet positions (Biersteker and Lewis, 1997).

But one of the worst uses of religion by the Nigerian ruling elite occurred during the regime of General Babangida when, in collaboration with others, he unilaterally enrolled Nigeria as a member of the Organization of Islamic Conference (OIC) (Suberu, 1997). The OIC imbroglio decisively threatened the unity of the nation and created a very hostile environment for public policy implementation. The president was distrusted by a large section of the country's population and he lost huge political capital and credibility. The president secretly and unilaterally admitted Nigeria into the OIC in an attempt to revamp its waning legitimacy and popularity in the far Northern part of Nigeria rather than because he had some specific conviction about the issue. In any case, the issue is not whether Nigeria should or should not be a member of the OIC but, rather, how the decision to join the OIC should have been made. By admitting Nigeria into the OIC, Babangida was trying to garner the support of northern Muslims in particular and Muslims of the country in general. Nigeria's case was a classic example of a regime that is bankrupt and incompetent and which could not legitimize itself through unifying public policies that have universal appeal but, by using Islam, it could divide and rule the country. Instead of using Islam in a way that would, among other things, bring desirable change, especially in Northern Nigeria which significantly lags behind in development, the Nigerian ruling elites were satisfied with manipulating religion to divide and rule the country.

In these two cases, we find ruling elites using the same religion in different ways. Rural Muslims in Northern Nigeria constitute a significant proportion of the poor people in the country, and any attempt to transform them and their conditions will have to start with Islam engaging critically with modernity. This is the major challenge that Northern Nigeria faces. Prime Minister Mohamad of Malaysia realized the need to undermine the equilibrium of traditional Islam and therefore effectively embarked on an open campaign to discredit Islam as failing to enable people to live competitively in the modern world of the twenty-first century.[3] Indeed, based on the literature on comparative religion, one can assert that Islam has been used to serve and legitimize different political and development agendas in the contemporary world in much the same way as Christianity (Milton-Edwards, 2004; see also Emerson and Smith, 2000). Meyer clearly articulates the need to see how Islam has been used for either conservative or progressive causes in different societies, at different times and by different types of ruling elite coalitions. She asserted that:

> In some cases, support for returning to the Shari'a could mean that Muslims are calling for the realization of political and economic goals such as honest and democratic government, accountability of public officials, social justice, and the redistribution of wealth, or the establishment of an egalitarian society. In another context, calls for Islamization could signify a pattern of hostile reactions to modernization measures and a commitment to buttressing the patriarchal family, expanding religious instruction in public schools, imposing discriminatory measures on religious minorities and Muslim dissidents, challenging the legality of land reform programs, or preventing women from working and serving in public office.

(Meyer, 1993: 111 cited in Billings and Scott 1994)

---

3   Although, I have provided useful information about Prime Minister Mahathir's critique of traditional Islam, it is not out of place to provide additional material to the assertion I am making here by quoting another of Mahathir's incisive critiques of traditional Islam. He asserted that "If Islam appears rigid and doctrinaire, it is because the learned interpreters make it so. They tended to be harsh and intolerant when interpreting during the hey-day of the Muslim Empires. And they and their followers brook no opposition to their writs once they were made. And so, long after the Muslims have lost their predominant position, long after the world environment has changed, the Muslims were exhorted to adhere to interpretations, which are no longer adequate or relevant or practicable.

What Muslims must do is to go back to the Quran and the genuine 'hadiths', study and interpret them in the context of the present world. It is Allah's will that the world has changed. It is not for man to reverse what has been willed by Allah. The faithful must look for guidance from the teachings of the Quran and 'Hadith' in the present context. Islam is not meant only for 7th Century Arabs. Islam is for all times and for every part of the world. If we Muslims understand this, then there will be less misunderstandings among us. If the non-Muslims appreciate the problems that the Muslims have in trying to adjust to modern changes, then they will not misunderstand Islam and the Muslims as much as they do now. And the world will be a better place if all these misunderstandings are removed" (Mahathir Mohamad, April 16th 1996: 21-22, speech delivered at the Oxford Center for Islamic Studies Oxford, United Kingdom).

Malaysia embarked on a generalized campaign of seeking to change sociocultural values and put significant emphasis on the need to transform traditional Islam while Nigeria has done neither. This distinction between the role of Islam in relation to economic development has significant implications for the cognitive orientation of public bureaucracies in the two countries. While public bureaucracies are formal organizations, the social processes going on within them as organizations are significantly shaped by the social environment, within which religious value play a key role.

Conclusion

Samuel Huntington (1984) argues that, in order to promote successful economic development and evolution of modern democratic institutions in the Third World, there are certain critical factors that have to be in place and which also play a decisive role. The factors are: historical choices made by Third World political elites; a socially differentiated social structure, i.e. civil society groups such as an autonomous bourgeoisie; the existence of a market economy; and favourable regional conditions. Finally, he stressed the role of cultural context and, under this rubric, he specifically stressed the role of religion in shaping political culture and development. He saw Protestantism as having the most favourable condition for the nurturing and thriving of democracy and economic development. On the other hand, the influence of Catholicism on democracy and economic development is at best moderate and delayed *vis-à-vis* Protestantism. He though that Hindu and Shinto culture do not play any negative role on democracy and, by implication, economic development. But he vehemently asserts that Islam, Confucianism and Buddhism are authoritarian (i.e. oriental despotism), and therefore anti-democratic and, by implication, serve to hinder modern development. He described Islam as a *'consummatory religious culture'* because it collapses the institution of religion and politics.

Huntington tries to provide an encompassing and universal generalization of the relationship between religion, politics and economic development. But the discussion in this chapter calls for greater caution about such generalizations. The chapter asserts that the same religion can have different cultural meanings and impacts on societies depending on time, historical context, geography, class and ethnicity. As I asserted above, no person familiar with the use of Protestant Christianity in the Southern part of the United States before and even after the Civil War and Reconstruction will deny that Christianity played a decisive and repressive role in legitimizing the state apparatus and social structures. Thus instead of identifying certain religions, ossifying their characteristics and generalizing about their existential reality across time and space, it is suggested here that we should pay attention to how geography, locality, class, ethnicity and historical contexts make the beliefs and practices of any religion contingent phenomena.

References

Andaya, B.W. and Leonard Y.A. (1982) *A History of Malaysia*, Basingstoke: Macmillan.

Biersteker, T. and Peter M.L. (1997) 'The Rise and Fall of Structural Adjustment in Nigeria', in Larry Diamond, Larry, Anthony Kirk-Green, Anthony, Oyediran, Oyeleye (eds) *Transition Without End: Nigerian Politics and Civil Society Under Babangida*, Boulder, Colorado: Lynne Rienner Publishers.

Billings, Dwight B. and Shaunna L. Scott (1994) 'Religion and Political Legitimacy', *Annual Review of Sociology* 20 173-201.

Birnbaum, N (1953) 'Conflicting Interpretations of the Rise of Capitalism: Marx and Weber', *British Journal of Sociology* 4 (41) 125.

Bloch, Marc (1961) *Feudal Society*, London: Routledge & Kegan Paul.

Crowder, Michael (1968) *West Africa Under Colonial Rule*, London: Huchinson University Library.

Emerson, Michael and Smith, Christian (2000) *Divided By Faith: Evangelical Religion and the Problem of Race in America,* New York: Oxford University Press.

Geertz, C (1963) *Peddlers and Prices: Social Development and Economic Change in Two Indonesian Towns*, Chicago and London: The University of Chicago Press.

Gerschenkron, Alexander (1962) *Economic Backwardness in Historical Perspective*, New York: Harvard University Press.

Hiskett, Mervyn (1973) *The Sword of Truth: The Life and Times of Shehu Usman Dan Fodio*, New York: Oxford University Press.

Huntington, Samuel P (1984) 'Will More Countries Become Democratic?', *Political Science Quarterly* 99 193-218.

Ifeka C. and G.T. Stride (1969) *Peoples and Empires of West Africa: West Africa in History 1000 - 1800.*

Kalberg, Stephen (1994) *Max Weber's Comparative Historical Sociology*, Chicago: The University of Chicago Press.

Kennedy, J.G. (1966) 'Peasant Society and the Image of the Limited Good', *American Anthropologist* 68 1212-1225.

Kennedy, R. F. (1962) 'The Protestant Ethic and the Parsis', *American Journal of Sociology* 68 (1) 11-20.

Lincoln, B. (ed.) (1985) *Religion, Rebellion, Revolution*, London: Macmillan.

Lubeck, Paul M. and Watts, Michael J (1994) 'An Alliance of Oil and Maize? The Response of Indigenous and State Capital to Structural Adjustment in Nigeria', in Bearman, Bruce J and Leys, Colin (eds) *African Capitalists in African Development,* Boulder, Colorado: Lynne Rienner Publishers, Inc.

Lugard, Flora (1929), Quoted in 'Great Britain and France in Northern Africa', *The Round Table Volume* 19(76).

Mahathir bin Mohamad (1970) *The Malay Dilemma*, Kuala Lumpur: Times International.

Mahathir bin Mohamad (1986) *The Challenge.*, Kuala Lumpur: Pelanduk Publications.

Mahathir bin Mohamad (1994) 'Improving Tolerance Through Better Understanding', in Alhabshi, Seyd Othman and Hassan, Nik Mustapha Nik (eds) *Islam and Tolerance*, Kuala Lumpur: Institute of Islamic Understanding Malaysia (IKIM).

Martindale, D (1971) *Foreword to Capitalists Without Capitalism*, by B. Nevaskar Westport, Connecticut: Greenwood Publishing Corporation.

Milner, Anthony (1995) *The Invention of Politics in Colonial Malaya*, Hong Kong: Cambridge University Press.

Milton-Edwards, Beverley (2004) *Islam & Politics in the Contemporary World*, Malden, Massachusetts: Polity Press.

Moore, Wilbert E (1963) *Social Change*, Englewood Cliff, New Jersey: Prentice Hall, Inc.

Murphy, Alexander B (1991) 'Regions as Social Constructs: The Gap Between Theory and Practice', *Progress in Human Geography* 15(1) 23-35.

Nafziger, E. W (1971) 'Indian Entrepreneurship: A Survey, in Kilby, Peter (ed.) *Entrepreneurship and Economic Development*, New York: The Free Press.

Nevaskar, B. (1971) *Capitalists Without Capitalism: The Jains of India and the Quakers of the West*, Westport, Connecticut: Greenwood Publishing Corporation.

Pieris, R. (1969) *Studies in the Sociology of Development*, Rotterdam: Rotterdam University Press.

Suberu, Rotimi T (1997) 'Religion and Politics: A View From the South', in Diamond, Larry, Kirk-Green, Anthony and Oyediran, Oyeleye (eds) *Transition Without End: Nigerian Politics and Society Under Babangida*, Boulder, Colorado: Lynne Rienner Publishers.

Weber, Max (1958) *The Protestant Ethic and the Spirit of Capitalism*, Upper Saddle River, New Jersey: Prentice Hall.

White, Jeremy (1981) *Central Administration in Nigeria, 1914-1948: The Problem of Polarity*, London: Frank Cass and Company.

White, Jeremy (1981) *Central Administration in Nigeria, 1914-1948: The Problem of Polarity*, London: Irish Academic Press, Dublin Frank Cass & Company.

Wuthnow, Robert (1980) 'World Order and Religious Movements', in Bergensen, A (ed.) *Studies of the Modern World System*, New York: Academic.

Chapter 11

Young Muslim Men's Experiences of Local Landscapes after 11 September 2001

Peter E. Hopkins

Introduction

The significance of the global geopolitical order, the idea of the nation-state, issues about borders and concerns around security and surveillance have been the focus of much discussion in human geography since the events of 11 September 2001 in New York and Washington (see for example, Anderson, 2002; Flint, 2002; 2003a; 2003b; Lyon, 2003). Several journals have also offered space to editorial board members to record their thoughts, emotions and reactions to the events (Mitchell, 2002; Qvorturp, 2002; Smith, 2001). There have been recollections of 'Shock. Anger. Fear' (Flint, 2002: 77), as well as reflections on the tensions and emotions of teaching students in the days after the events (Mitchell, 2002). Neil Smith (2001) commented on the ways in which the events and aftermath led to a struggle over various scales, and noted that, 'amidst the discursive hysteria after September 11, the silences are as important as the frenzy. National indignation fastened on the World Trade Center, while the destruction of one wing of the Pentagon fell from focus.' Certain issues remained silenced and fell from view, whilst others remained the focus of attention. This is an important point because the opinions and reactions of key geographers have been documented in various journal articles and books (some of which are cited above). However, the responses and experiences of certain social groups, apart from a few notable exceptions, appear marginalised in this growing literature.

The exceptions to this marginalisation include the experiences of racism, community responses and media biases outlined by research participants in Canada (Khalema and Wannas-Jones, 2003), and the 'feelings of sadness, fear, victimisation, anger, and sometimes blame' amongst Muslim students attending universities in New York (Peek, 2003: 282). Apart from this, the everyday experiences of people in the days, weeks and months after the events appear marginalised in the literature. There is therefore a need to include the voices of various groups, including Muslims, in this developing literature. Alongside this, the geographies and identities of young Muslim men in general are usually silenced, often unheard and frequently distorted. The majority of research about Muslims explores the experiences of women (e.g. Bowlby, Lloyd Evans and Mohammad 1999, Dwyer, 1998), and young Muslim men are often demonised as part of the 'Asian gang' (Alexander, 2000). Furthermore, few studies have considered the significance of religion, race and racism from a Scottish perspective, with Scotland often implicitly associated with whiteness.

This chapter challenges these inadequacies in the literature by building on a research project about the geographies and identities of young Muslim men, aged 16-25, who live in post-devolution urban Scotland (Hopkins, 2005) and, in so doing, seeks to explore the experiences of the young men following the events of 11 September 2001 in New York and Washington. This project involved consulting young Muslim men through eleven focus group discussions and twenty-two interviews, in which the main topics of conversation encouraged research participants to think about their local communities, Scotland and Scottishness, as well as thinking about being a young man and being a Muslim. All of the interviews took place in two contrasting urban communities in Scotland, Pollokshields in Glasgow and South Edinburgh. Overall, over seventy young Muslim men participated in this project, and all of their names have been changed in order to protect their confidentiality and anonymity. The majority of the participants were born in Scotland, identified with a Pakistani heritage and were reasonably middle-class compared with the samples of other project about young Muslim men (e.g. Alexander, 2000, Archer, 2003). Many of the discussions involved the young men recollecting their experiences and emotions after 11 September 2001.

Everyday Local Lives

The crisis unleashed by the events of 11 September is one that is global and all-encompassing. It is global in the sense that it binds many different countries into conflict, most obviously the USA and parts of the Muslim world. It is all-encompassing in that, more than any other international crisis yet seen, it affects a multiplicity of life's levels, political, economic, cultural and psychological (Halliday, 2002, p. 31).

Although the events and aftermath of 11 September 2001 can be seen as international, 'global' and 'all-encompassing', they also influenced various aspects of individuals' everyday lives including, and in particular, the negotiations and interactions that are important to daily routines and practices. These everyday experiences are often taken-for-granted and so may appear dull and uninteresting. However, the everyday 'provides the unquestioned background of meaning for the individual' (Eyles, 1989: 103), and so grants researchers access to deeper understandings of people's lives. Despite this, 'it is apparent that many human geographers have neglected the everyday in their enthusiasm to document the exceptional, the new and the exotic' (Holloway and Hubbard, 2001: 36). In particular, accounts of the geographies of everyday life have not adequately reflected on issues of masculinity and religious identities, and the intersection between these, in the context of local experiences. The events that Halliday (2002) alludes to have often had the most negative impact on the everyday lives of those who are perceived to be of Muslim faith, as they(Hopkins 2007a) increasingly 'became the victims of discrimination, harassment, racial and religious profiling, and verbal and physical assault' (Peek, 2003: 271).

My work shows that Muslims in Scotland have also experienced increasing levels of harassment, violence and scrutiny since 11 September 2001, particularly during the months shortly following the events. In order to demonstrate this, I focus upon the young men's negotiations of local spaces and networks, such as the mosque and peer-group (including sport and leisure time) and, in particular, their use and management of the street. In doing so, I highlight the racist exclusion that the young men experienced, along with the ways in which the anchor points of their everyday local negotiations changed as a result of their often intense and anxious circumstances and experiences. In particular, the events and aftermath of 11 September 2001 have influenced the markings on the young men's bodies, the character of the street, the engagement between the two sites or sights, and the young men's sense of self and community.

The Muslim boys in Archer's (2003: 88) research 'talked about hanging around with their friends, playing football, going shopping, watching TV and listening to music'. Similarly, the young Muslim men in this research talked about their peer group, playing football, going to the mosque, and hanging about. Consider Saeed's account:

Saeed: Yeah, wake up in the morning, normal kind of thing, and I do my morning prayer and then I might go back to sleep, that's at about four or five in the morning ... and then I wake up again about seven or eight o'clock, have breakfast and get ready to go to work ... and then go home, and then either go home for prayer or go to the mosque for prayer, sit with the family, have dinner, talk and do things and then it's time to go back to bed. I try to split my time between work and family and mosque ... and at night I do my night prayer and then go to sleep and start again in the morning ... so a normal day is like that.

(Interview, Edinburgh, 14th June 2002)

Saeed's comments demonstrate that the key anchor points for his everyday local negotiations are the home and family, the mosque and his workplace. All of the young men consulted in this research experience these local frameworks in a range of diverse ways and their accounts highlight how they use, manage and resist these networks, all of which contribute to their experiences of local landscapes. In particular, the young men discussed their peer groups and leisure spaces and times, and the mosque as key frameworks in their negotiations of local life (alongside the home and school / work). For the remainder of this chapter, I focus on the importance of the mosque, peer-group, and leisure and sport in the young men's everyday local lives highlighting the contribution that these make to the young men's senses of identity. After this, I focus on the spaces of the street to highlighting how these local anchor points have changed since 11 September 2001.

Sport, Peer-group and Mosque

During the focus group and interview discussions with young Muslim men, their local lives, everyday activities and negotiations of the spaces of the local community were regularly discussed. The peer-group, sport and leisure activities and the mosque were regular features of such discussions. These local anchor points are important reference points for the young men's constructions of their Muslim identities and masculinities, and to their senses of personhood and belonging.

There are strong linkages between sport, in particular football, and the performance of hegemonic masculinity (Connell, 2000, O'Donnell and Sharpe, 2000). Football is 'understood by many boys not only as a masculine activity but as something which make boys masculine', and so helps them to emphasise gender differences (Pattman *et al.*, 1998, in O'Donnell and Sharpe, 2000: 18). Sport is therefore a key activity in the social construction of a masculine identity, and as 'a form of physical culture, sport has a particular corporeal resonance in making visible those aspects of social life that often remain hidden and submerged in other domains' (Carrington, 2004: 2). This research project found that football and cricket were important in the formation of youthful Muslim masculinities. The significance of sports, football and cricket in particular, in the lives of young Muslim men was recognised as an aspect of their everyday lives that had a direct impact upon their local negotiations. Shafqat states that "football is my life" (Interview, 17th June 2003) and similarly when I asked Ishmail about the kind of things he does on a daily basis, he noted that he likes to "play football and hang about" (Interview, Glasgow, 12th July 2002). Faruk notes that "guys tend to be out playing football and not really giving a fuck generally" (Interview, Glasgow, 25th June 2003). Many boys tend to regard sport as synonymous with being masculine, and so gain respect for participating in aggressive sporting activities (Furlong and Cartmel, 2001). The young men's accounts suggest that sport is important to their everyday senses of possessing an appropriate masculine identity and a significant aspect of being a young Muslim man.

Louise Archer (2003: 86) notes that 'the boys constructed 'locally' hegemonic masculine identities by associating Muslim masculinity with power, privilege, 'being the boss,' hardness and hyper-heterosexuality' and, to an extent, this exploration of the young men's views highlights similar constructions. Physicality, toughness and sport were important to many of the young men. The majority of the young men acknowledged that their participation in sport and inclination to 'muck about' were important to their sense of identity, feeling of belonging and everyday lives. Participating in sport often involved the young men belonging to loosely defined peer groups and, from many of their accounts, sport is an important aspect of the young men's local frameworks and everyday lives.

Consider Anwar and Sabir's accounts:

Anwar: A typical day in my life would be just like getting up for uni ... I'm at uni ... and then after that just sort of come home, maybe I walk to a friend's house, so I might stay there till later ... go to the cinema and things like that ... then weekends, like some weekends we go out or something, you know ... to a club or something like that.

(Interview, Edinburgh, 17th December 2002)

Sabir:... I'll go to the library. If I've got lectures it's not normally nine o'clock ... when I'm finished there I'll go home, go to my friend's house, watch a DVD or watch a video, play the computer and mess about.

(Interview, Edinburgh, 10th December 2002)

Alongside university, going out or watching TV, Anwar and Sabir both mention visiting or meeting friends as part of their everyday lives. Many of the young men discussed the importance of their friends during interviews, offering them a sense of identity and belonging. The importance of friends to many of the young men is highlighted by the fact that they are willing to travel (frequently) across the city or into the city centre in order to meet up with friends and participate in a range of leisure and sporting activities.

The young men emphasise the importance of sport, peer-group, hanging about and having a laugh in their accounts of their everyday lives, and so the street and the sports pitch are important spaces of the local community for the young men. Alongside this, the mosque is also a key aspect of the young men's local everyday lives, and therefore an important aspect of their Muslim identities. As Saeed mentioned earlier, and as Ifty notes, a strong sense of attachment, belonging and purpose can be obtained through going to mosque:

Ifty: I just like hang around with my friends and that, and have a good time ... maybe watch a film or something like that. I definitely go to mosque ... so I try to go five times a day, but I normally go four times a day at least. I play football ... I love football and cricket so I play quite a bit of that.

(Interview, Glasgow, 16th July 2002)

Not all of the young men talked about attending mosque in this way. Most aspired to attend mosque and pray five times a day, however educational and employment commitments often prevented them from doing this. However, regardless of whether or not they actually visit the mosque, the young men's religious faith has an important place in their everyday lives, be this real or imagined. Linking back to the discussion about the significance of peer-group, Arif highlights the importance of having Muslim friends and signals that having access to other people who share his religious faith is an important aspect of his Muslim identity. Alongside this, Arif also highlights the diversity within the Muslim community:

Arif: Well, the thing is, Muslims like other people, have differences of opinion, views. However, we have this common goal, this common belief, so you can put these differences aside so that you can still get on with each other. But with non-Muslims, if you have a difference of opinion, it is difficult to then form a relationship in other areas ... so, with Muslims, we can be more flexible ... I actually spend more time with Muslims after starting university because I came from an area that had fewer Muslims. It had its advantages and disadvantages. Obviously the disadvantages are that I didn't have people that I could get really close to, and see things from a similar view. However, it made me realise the importance of being a good Muslim, because people may possibly be looking and questioning your actions. Coming to university, especially being away from home, I think it is important that you, even if you don't have lots of Muslim friends, you should at least have one or two ... so at the end of the day you have someone you can go to for help.

I mean I'm not saying that you can't go to non-Muslims, but perhaps it would be better going to a Muslim because you will have similar goals at the end of the day.

(Focus Group, Edinburgh 30th April 2003)

In these narratives about the importance of peer group and mosque, most of the statements are gendered, and it is clear that the mosque is experienced as a masculine space. Mohammed noted during an interview, "... well, one thing is that men have to go to the mosque and pray, but the mosque for the women is in the home" (Interview, Edinburgh, 16th May 2002). As well as emphasising the connections between women and home, Mohammed is also claiming the mosque as a space for men. The mosque and the peer group are therefore important to the young men in their construction of Muslim identities and masculinities.

Although participating in sport and leisure activities and attending mosque are important in the construction of the young men's everyday lives, they also serve different purposes in terms of the construction of the young men's religious identities and masculinities. For example, Latif articulates his everyday life in the context of how it differs from other young men his age, and so places it in opposition to the lives of young white men:

Latif: I do typical stuff like sports and like clubs after school, and like going out with my mates. I would say that what isn't typical is the fact that I pray five times a day, and I follow the five pillars of Islam, you know what I mean.

(Interview, Edinburgh, 25th March 2003)

The fact that he identifies as a Muslim and so tries to pray regularly and follow the pillars of Islam makes him different from non-Muslim young men his age. In this respect, Latif sees certain aspects of his daily routine, such as sport and 'going out with my mates' as according with the hegemonic (white) youth culture, whilst his religious faith and practice are part of a marginalised youth culture and so make him not 'typical'. It could also be that Latif is responding to what he perceives as my whiteness, and so is making assumptions about what my everyday life would have been like when I was his age. However, Latif's sentiments suggest to me that, whilst participating in sport and leisure activities with your peer group and attending the mosque (or having it as a focal point) are important to the young men, following their religion and thinking about the mosque speak to their religious identities, and the peer group identifies them with their age group and masculinity.

Exploring the everyday lives of young Muslim men may conjure up images of the 'Asian gang' (Alexander, 2000), which sees young Muslim men as the 'ultimate 'Other' ... undesired, irredeemable, alien', however, I think it is important to note that this did not feature in the young men's account of their everyday lives. A couple of the young men mentioned that nobody "messed with them", yet there was never any mention of gang membership or violence in their articulations of their everyday lives. I was put in touch with one young Muslim man, having being warned by a local voluntary sector worker that he was a "problem" and "involved with gangs". His account of his everyday life did not mention such activities, and my conversations with other local people as well as other young Muslim men did not include his name being mentioned as a 'trouble-maker'. Perhaps the young men did not tell me about their 'Asian gang', however, I am inclined to agree with Alexander, (2000: 251) when she states that the young men she spoke to 'do not, in any way, constitute 'a gang''.

Under Scrutiny After 11 September 2001

So far I have highlighted the importance of mosque, peer-group, and sport and leisure in the young men's everyday local lives and the ways in which these anchor points relate to the construction of the young men's masculine and religious identities. It is also important to think about where these interactions take place. The mosque is often a purpose-built religious centre, and some Muslims choose to conduct prayers in a large house or flat. The young men may visit local sports centres, football pitches or clubs in order to participate in leisure activities. Participation in activities such as visiting the mosque, going to the sports centre, and visiting friends nearly always requires the young men to negotiate the streets of their local community. This may involve walking along the street or getting the bus to the mosque, crossing roads and winding down side streets to a friend's house or parking the car and walking along the road to the entrance of the sports centre. Highlighting the significance of the geography associated with the young men's everyday local negotiations makes it clear that the young men have had to negotiate radically transforming urban geographies since the events of 11 September 2001, and these changes have impacted most directly on the young men's experiences and negotiations of the street.

Whilst the division of public and private space has been recognised by geographers as problematic (see for example, Staeheli, 1996; Bondi, 1998), the street is often perceived to be a public space that is inclusive, democratic and so can be used as a site of protest and political action. However, the street is also a potentially feared space that needs to be policed, and there is ongoing debate about the end of public space (Mitchell, 2003). As Nicholas Fyfe (1998: 1) notes 'streets are the terrain of social encounters and political protest, sites of domination and resistance, places of pleasure and anxiety'. Much of the work about the ways in which the street is constantly under surveillance and control has focused either on various forms of technological surveillance such as CCTV (see for example Fyfe and Bannister, 1998), or on the subtle exclusion and marginalisation of people who are deemed to be out of place (Holloway and Hubbard, 2001). Such perceived transgressions can create 'a moral panic about a particular group or practice which acts as a trigger to new forms of social and spatial control' (Holloway and Hubbard, 2001: 214), new mechanisms of surveillance and therefore constantly changing experiences of place.

The young men I spoke to saw the street as a place where they are likely to experience racism, harassment and discrimination. Moreover, they suggested that the possibility of this occurring had increased since 11 September 2001. For example, Ifty notes:

Ifty: ... I think that when people see a Muslim walking down the street they think that is good, nice and friendly and things like that, but now I think that there is more racism and things like that...

Peter: So you think that there have been more problems for Muslims since September 11th?

Ifty: Yeah, definitely ... racism has increased; definitely ... there is lots of fighting like white youths and black youths and stuff

(Interview, Edinburgh, 16th July 2002)

Ifty suggests that racism has increased since 11 September 2001, and the street is the place where these experiences are most likely to take place. In particular, it is interesting to highlight that Ifty notes that "when people see a Muslim..." thereby suggesting that Muslims are immediately identifiable according to their physicality, appearance or dress. 'This would suggest that Muslims who openly display markers of their religious identity are more likely to experience exclusion than Muslims who restrict displaying markers of 'Muslimness" (Hopkins, 2004: 263). This also means that people may be mistaken for being Muslims and may suffer as a result of this, and there is evidence to suggest that a range of black and minority ethnic and religious people have been mistakenly identified as Muslims and experienced racism as a result (Scottish Executive, 2002). However, the majority of the young men consulted in this project experienced changes in their local lives, and some even felt compelled to try to mask their Muslim identities. This suggests that it is likely that there has been (and is) a moral panic about Muslim men in public spaces and their potential threat to the order of the street. During one of the focus groups, a couple of the participants mentioned how they had contemplated shaving their beards in order to reduce the extent to which they appeared to look like Muslims. Yet, for some of the young men, keeping a beard is an important part of being a 'proper' Muslim as they strive to follow the example of the Prophet Mohammed. Similarly, Asadullah recalls an incident where he felt isolated, ashamed and embarrassed by his religious faith (Hopkins, 2004: 264):

Asadullah: ... after it, all of these guys started shouting things out of a van at me, saying Osama bin Laden and all that.

(Focus Group, Glasgow, 3rd April 2003)

Asadullah, along with other young men involved in this project, talked about the increasing experiences of racism, discrimination and marginalisation after 11 September 2001. The fear and expectation of experiencing racism, led them to use the streets as little as possible, and this had direct consequences for their access to and use of the mosque, peer-group and leisure activities.

Withdrawal from religious practice was also an action that some of the young men, such as Abdul decided to take.

Ahmed: I think a lot of people stopped going to mosque

Abdul: I used to go with him but I don't now

(Focus Group, Edinburgh, 19th June 2002)

This was not just because of fear of racism, but also because of the threat that many mosques faced following the events of 11 September 2001. For example, the Annandale Street mosque in Edinburgh was firebombed causing £20,000 worth of damage (Hopkins, 2004). Mohammed (Interview, Edinburgh, 16th May 2002) showed me the smashed window of an Edinburgh mosque. Babar (Interview, Glasgow, 24th June 2003) explained that after 11 September 2001, money was regularly stolen from the mosque he attended at university. The sister of Kabir's friend was spat at in the underground (Interview, Edinburgh, 12th December 2002) and Michael recalled eggs being thrown at the central mosque in Glasgow (Focus Group, Glasgow, 3rd April 2003). Overall, the young men either decided to refrain from attending mosque, or had to carefully negotiate the local streets in order to be able to attend the mosque and fulfil an important aspect of their Muslim identities. This may not appear to be a major change to the young men's everyday lives. However, for some of the young men to restrict their use of the mosque may leave them feeling neglected and fragile in an increasingly racist post-September 11 world, especially given the senses of belonging, identity and community that attending the mosque gives them.

As well as restricting their use of the mosque (or having to carefully negotiate their route to the mosque), some of the young men withdrew from social networks that required them to negotiate the local streets to visit friends, youth groups or other activities. Others would only go out into the streets as a group or with family in the hope that a group identity might discourage potential racists. Given the increasing significance of peer group and leisure time in young men's lives (Furlong and Cartmel, 2001), these changes to their everyday routines have had a major impact on their personal identities, political futures and senses of self and community.

It may well be easy to overlook the emotional geographies of the young men's experiences. However, Anderson and Smith (2001: 7) note that 'at particular places and at particular times, there are moments where lives are so explicitly lived through pain, bereavement, elation, anger, love and so on that the power of emotional relations cannot be ignored'. The experiences of racism and exclusion, coupled with fear and apprehension have had, and continue to have, marked emotional and psychological influences on young Muslim men, as well as the wider Muslim community. Consider Kabir's comments:

Kabir: I felt upset, maybe I felt angry, probably, a little bit worried and insecure about what might happen to our community. You know, you worry about what may happen to your own family, and I was walking down the street after and I just didn't feel very safe walking around and it was a terrible feeling where you somehow feel guilty for something that you shouldn't feel guilty about.

(Interview, Edinburgh, 12th December 2002)

Like others, Kabir experienced waves of different emotions after the events of 11 September 2001. The young men recollected their initial feelings of shock and anger; however, the speed at which Muslims were identified as the main threat soon changed the young men's emotions to those of worry, stress and insecurity. Kabir suffers from confusion because he feels guilty for something that he should not be feeling guilty about, and the transcripts of other focus group and interview discussions are littered with comments about the young men's feelings of fear, guilt, anger, stress and tension. In various ways, these reactions led the young men to restrict their use of everyday local frameworks at certain times. In addition, these reactions and restrictions encouraged several of the young men to try to take some responsibility for world events and the influence that these have had on the young men's experiences and the demonisation and radicalisation of their religious faith (Hopkins 2007b).

An important aspect of the young men's construction of appropriate masculinities relates to how they interact and negotiate their peer group's relationships. Other research has noted that young men may be more likely to disclose emotions during individual interviews, yet are more likely to perform a 'macho' masculinity during focus group discussions (Phoenix, Frosh and Pattman, 2003). Although my research involved consulting young men who were older than those in such studies, the emotional accounts of discrimination, racism and victimisation overwhelmingly took place in individual interviews, with the focus groups being left for the less personal aspects about being a young Muslim man in urban Scotland.

Conclusion

In conclusion, this chapter has explored the ways in which the events and aftermath of 11 September 2001 have had a negative influence on the everyday lives of young Muslim men in Scotland. Focusing on the anchor points of the young men's local lives – mosque, peer group and sport and leisure activities – I have demonstrated the importance of these local networks to the construction of the young men's religious and masculine identities, and senses of personhood and belonging. In participating in recreational activities as well as seeking out their peer group and attending mosque, the young men have to frequent the local streets, and it is in such places that they come under scrutiny.

After 11 September 2001, the experience and negotiation of the street changed for the majority of the young Muslim men consulted in this research. Many suffered from increasing levels of racial harassment in the days and weeks following the events. Others felt uneasy about attending their local mosque due to fear of racist attack because their bodies marked them out as different, and others still were anxious about the possibility of the mosque building being attacked. This restriction on the young men's use of the local community has a direct impact upon their emotional geographies, senses of self-esteem and everyday experiences.

It is important to think about whether or not young Muslim men are still experiencing similar levels of racism and harassment? The racism may have decreased slightly since the events of 11 September 2001, however the bombings in London on 7 July 2005 also led to a heightened sense of unease, discomfort and insecurity among young Muslim men. Alongside this, we are still inundated with news reports about the liberation of Iraq, the 'war on terror', and the detention of threatening 'terrorists' who are almost always associated with Islam or assumed to be 'dangerous Muslim men (Archer, 2003: 1). Many young people hear discourses and either use these as a strategic resource against others or feel threatened and marginalised in their attempts to negotiate their local networks. Perhaps more accurate media coverage coupled with campaigning against religious intolerance and racism may help young Muslim men to experience a more tolerant and diverse society in which they can openly negotiate their religious identities.

References

Alexander, C. (2000) *The Asian Gang: ethnicity, identity, masculinity*, Oxford: Berg.

Archer, L. (2003) *Race, Masculinity and Schooling: Muslim Boys and Education*, Maidenhead: Open University Press.

Anderson, J. (2002) 'Borders after 11 September 2001', *Space and Polity* 6(2) 227-232.

Anderson, K. and Smith, S.J. (2001) 'Editorial: Emotional Geographies', *Transactions of the Institute of British Geographers* 26(1) 7-10.

Bondi, L. (1998) 'Gender, Class and Urban Space: Public and Private Space in Contemporary Urban Landscapes', *Urban Geography* 19(3) 160-185.

Bowlby, S. Lloyd Evans, S. and Mohammad, R. (1998) 'The Workplace: Becoming a Paid Worker: Images and Identity', in Skelton, T. and Valentine, G. (eds) *Cool Places: Geographies of Youth Cultures* London: Routledge, pp. 229-248.

Carrington, B. (2004) 'Introduction: Race/Nation/Sport', *Leisure Studies* 23(1) 1-3.

Connell, R. (2000) *The Men and The Boys*, Cambridge: Polity Press.

Dwyer, C. (1998) 'Contested Identities: challenging dominant representations of young British Muslim Women', in Skelton, T. and Valentine, G. (eds) *Cool Places: Geographies of Youth Cultures*, London: Routledge, pp. 5-65.

Eyles, J. (1989) 'The Geography of Everyday Life', Gregory, D. and Walford, R. (eds) *Horizons in Human Geography*, London: MacMillan Education Limited, pp. 102-117.

Flint, C. (2002) 'Initial thoughts towards political geographies in the wake of September 11th 2001: an introduction', *Arab World Geographer*, 4(2) 77-80.

Flint, C. (2003a) 'Political Geography II: Terrorism, Modernity, Governance and Governmentality', *Progress in Human Geography*, 27(1) 97-106.

Flint, C. (2003b) 'Political Geography: context and agency in a multiscalar framework', *Progress in Human Geography*, 27(5) 627-636.

Furlong, A. and Cartmel, F. (2001) *Young People and Social Change: Inidvidualization and risk in late modernity*, Buckingham: Open University Press.

Fyfe, NR. (1998) 'Introduction: Reading the Street', Fyfe, NR. (ed.) *Images of the Street: Planning, Identity and Control in Public Space*, London: Routledge. 1-12.

Fyfe, NR. and Bannister, J. (1998) 'The Eyes Upon The Street': closed-circuit television surveillance and the city', in Fyfe, NR. (ed.) *Images of the Street: Planning, Identity and Control in Public Space*, London: Routledge pp. 254-267.

Halliday, F. (2002) *Two Hours that Shook the World: September 11, 2001: Causes and Consequences*, London: Saqi Books.

Holloway, L. and Hubbard, P. (2001) *People and place: the extraordinary geographies of everyday life*, Harlow: Pearson Education Limited.

Hopkins, PE. (2004) 'Young Muslim men in Scotland: inclusions and exclusions', *Children's Geographies* 2(2) 257-272.

Hopkins, PE. (2005) *Young Muslim men in Scotland: scales of in/exclusion and the location of identity*, Unpublished PhD thesis, University of Edinburgh.

Hopkins, PE. (in press), 'Global events, national politics, local lives: young Muslim men in Scotland', *Environment and Planning A*.

Hopkins, PE. (2007a) Young people, masculinities, religion and race: new social geographies, Progress in Human Geography. 31 (2), 163-177.

Hopkins. PE. (2007b) Global events, national politics, local lives: young Muslim men in Scotland, Environmental Planning A, 39 (5), 1119-1133,

Khalema, NE. and Wannas-Jones, J. (2003), Under the Prism of Suspicion: Minority Voices in Canada Post-September 11', *Journal of Muslim Minority Affairs* 23(1) 25-39.

Lyon, D. (2003) Technology vs 'Terrorism': Circuits of city surveillance since September 11th', *International Journal of Urban and Regional Research*, 27(3) 666-678.

Mitchell, D. (2002) 'Commentary: About time', *Environment and Planning A*, 34(1) 1-5.

Mitchell, D. (2003) *The Right to the City: Social Justice and the Fight for Public Space*, New York: The Guilford Press.

O'Donnell, M. and Sharpe, S. (2000) *Uncertain Masculinities: Youth, Ethnicity and Class in Contemporary Britain*, London: Routledge.

Peek, LA., (2003) 'Reactions and Response: Muslim Students' Experiences on New York City Campuses Post 9/11', *Journal of Muslim Minority Affairs*, 23(3) 271-283.

Pattman, R. Frosh, S. and Phoenix, A. (1998) 'Lads, Machos and Others: Developing 'Boy-Centred' Research', *Journal of Youth Studies*, 1(2) 125-142.

Phoenix, A. Frosh, S. and Pattman, R. (2003) 'Producing Contradictory Masculine Subject Positions: Narratives of Threat, Homophobia and Bullying in 11-14 Year Old Boys', *Journal of Social Issues*, 59(1) 179-195.

Qvorturp, Jens, (2002) Editorial: September elevens and invisible enemies. *Childhood,* 9(2) 139-145.

Scottish Executive (2002) *Tackling Religious Hatred*, Edinburgh: Scottish Executive.

Smith, N. (2001) 'Editorial: Scales of Terror and the Resort to Geography: September 11, October 7', *Environment and Planning D: Society and Space,* 19(6) 631-637.

Staeheli, LA. (1996) 'Publicity, Privacy and Women's Political Action', *Environment and Planning D: Society and Space*, 14(5) 601-619.

Index